AF673962

FOREWORD TO REVISED AND EXPANDED EDITION

This book is a revised and expanded edition of the publication that accompanied the first complete retrospective of Indian silent films in Le Giornate del Cinema Muto, Pordenone, October, 1994. In the Foreword to that edition I explained the circumstances in which it was written. In the years that followed many scholars working on their dissertations in the National Film Archive of India (NFAI)'s library in Pune remarked that *Light of Asia*–along with Ashish Rajadhyaksha and Paul Willemen's *Encyclopaedia of Indian Cinema* published in the same year–provided a starting point for a new phase in the writing of the history of Indian cinema. Even as the latter continues to be an essential reference work, *Light of Asia* has also remained in constant demand. Numerous historians and researchers have thumbed through the few available copies in various libraries, and I have often had occasion to send photocopies to friends and colleagues in different parts of the world. Thus the suggestion frequently came up in conversation and correspondence that there Is a need for a new edition.

This idea has finally taken shape and preparation of the expanded and revised edition began on the eve of the centenary of India's first feature film *Raja Harishchandra* released in 1913. As prime mover and curator of the Pordenone retrospective and editor-contributor of the companion book, it is a great pleasure for me to return to it and make it available with added materials for a new generation of historians and researchers. And since interest in Indian cinema is more widespread than before, one hopes that the larger public will also find it a useful entry point to the rich and complex legacy of Indian cinema.

In Part One, the first chapter 'Before Our Eyes: A Short History of India's Silent Cinema' has been slightly modified in the light of recent research. However, I have added a separate bibliographical essay to supplement the notes appended to the chapter. This essay summarises the work done by various authors since 1994. Acknowledging this significant body of research and interpretation is another reason for bringing out a new edition.

A refrain among historians and aficionados of Indian cinema has always been the scarcity of surviving silent films. Thus, in retrospect, the discovery of reels from three 1920s mythologicals–*Maya Bazar, Sati Savitri and Muralivala*–by the great Baburao Painter was perhaps the most notable event in my tenure at the NFAI. They were found in extraordinary circumstances which I wrote about in the Fédération of International Film Archives' *This Film is Dangerous: A Celebration of Nitrate Film* (FIAF, Brussels, 2002). The essay titled 'The Cobra's Hoard' is reprinted here along with a new chapter called 'The Hoard: Three Films by Baburao Painter' which completes the inventory of all extant Indian silent films currently available with the NFAI. It should be read along with the partially reworked chapter 'The Indian Silent Cinema Retrospective, Pordenone, 1994' which included only the silent films available in 1994.

Ashish Rajadhyaksha's 'India's Silent Cinema: A "Viewer's View"' in the first edition was perhaps the first essay on the subject from the perspective of film studies methodology. For reasons of space it is not included in this edition, but he has written a new chapter which masterfully answers the question 'what, since Suresh Chabria's collaboration with Paolo Cherchi

Usai, the publication of *Light of Asia* and the programming of the Pordenone festival, has happened in relation to *research* on the silent cinema?' Rajadhyaksha, arguably the foremost Indian film theorist, comments on some of the subsequent work in the field and adds his own thoughts about the direction and areas of further research. Also, his discussion of Painter's *Muralivala*, written in a characteristically thought-provoking manner, opens the way for a novel interpretation of the mythological and other major genres of Indian silent cinema.

Part Two again contains Virchand Dharamsey's 'Filmography of Indian Silent Cinema' which was fundamental material for later scholarship, and it now perhaps receives its definitive form. It has been updated with additional information which he uncovered since 1994. The main changes or additions are in the credit lists of the films, names of some actors and other personalities and alternative film titles. He has also added information and remarks about censorship problems, the literary sources of the scripts and stories and the production history of some important films. Significant examples are the conclusive dating of the surviving reels of Phalke's *Raja Harishchandra* to 1917 and the surprising fact that Painter's *Maya Bazar* is actually a re-release of *Surekha Haran* originally made in 1921. The recorded beginnings of feature film production in South India can now also be safely pulled back by almost two years: the pioneer Nataraja Mudaliar made *Gopal Krishna* in 1915 (length unknown) and *Keechak Vadham* was in fact made and released in 1916 and not in 1917. Everyone interested in Indian silent cinema owes Dharamsey an immense debt of gratitude.

Finally, I recall that in the earlier Foreword I referred to India's silent cinema as 'a lost cinematic paradise'. It will perhaps always remain so. But its vivid traces and lasting legacy summed up in this revised edition will hopefully provide some consolation and a solid foundation for others to build upon.

Suresh Chabria
Pune
February, 2013

FOREWORD TO THE FIRST EDITION (1994)

For enthusiasts and historians of Indian cinema, it has always been a matter of deep pain and regret that our entire silent film heritage has virtually perished. One reason for this is that the Indian silent cinema—as also the first fifteen years of the sound era—coincides with the last decades of colonial rule. Though some far-sighted Indians like the producer-director J.B.H. Wadia had already realised the need for preserving films, without self-rule the institutions required to do so could not be set up before Independence.

Hence it is largely due to the efforts of the National Film Archive of India established in 1964–and a lot of luck–that a handful of silent films has survived. These give us a glimpse of that artistically special art form as it evolved on Indian soil with its distinct culture and traits.

However, even as the process of nitrate decomposition, climatic stress, poor storage conditions and the indifference and apathy of the film industry were playing their part, several historians and cinema buffs individually and with the help of the NFAI carried on the work of scouting for films and compiling and collecting information, filmographies, stills, booklets, posters etc. Thanks to all of them many pieces from the gigantic jigsaw puzzle of silent Indian cinema have been put together with the unfortunate exception of several of the key films themselves.

When I joined the NFAI in 1992 I was very keen on trying to renew and further develop the interest and search for our silent films both in India and abroad. Coming from the ranks of cinephiles born long after the passing of that era, the romantic nostalgia for a lost cinematic paradise had always beckoned me. This emotion was further stirred by my admiration for the great and more extensively preserved achievements of the silent cinema in other parts of the world. Thus in the 1970s and 1980s when one heard so much about the presentation of restored silent films with music accompaniment and silent speed projection in Europe and America, I began to dream about how our own silent films could be presented in a similar manner. It was also at that time that I first heard with a thrilling sense of kinship about a festival which is wholly dedicated to rehabilitating the culture of silent cinema. To us, in India, the name of Pordenone was an obscure one, but it soon became a name which evoked a sense of heroic purpose, the romance of fabulous rediscovered treasures, the gateway to unknown and undreamt of cinematic treats. As the festival and its legend grew it became a kind of reference point, the end of a voyage one wanted to undertake again and again.

This is why I immediately proposed an Indian silent cinema retrospective to the Board of Directors of the Pordenone Silent Film Festival. My argument was that the festival had become a largely Eurocentric affair and that on the eve of the cinema centenary its programme would immensely benefit from the presentation of our silent films. With the help of like-minded film scholars such as Stephen Bottomore and Martin Loiperdinger who visited Pune at the time I was able to contact Paolo Cherchi Usai, and the NFAI was invited to present the retrospective in 1994.

However, this retrospective and the book which accompanies it is ultimately a realisation of the efforts of many other people before me. To list all of them would be an impossible feat, but I must mention some of the writers, teachers, researchers, journalists, film enthusiasts, memorabilia collectors and others who at various anniversaries of the founding of Indian film industry and often without any such circumstance to inspire them charted the history of India's early cinema—B.V. Dharap, Firoze Rangoonwalla, P.K. Nair, Satish Bahadur, Abdul Ali, Shashikant Kinikar, A.V. Damle, B.D. Garga, Bagishwar Jha, Erik Barnouw, S. Krishnaswamy, T.M. Ramachandran, S. Theodore Baskaran, Narmada Shahane, V.P. Sathe and others; the short-lived but extremely important journal *Cinema Vision India* and film industry organisations such as the South Indian Film Chamber of Commerce and the Film Federation of India. And, finally, I thank the staff of the NFAI who over the last thirty years of its existence have worked tirelessly and against very great odds.

My gratitude is also due to the Board of Directors, Le Giornate del Cinema Muto, for providing us an opportunity of showing our silent cinema heritage to a larger international community of film scholars and others dedicated to the cause of the silent film. I hope that this encounter will be an enriching one for them and that they will join us in the search for unknown and lost Indian films in different parts of the world.

Suresh Chabria
Director
National Film Archive of India
Pune

ENGAGEME
ALEXANDRA
LOHAR STREET........
TO-NIGHT !
8-30......TO

PART ONE

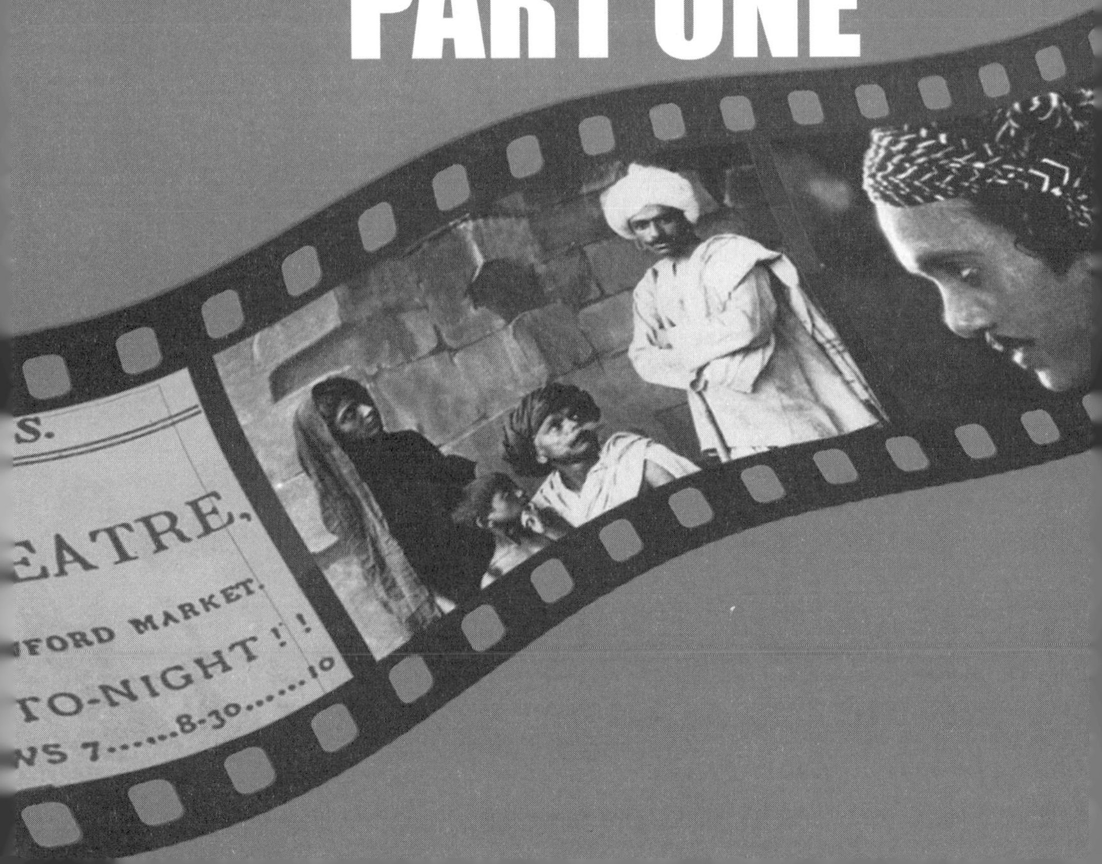

▲ Magic lantern slide

BEFORE OUR EYES

A SHORT HISTORY OF INDIA'S SILENT CINEMA

Suresh Chabria

The chief forerunners of the moving image in India are perhaps the ancient ritual art of shadow puppetry and the folk tradition of *pat* painting. In the latter, pictures were painted in a series on a long scroll and the *chitrakathi* or painter-cum-narrator recited alongside. Their repertoire consisted of illustrations of proverbs, folk tales and mythology. A variation on this is the *Pabuji ka phad* or Pabuji scroll of Rajasthan. Here the entire narrative of a traditional heroic saga is painted on a large sheet of cloth and during the nocturnal performances it is lit in segments as the stories are narrated by a *bhopa* over hours for a period of several days.

The stills camera came to India in 1840, barely a year after its introduction in the West. Indian photographers, like their British counterparts, used it for making portraits and 'documentary' style views. But in both genres they drew from native visual conventions. Thus portraits were directly painted on and a similar planar flatness emphasising frontality was also incorporated into the views. These practices were distinct from the Western preference for depth, perspective and symmetry[1].

Magic lantern shows made an appearance in the middle of the 19th century but the showmen, content and clientele were almost entirely British. In 1892 the Indian version of the magic lantern–called *shambarik kharolika*–was presented by Mahadeo Gopal Patwardhan of Kalyan, a suburb of Bombay. After his death in 1902 his sons travelled with their shows to different parts of India. The programmes included stories from the Hindu epics, thus anticipating the mythologicals of early silent Indian cinema by about a decade. Very much a family affair, the shows were discontinued in 1918[2]. By then the popularity of both imported and Indian silent films had made the magic lantern obsolete.

Entry of Cinématographe

Marius Sestier, representative of the Lumière Brothers, presented the *Cinématographe* at Bombay's Watson's Hotel on 7 July 1896—the same day on which a special show was being held for the Czar of Russia in St. Petersburg. Advertised as 'the marvel of the century' and 'the wonder of the world' among the six 'living photographic pictures' screened were *Entry of Cinématographe, Arrival of a Train* and *Leaving the Factory*.The city's elite–both Indian and European–flocked to the first film exhibitions. Thus the cinema arrived in India barely six months after the first public screenings at the Salon Indien of the Grand Café in Paris. A week later the programme with several additions from the Lumière repertoire was shifted to a regular theatre with a separate section for women and a range of ticket prices for different classes.

Other visiting showmen followed after an interval of a few months. Stewart's 'Vitagraph' was presented in early 1897 and was followed in quick succession by Hughes' 'Moto-Photoscope', Prof. Anderson's 'Andersonoscopograph' and a certain 'Biurnial Optical Diorama'. The venues ranged from prestigious public halls to tent cinemas set up in playgrounds and *maidans* and the shows travelled to the other two major cities of colonial India, Calcutta in the east and Madras in the south[3].

Before long Indian material shot by foreign operators began to feature in the programmes—'exotic' views of monuments, bazaars, religious processions

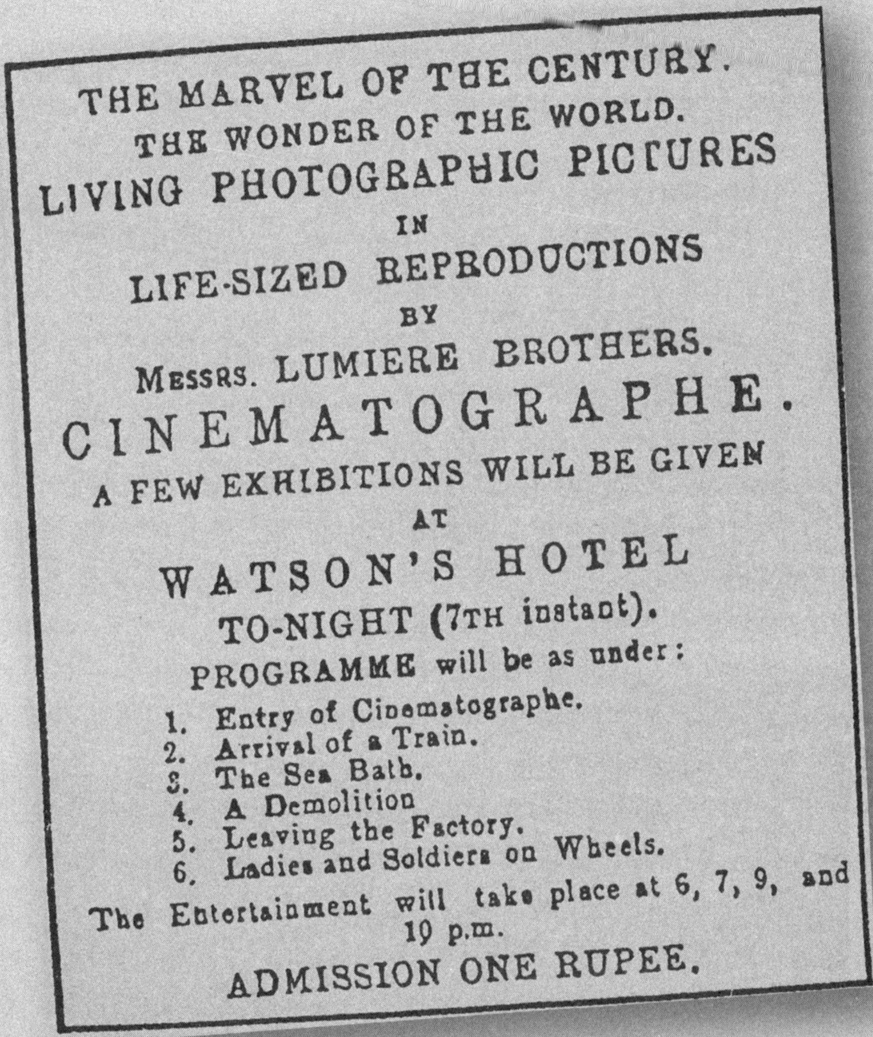
THE MARVEL OF THE CENTURY.
THE WONDER OF THE WORLD.
LIVING PHOTOGRAPHIC PICTURES
IN
LIFE-SIZED REPRODUCTIONS
BY
MESSRS. LUMIERE BROTHERS.
CINEMATOGRAPHE.
A FEW EXHIBITIONS WILL BE GIVEN
AT
WATSON'S HOTEL
TO-NIGHT (7TH instant).
PROGRAMME will be as under:

1. Entry of Cinematographe.
2. Arrival of a Train.
3. The Sea Bath.
4. A Demolition
5. Leaving the Factory.
6. Ladies and Soldiers on Wheels.

The Entertainment will take place at 6, 7, 9, and 10 p.m.
ADMISSION ONE RUPEE.

▲ Advertisement for the Lumière Brothers show at Watson's Hotel Bombay, *The Times of India*, 7 July 1896

and a few filmed theatre items. The lead seems to have been taken by two Englishmen, Mr Stephens and Mr Hudson, who separately exhibited 'bioscope' shows to an enthusiastic public in Calcutta. *Train Arriving at Bombay Station* and *Poona Races '98* attributed to Prof. Anderson are among the earliest 'local scenes' known to have been screened all over India.

The first Indian to venture into filmmaking was Harishchandra S. Bhatvadekar, better known as Save Dada. A stills photographer and photographic equipment dealer, he started by exhibiting imported films in 1898. Soon he acquired his own camera–a Riley–from England and photographed popular early cinema subjects like a wrestling match at Bombay's Hanging Gardens in 1899. Establishing the cinema's relation with the rising tide of Indian nationalism, in December 1901 he filmed the reception given to R.P. Paranjpye, a student who had won top honours in mathematics at Cambridge. This lost film is commonly accepted as the first Indian newsreel.

▼ **Curious Scenes in India**—still from an early actuality shot by a foreign cameraman

At the same time Hiralal Sen, another film enthusiast and pioneer began to photograph well-known stage plays performed at the Classic Theatre in Calcutta. These were screened as an added attraction after the live stage performances and were sometimes exhibited as independent programmes. Sen also made some advertisement shorts and newsreels for his Royal Bioscope Film Co. set up in partnership with his brother Motilal Sen.

Like Bombay and Calcutta, Madras had a lively touring cinema exhibition scene at the end of the 1890s and the early 1900s that catered primarily to the European residents[4]. But perhaps more significant was the impact of the travelling cinemas which toured the entire region bringing foreign and Indian films to the early filmgoers. These shows and the earlier entry of the gramophone and the printing press were harbingers of a tremendous upheaval which transformed the orthodox and tradition-bound society of southern India after centuries of resistance to change[5].

Travelling Cinemas and Picture Palaces

Thus the turn of the century saw the rise of India's equivalent of the 'travelling picture show man'. Equipped with films for two or three programmes the early film exhibitors travelled from city to city and even ventured into remote rural areas. With poor communications and without locally available electricity, they followed in the footsteps of the theatre companies which were touring at the same time with their popular folk theatre and other entertainment forms.

The most prominent film pioneer to emerge from this phenomenon was Jamshedji Framji Madan in Calcutta. Already a major theatre company owner and wealthy businessman, around 1902 he started his 'bioscope' shows (as the cinema was popularly called in India until the arrival of the 'talkies'). Within a few years he presided over Madan Theatres Ltd., a film production-distribution-exhibition empire spread over the whole of British India. Soon he was joined by Abdulally Esoofally of Bombay who toured Southeast Asia before putting up his travelling cinema shows in India. His stock-in-trade was a projector, a folding screen, a tent and a staff of twenty-five workers[6]. Propped up by four pillars the 100 ft. long and 50 ft. wide tent could accommodate more than 1000 spectators at each show.

Among the most popular attractions exhibited by the travelling cinemas were actualities like the famous Boer War films, Queen Victoria's funeral and the earliest story films of the cinema. After Madan built the Elphinstone Picture Palace in Calcutta in 1907, Esoofally set up his own permanent cinema halls in Bombay in the early 1910s. These 'picture palaces' showed films from every major foreign company—Pathé, Gaumont, Éclair, Ambrosio, Biograph, Lubin, Vitagraph, Nordisk, Messter, Warwick and Urban.

With access to a growing exhibition and distribution network, Indian filmmakers of the pre-studio era were encouraged to make a large number of actualities. The pomp and pageantry of the Delhi Durbar and the British royal family's visits to Bombay and Calcutta in 1911 were photographed by Hiralal Sen, S.N. Patankar, Madan Theatres and others alongside numerous foreign operators. Among the Indian-owned concerns, Madan Theatres dominated the production of short actualities for several years. The films included both local scenes and newsreels which recorded many of the major historical and political events of the period.

Dadasaheb Phalke and Friends

At this stage of our chronicle the focus shifts to the beginnings of the Indian feature film industry. Newspapers of the time carry advertisements for a wide range of early silent cinema from every part of the filmmaking world. Méliès' *A Trip to the Moon* and *Gulliver* and Porter's *The Great Train Robbery* and *Uncle Tom's Cabin* toured all over the country for several years. French and Italian Film d'Art productions jostled with the comedies of André Deed and Max Linder. The logos of Pathé and Gaumont were widely recognised by avid moviegoers, and even early Russian films were shown. Therefore, it was only a matter of time before the indigenous story film made its appearance.

The first Indian story film is *Pundalik* made in Bombay and released at the Coronation Cinematograph on 18 May 1912. Based on a Marathi play about

◀ Title card from **The Great Train Robbery**

the eponymous Hindu saint, it was a joint venture of N.G. Chitre and R.G. Torney. Made with the help of Mr Johnson of Bourne & Shepherd (the oldest and most important stills photography dealers in British India) it was screened as part of a double bill with a foreign film entitled *A Dead Man's Child.* Though the press reviews praised the film it seems to have been crudely filmed theatre—a fact that has somewhat obscured its pioneer status.

In the same year, newspaper advertisements announced *Savitri* made jointly by S.N. Patankar, V.P. Divekar and A.P. Karandikar, who later formed Patankar Friends & Co., one of the founding institutions of Indian cinema. However it could not be released since the developing was found defective.

Cecil B. DeMille's famous remark 'And so we came to the fateful year of 1913', has a significance for Indian cinema as well. For it is in 1913 that after a preparation of three years Dhundiraj Govind Phalke (affectionately known as Dadasaheb Phalke) released *Raja Harishchandra.* Like the stories about Méliès' accidental discovery of trick photography, Griffith's 'invention' of the close-up or Chaplin's creation of the character of the Tramp, the story of Phalke's entry into the cinema has often been retold and has something of the quality of an originary myth or founding legend in Indian film histories. For not only have fragments of some of his most important films actually survived, his impact on Indian popular art in this century can only be compared with that of his predecessor, the vastly influential painter, Raja Ravi Varma[7].

Born in a Maharashtrian Brahmin family in 1870, Phalke was educated in two of the major art schools of the colonial period—the J.J. School of Arts in Bombay and Kalabhavan in Baroda. Here he learned drawing, photography, lithography, architecture, and molding and participated in stage dramas as an amateur actor. He also taught himself magic, which he later considered an essential qualification for a filmmaker. After a stint as a draughtsman and photographer with the Government of India's Archaeological Department he set up his own printing and engraving works. Here he brought out oleographs based on the paintings of Ravi Varma whose style and content he was to further extend by carrying them over into his own films.

In 1910, he saw a film entitled *The Life of Christ* and describes its impact on him in the famous passage written in 1917:

> I must have seen films on many occasions before this but that day, that Saturday in Christmas, marked the beginning of a revolutionary change in my life. That day also marked the foundation in India of an industry which occupies the fifth place in the myriad of big and small professions that exist ... While the life of Christ was rolling fast before my eyes I was mentally visualising the gods, Shri Krishna, Shri Ramchandra, their Gokul and Ayodhya ... Could we, the sons of India, ever be able to see Indian images on the screen?[8]

What Phalke was pointing out is that under British rule a combination of political, historical and economic factors had prevented the emergence of a genuine indigenous film industry. Participation in the modern sectors of the economy by Indians at the turn of the century was only a couple of decades old; and that too in a limited and rather tentative manner. Thus, as far as cinema was concerned, aside from the large production of actualities,

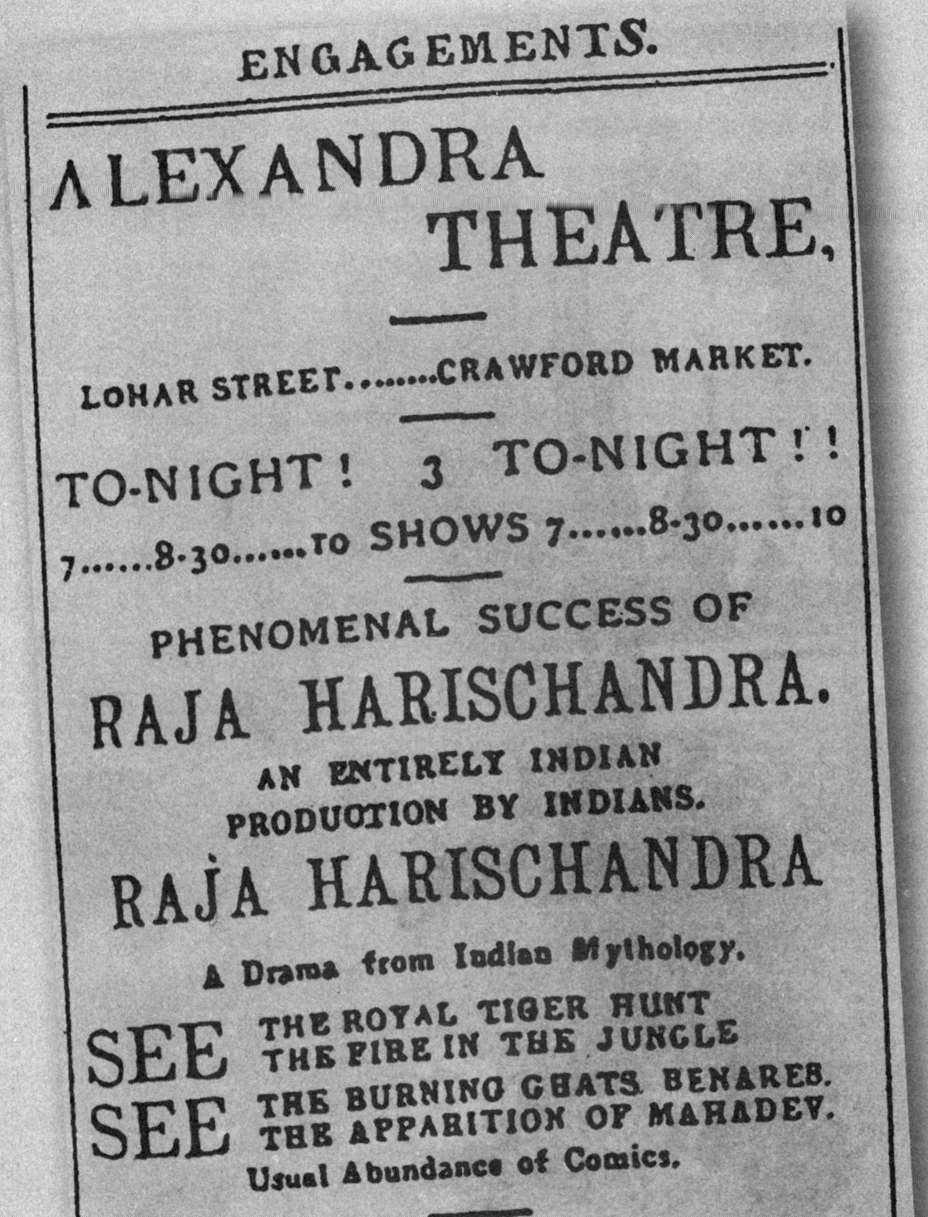

ENGAGEMENTS.

ALEXANDRA THEATRE,

LOHAR STREET........CRAWFORD MARKET.

TO-NIGHT! 3 TO-NIGHT!!

7......8-30......TO SHOWS 7......8-30......10

PHENOMENAL SUCCESS OF

RAJA HARISCHANDRA.

AN ENTIRELY INDIAN PRODUCTION BY INDIANS.

RAJA HARISCHANDRA

A Drama from Indian Mythology.

SEE THE ROYAL TIGER HUNT
THE FIRE IN THE JUNGLE

SEE THE BURNING GHATS BENARES.
THE APPARITION OF MAHADEV.

Usual Abundance of Comics.

NO ADVANCE IN PRICES.

28 JUNE 1913

▲ Advertisement for *Raja Harishchandra*

Indian entrepreneurs preferred to distribute and exhibit the finished product imported from abroad. Fascination with the medium of cinema and the rising sense of nationalism and anti-colonial sentiment fused in the mind of Phalke. As a result from the very beginning he consciously gave his work a political dimension by viewing it in the context of the Swadeshi movement (or the nationalist programme of self-reliance).

To return to the making of *Raja Harishchandra*, Phalke first made a trick film entitled *Growth of a Pea Plant*.This helped him raise finance and travel to England in 1912. There he familiarised himself with film technology, purchased a Williamson camera, Kodak stock and a perforator. He also met Cecil Hepworth who invited him to visit his studio at Walton-on-Thames and see for himself the results of his new equipment.

On his return to Bombay he launched his own production company Phalke's Films and made *Raja Harishchandra*—released at the Coronation Cinematograph on 3 May 1913. The 90-minute programme also featured Miss Delmar in a duet and dance number, a comical sketch by the McClements, Alexandroff, the Foot Juggler and Tip-Top Comics. The programme must have had the full flavour of colonial India with even more colour added by the fact that the female roles in *Raja Harishchandra* were enacted by men since no 'decent' Indian woman would consider acting in a film.

Raja Harishchandra was a tremendous success. Though largely ignored by English-language newspapers and the audiences which frequented Western films, it reached the native audience almost immediately. The 'Indian images' which Phalke had imagined three years earlier struck a deep chord in the psyche of the spectators. They recognised and welcomed his integration of India's centuries-old traditions and culture with the new medium of the cinema, finding in it a new 'self' or identity in the modern context[9].

In fact, it would not be an exaggeration to say that ever since Phalke, the cinema's hold over the average Indian's imagination can only be compared with some of the traditional cultural and art forms which are similarly inscribed with the ancient legends and myths which have intermingled for generations with religious and folk festivals and the daily life of the people[10].

A Film Industry Takes Off

After *Raja Harishchandra* Phalke shifted to Nasik–180 kilometres from Bombay–which he preferred because of easy access to scenic locations and several famous shrines which he considered essential for his mythologicals. In *Bhasmasur Mohini* (1913) he could finally cast two stage actresses–Durgabai and Kamalabai–and in the same year he revisited England to update his equipment and also exhibit his films there.

On his return to India he faced difficulties caused by the outbreak of World War I. Financiers backed off from the new adventure of filmmaking during the crisis. But with the huge success of *Lanka Dahan* in 1917 and the founding of his Hindustan Cinema Film Co. the following year, the foundations of Indian cinema were finally secured.

Phalke's example was quickly followed by pioneers in the other two major traditional filmmaking centres of Calcutta and Madras. To quote Barnouw and Krishnaswamy's vivid and succinct account of the infancy of Indian cinema:

> In due time Phalke, like other producers of this period, became an exhibitor and travelled far and wide by bullock cart, with projectors, screen and films. The people who came were seldom two-rupee customers. Most paid four annas, two annas, or even one anna, and most of them sat on the ground. The revenue was in coins. The weight of the coins, on the homeward trip, could be enormous[11].

Cinema was already becoming an inseparable part of the Indian cultural landscape and adding to its immense complexity by bringing in more rapid change and a new expression of the modern.

A Painter's Signature

Decisively leaving behind the artisanal and somewhat improvised methods of the pioneers of the pre-studio era–Phalke, Patankar Friends & Co., Suchet Singh and others–the period from 1917 onwards saw the rise of a number of studios and filmmakers in other parts of India whose almost entirely lost work is the stuff of India's silent cinema legend[12].

Perhaps the most illustrious among these are the names of Baburao Painter and his Maharashtra Film Co. which he set up in Kolhapur with the help of the local nobility in 1918. Born Baburao Krishnarao Mestri, he was a painter by profession (hence his assumed name) and like his contemporary, Phalke was a consummate craftsman and a technical genius conscious of Swadeshi philosophy. Redesigning an old camera, using artificial lights, painting the sets to get a particular shade of grey on film, devising and using filters with tinted glass for the first time—the stories about him are legion.

Among his most famous early films are *Sairandhri* (1920), *Sinhagad* (1923), *Kalyan Khajina* and *Sati Padmini* (both 1924). The subjects of these films were drawn from mythology and Maratha history; but his most celebrated film is the lost *Savkari Pash* (1925) a realist social about rural exploitation which has a status akin to that of *Greed* in the history of Indian cinema. Critics noted the poetic combination of visuals evoking sound and light and J.B.H. Wadia later praised the 'artistry and excellence' of both the silent and sound versions of the film[13]. Perhaps the most important acquisitions of the NFAI since the Pordenone retrospective are some reels from Painter's mythologicals *Maya Bazar, Sati Savitri* and *Muralivala,* which are discussed for the first time in this edition.

Painter had the manner and outlook of a traditional guru and among his important disciples are some of the most renowned filmmakers in Indian cinema. These include V. Shantaram, Keshavrao Dhaiber, V. Damle and S. Fattelal who formed Prabhat Film Co. in 1929. Sharing the patronage of the Maharaja of Kolhapur with Painter's company, Prabhat's silents–mythologicals and historicals–were made with an eye for detail and high

▲ **Jugari Dharma** (1927)

▼ Zunzharrao Pawar and V. Shantaram in **Savkari Pash** (1925)

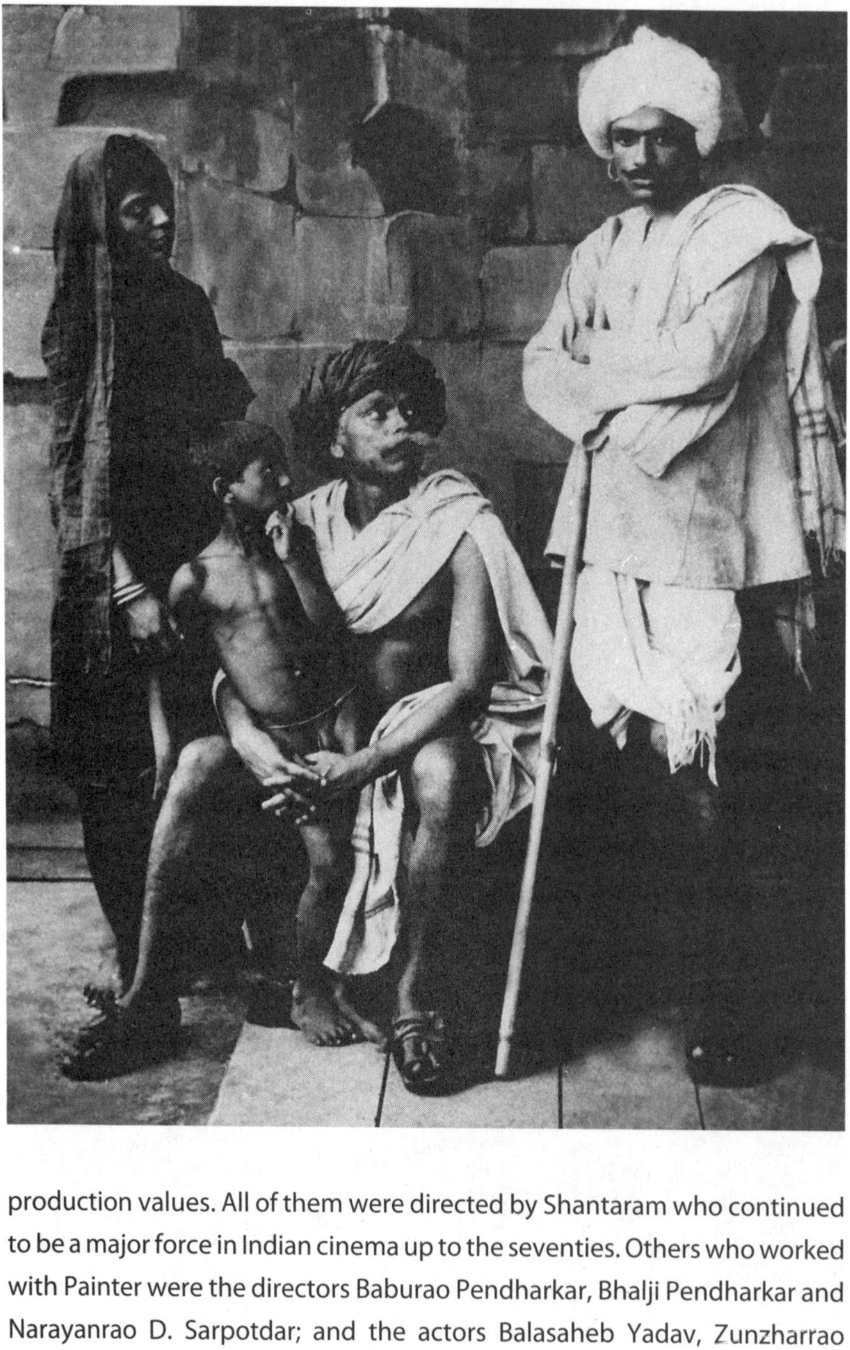

production values. All of them were directed by Shantaram who continued to be a major force in Indian cinema up to the seventies. Others who worked with Painter were the directors Baburao Pendharkar, Bhalji Pendharkar and Narayanrao D. Sarpotdar; and the actors Balasaheb Yadav, Zunzharrao Pawar, Master Vithal and Ganpat Bakre.

Made in India: A Large Industry for a Large Country

The first feature films made in Calcutta were *Satyawadi Raja Harishchandra* (1917) and *Bilwamangal* (1919) produced by Madan's Elphinstone Bioscope Co. and directed by Rustomji Dotiwala. Like many of the subsequent films made by Madan Theatres (as the company was renamed) directed by Camille de Grand–a former Pathé photographer–and Jyotish Bannerjee, these were adaptations of popular plays in the Parsi theatre style. In a bid to enter the international market Madan Theatres also hired the services of the Italian director Eugenio de Liguoro and several European actors in *Nala Damayanti* (1920) and *Dhruva Charitra* (1921). This led to a co-production with Cines called *Savitri* (1924) directed by Giorgio Mannini and featuring the famous Italian stars Rina de Liguoro and Angelo Ferrari. The Calcutta newspaper advertisement of the film boasted that it was shot in world-renowned locations in Rome and the Cines Studios where *Quo Vadis* was filmed, and that 'Hindu mythology (is) at last produced with all its sweet simplicity and magnificence.' However, with frequent international collaboration and the consistent use of a Westernised theatrical idiom, Madan Theatres was accused by their Calcutta rivals of merely making films in Bengal and not Bengali films.

The most famous Bengali production of its time was Indo-British Film Co.'s *Bilet Pherat* aka *The England Returned* (1921) directed by Nitish C. Lahiri and starring Dhirendranath Ganguly. It was a satire on a young Indian who mimics European manners and values and 'startles everybody with his quixotic notions of love

◀ Dhirendranath Ganguly in **Bilet Pherat**

and matrimony'. Ganguly was a multi-faceted personality who besides producing and acting in films was also a portrait painter and experimented with photography, famously producing two photo-montage collections in which he appeared in several roles. After a stint in Hyderabad at the invitation of the local ruler he returned to Calcutta and, together with P.C. Barua, started British Dominion Films in 1929.

As early as 1911, Anadi Bose founded Aurora Cinema Co. which shifted from exhibition and production of short films to feature filmmaking with *Ratnakar,* released in 1921. Though the company successfully made features for several years it is perhaps better remembered for its news review called *Calcutta Film Gazette.* Another major Calcutta company of the early 1920s was Taj Mahal Film Co. for which Sisir Bhaduri made *Andhare Alo* (1922). This film was adapted from a novel by Saratchandra Chatterjee, one of the literary giants of Bengal. Thereafter, Bengali filmmakers drew frequently from their rich theatre and literary traditions to consciously create an indigenous cinematic idiom that was distinct from the foreign influenced style of Madan Theatres.

In Madras Nataraja Mudaliar, an automobile spare parts dealer, made *Gopal Krishna* (1915) and *Keechak Vadham* (1916) which are the first feature films made in the south. He trained as a cameraman under Stewart Smith, an official photographer in Poona, before returning to Madras to establish the Indian Film Co. with its own film studio. Mudaliar was soon followed by R. Venkaiah, a wealthy exhibitor and cinema owner who sent his son Raghupati S. Prakash to Europe to learn filmmaking. During his travels Prakash is said to have seen Murnau at work in Germany. On his return to Madras he set up a well-equipped studio for the Star of the East Film Co. started by his father. Their debut production *Bhishma Pratigna* (1921) was a big success. Like their subsequent films it was released all over India, Burma and Ceylon. It was in their roles as the movie moguls of the south that the Irish missionary T. Gavan Duffy contacted Venkaiah and Prakash to help him make his Catholic propaganda film, *The Catechist of Kil-Arni*[14].

Aside from the fact that it was praised by a contemporary reviewer as an authentically south Indian film, little is known about the highly successful *Valli Thirumanam* (1921) made by Whittaker—probably a Maharashtrian filmmaker. The latter half of the 1920s saw the emergence of several other important companies in the region including General Pictures Corporation founded by A. Narayanan and R. Padmanabhan's Associated Films Ltd. For the latter, Bombay star Raja Sandow directed and acted in a number of films such as *Sati Ushasundari* (1930) and *Pride of Hindustan* (1931). Other filmmaking concerns mushroomed in Bangalore, Hyderabad and the relatively smaller town of Nagercoil where P.V. Rao made *Marthanda Varma* (1931), which is the only surviving south Indian silent film.

▲ Raja Sandow

The Movie Moguls of Bombay

In the silent era, as it would also be in later decades, the Bombay film industry was the leader; the ultimate badge of success was to have made it there. In the 1920s 'Bollywood' or *masala* cinema was already being created. It was partly, of course, the product of Bombay's cosmopolitan character and partly an offshoot of its commercial dynamo which made capital more accessible.

Arguably the most important production company was Dwarkadas Sampat's Kohinoor Film Co. established in 1919. It made the largest number of films in the silent period and launched some of its most famous stars like Raja Sandow, Khalil, Gohar, Sulochana, Sultana, Zubeida and Fatma Begum (who became the first woman director in Indian cinema); and directors like Homi Master, Mohanlal G. Dave, Chandulal Shah, Kanjibhai Rathod and Mohan Bhavnani.

◀ Sulochana (Ruby Myers)

▼ Dinshaw Bilimoria (left);
Gohar (right)

With Rathod's *Bhakta Vidur* (1921) Kohinoor was involved in the most famous censorship row of the silent era. After a successful run in Bombay it was banned for being 'a thinly veiled resume of political events in India, Vidur appearing as Mr Gandhi clad in a Gandhi cap and *khaddar* shirt'[15]. Sensationalist content may have helped some of the studio's realist socials made by its most energetic director Homi Master, but several of Kohinoor's legendary hits needed no such hype. These included the immensely popular folk fantasy *Gul-e-Bakavali* (1924) and the path breaking socials *Cinema Queen* (1925), *Telephone Girl* (1926) and *Gunasundari* aka *Why Husbands Go Astray* (1927). Unfortunately, only one Kohinoor film has survived—the extraordinary mythological *Sukanya Savitri* (1922) directed by Rathod.

Kohinoor's chief rival was Ardeshir M. Irani's Imperial Film Co. founded in 1926. After a string of enormous successes such as *Gamdani Gori* aka *Village Girl* and *Wild Cat of Bombay* (both 1927) and *Cinema Girl* (1930), Imperial produced the first Indian talkie, *Alam Ara* in 1931. In the last years of the silent era it was home to the leading romantic star couple, Sulochana and Dinshaw Bilimoria.

Another major studio was Sharda Film Co. established by Bhogilal Dave and Nanubhai Desai in 1925. Its speciality was the bunch of stunt movies starring Master Vithal who was promoted as the 'Indian Douglas Fairbanks'. Derived equally from *Arabian Nights* exotica and Rajput tales of valour, they introduced fast editing and the chase to Indian cinema. Master Vithal, like other 'stunt pullers' of the era, was famous for doing his own stunts.

Working his way through the 1920s from stockbroker to film director and movie mogul was Chandulal Shah who set up Ranjit Film Co. in 1929. His early films were made for Kohinoor with Gohar—an association which continued at Ranjit and is among the most famous director and star teams in Indian film history. Ranjit soon became one of Bombay's elite studios and gathered under its banner other stars like Sulochana, Madhuri, Zubeida, Sultana and Shantakumari, and big league directors like Jaswantlal, Nanubhai Vakil, Jayant Desai and Nagendra Mazumdar.

After a fire destroyed all the Kohinoor negatives in 1923, Maneklal Patel–one of the founding partners–inherited the surviving prints which helped him to set up his own Krishna Film Co. Its trademark was that it commissioned scripts from a large number of well-known authors of the time—a trend analogous to the numerous literary adaptations being made in Bengal. The most eminent among these authors was the stalwart politician and writer K.M. Munshi whose reformist novels were adapted into *Jay Somnath* and *Kono Wank* aka *Whose Fault* in 1929.

Finally, one must mention the Surya Film Co. set up in Bangalore by the Bombay-based Haribhai R. Desai in 1929. Surya pooled together talents from various companies in Bombay, Poona and Kolhapur to become one of the biggest production companies in the south during the last years of the silent era[16].

Have You Seen An Indian Silent Film Recently?

Thus by the mid-1920s India had a large and flourishing studio system based in the three leading economic zones and urban centres of British India. Reflecting the culture and ethnic character of each region, films were made in nine broad genres—mythologicals, devotionals, socials, historicals, costume films, stunt movies, comedies, literary adaptations and crime films.

Though many of the production companies were short-lived with brittle partnerships and shifts in financial backing constantly leading to realignments and the setting up of new concerns, the annual production remained high throughout the period.

At least the dozen or so companies discussed above survived long enough to account for more than half of Indian silent cinema's total output of more than 1300 films. Like their counterparts in other parts of the world these studios nurtured the careers of India's best-known silent movie stars, directors, scriptwriters and technicians.

The Report of the Indian Cinematograph Committee, 1927-28, gives an invaluable and vivid description of the silent era. It is ironical that while hardly any of the films themselves have survived, this 3300 page report written with classical British bureaucratic thoroughness, has exhaustively documented virtually every aspect of India's silent cinema[17].

In the peak year of 1926-27 more than 100 films were made but the Committee found that the studios were generally ill equipped. The use of artificial lights was still rare, and processing could be a dangerous and hazardous affair. It took four to six weeks to complete a film and the average cost ranged from twenty to thirty thousand rupees (US $7000–10,000). Shortage of capital was a perennial problem; loans at high interest from moneylenders often saved the day even for the major studios. Most of them maintained a permanent staff of technicians and stars. The female stars were still largely drawn from among 'dancing girls' and women of Jewish origin or Anglo-Indians like Sulochana (Ruby Myers), Ermeline and Patience Cooper.

▼ Patience Cooper

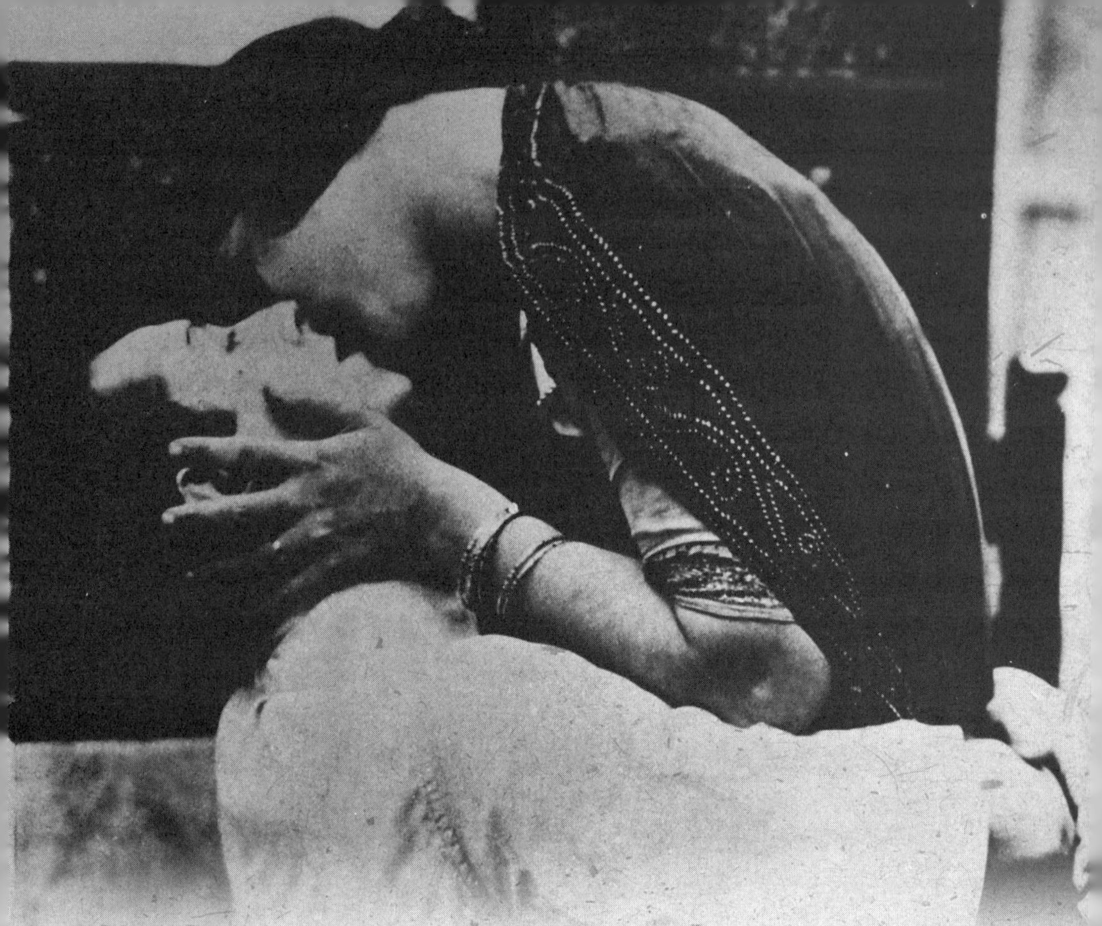

▲ Sulochana and Jal Merchant in **Amarun Hindustan** (1930) - a 'passionate love scene'

As compared with the big American film distributors, Indian producers demanded higher rates from the exhibitors in order to recover their investment. 'Block booking' was common and the best theatres in the major cities were reserved for American films patronised by the Indian and European elite. Nevertheless, the larger audience showed a marked preference for indigenous films notwithstanding poor exhibition conditions and higher ticket prices.

As regards censorship, the main preoccupation of the British censor was not the 'passionate love scenes' then common in Indian cinema, but the ever-present threat of communal discord and expression of nationalistic sentiments. In a reference to the problems caused by India's diverse and pluralistic society–which persist to this day–the Committee advised the

▲ A scene in frontal style from **Pitru Prem** (1929)

censors not to 'encourage individuals who in their private or representative capacities object to film plots or incidents'[18].

Now for a few words about some of the other features of the silent film in India. One is the use of multi-lingual titles. These were generally in English and in one or more of the major Indian languages depending on the linguistic composition of the audience. For instance, titles in four languages–English, Hindi, Gujarati and Urdu–were frequently used for many Bombay releases. In several theatres a commentator read out the titles for the illiterate among the audience and also 'dubbed' for the actors.

Music accompaniment usually consisted of an orchestra of harmonium, *tabla* and sometimes a *sarangi* or a violin. (Foreign pictures were generally accompanied by a piano and violin). The musicians were also expected to provide dialogue and live sound effects for the most exciting action scenes[19]. Since the practice of written scores did not exist, the music accompaniment for a film could greatly differ from region to region, bringing in the local folk and popular music styles. Thus songs and musical sequences–the most common elements in our sound films–were in a sense, already a part of the silent film viewing experience.

Serials based on mythological and costume fantasy themes were very popular—the most famous being *Ram Vanvas* (1918) produced by Patankar Friends & Co. and Krishna's *Hatimtai* (1929). The latter was an *Arabian Nights* costume fantasy which was remade several times in the sound era.

However, the much talked about orientalist Indo-German films of Himansu Rai and Franz Osten–*Prem Sanyas, Shiraz* and *Prapancha Pasha*–did not enjoy the same success in India as in Europe. The majority of the audience preferred the indigenous idiom of frontal style, a looser narrative development and homegrown genre cinema conventions and stars. In contrast, imported American films were much more influential. Stars were promoted by giving them soubriquets like 'Indian Mary Pickford' (Ermeline) and 'Indian Eddie Polo' (Nandram). The popular stunt movie genre was almost single-handedly launched by the success of Fairbanks and Walsh's *The Thief of Baghdad* and American comedies were much imitated in the last years of the silent era.

But ultimately the Hollywood influence was only one element which blended with and added a new spice to Indian silent cinema. India's own popular visual and performing arts (specially the folk and company theatre forms) remained the chief stylistic source and inspiration. The silent film borrowed from them some of its most typical traits which give it a distinct character and resonance—the previously mentioned frontal style, direct address to the spectator, storylines, set design, acting styles, narration provided by the commentator, and of course, live music. As soon as sound technology arrived these influences received their definitive transformation into yet another cinematic expression—the all-talking, all-singing, all-Indian sound film.

NOTES

1. See Judith Mara Gutman, *Through Indian Eyes, 19th and Early 20th Century Photography from India,* New York: Oxford University Press, 1982.
2. R. Washikar, 'Shambarik Kharolika', in Firoze Rangoonwalla (ed.), *Phalke Centenary Souvenir*, Bombay: 1970, pp. 117-119.
3. Among the main sources of information on early film exhibition and India's silent cinema used for this chapter are Firoze Rangoonwalla, *75 Years of Indian Cinema*, New Delhi: India Book Company, 1975; T.M. Ramachandran (ed.), *70 Years of Indian Cinema (1913-1983), Bombay: Cinema India—International*, 1985; and *Cinema Vision India*, Bombay: vol. 1, no. 1, 1980.
4. Stephen Putnam Hughes, 'When Film Came to Madras', *BioScope: South Asian Screen Studies*, vol.1, no. 2, 2010, pp. 147-148. In the first edition it was erroneously stated that Madras was reputed to have had its first permanent cinema house as early as 1900. Hughes' research has since established that this was not so and that the Electric Theatre was built only in 1913.
5. S. Theodore Baskaran, *The Message Bearers: The Nationalist Politics and the Entertainment Media in South India, 1880-1945*, Madras: Cre-A: 1981. This book contains an excellent chapter on the silent period in south India.
6. See 'Half a Century in Exhibition Line: Shri Abdulally Recalls Bioscope Days', in *Indian Talkie, 1931-56*, Silver Jubilee Souvenir: Bombay, 1956, pp. 121-122.
7. All biographical information about D.G. Phalke is from B.V. Dharap, 'The Phalke Saga', in *Phalke Centenary Souvenir*, op. cit., pp. 49-65. See also my essay 'D.G. Phalke and the Méliès Tradition in Early Indian Cinema', *KINtop 2*, Frankfurt am Main: 1993, pp. 103-115. For biographical and critical texts on Raja Ravi Varma see R.C. Sharma (ed.), *Raja Ravi Varma: New Perspectives*, New Delhi: National Museum, 1993. Also see Geeta Kapur, 'Ravi Varma: Representational Dilemmas of a Nineteenth Century Indian Painter', *Journal of Arts & Ideas*, nos. 17-18, New Delhi: June 1989, pp. 59-80. Raja Ravi Varma (1848-1906) created the model for a modern Indian identity and imagery within the oil and easel format of European academic painting. He later extended this to the field of mass produced oleographs. His work is thus analogous to that of his contemporary, Lala Deen Dayal, the pioneering stills photographer; the Parsi theatre which was the proscenium style theatre introduced from the West in the latter part of the 19th century; and later, of course, the films of Phalke.

8. D.G. Phalke, essays on the Indian Cinema, 'Bhartiya Chitrapat' in *Navyug*, Bombay: Nov 1917.
9. For a detailed discussion of this see Ashish Rajadhyaksha, 'Neo-Traditionalism: Film as Popular Art in India', *Framework*, nos. 32/33, London: 1986, pp. 20-67. See also various essays in Tejaswini Niranjana, P. Sudhir, and Vivek Dhareshwar (eds.), *Interrogating Modernity, Culture and Colonialism in India*, Calcutta: Seagull Books, 1993.
10. For essays on this approach see 'Indian Popular Cinema: Myth, Meaning and Metaphor', *India International Centre Quarterly*, Special Issue, New Delhi: March 1981; and Beatrix Pfleiderer and Lothar Lutze (eds.), *The Hindi Film : Agent and Re-agent of Cultural Change*, New Delhi: Manohar, 1985.
11. Erik Barnouw and S. Krishnaswamy, *Indian Film*, New York and London: Columbia University Press, 1963, p.15.
12. In the following brief survey of the major studios and personalities of Indian silent cinema I have given only the essential chronological and biographical details. For additional information see Ashish Rajadhyaksha and Paul Willemen (eds.), *Encyclopaedia of Indian Cinema*, new revised edition, New Delhi: Oxford University Press, 1999.
13. J. B. H. Wadia, 'The Indian Silent Film', in Ramachandran, op. cit., p. 27.
14. From Gerard Brady's unpublished biography of Thomas Gavan Duffy.
15. Report of the Indian Cinematograph Committee, 1927-28, Evidence, vol. IV, p. 375.
16. Among the production companies which briefly thrived near Bombay were Pandurang S. Talegiri's Deccan Pictures Corporation and Bharat Cinema Film Corporation, both in Poona, and United Pictures Syndicate in Kirkee. Deccan Pictures made the influential historical *Poona Par Hallo* aka *Poona Raided* (1924) directed by Mama Varerkar which was about the great 17th century Maratha warrior Chhatrapati Shivaji.
17. For a short summary of the objectives, recommendations and evidence presented before the Committee, see Rani Burra (ed.), *Looking Back: 1896–1960*, New Delhi: The Directorate of Film Festivals, 1981, pp. 26-31.
18. Report of the Indian Cinematograph Committee, 1927-28, p. 119.
19. Bhaskar Chandavarkar, 'Sound in a Silent Era', in *Cinema Vision India*, op. cit., p. 118.

THE INDIAN SILENT CINEMA RETROSPECTIVE

PORDENONE, 1994

Suresh Chabria

BANGA DARSHAN

aka Travels in Bengal

(The Eastern Bengal Railway, year unknown)

Directed and edited by William J. Moylan. Photographed by C.Marconi.

Length: 989 feet. 35 mm. English and Bengali titles.

The main credit title of this beautifully photographed travelogue includes credits for narration and sound recording. But since the print available with the National Film Archive of India is in the silent full gate format, it may have been planned and shot as a silent film and later released with an added sound track in the early talkie era.

The introductory title states: 'The Eastern Bengal Railways respectfully dedicates this film to the people of Bengal whom it has served for 80 years carrying men, women and children far and near for their business, pleasure or religion as the case required'.

▲ **Banga Darshan**

The film then takes the viewer on a journey through Bengal. Beginning with the famous sights of Calcutta, we leave by train from Sealdah Main Station first for the Darjeeling hills dominated by the superb Kanchenjunga, and then to some of the major temples of north Bengal.

BHAKTA PRAHLAD

(Hindustan Cinema Film Co., 1926)

Directed and scripted by D.G. Phalke. Photographed by Anna Salunke. Cast: Gangaram Nhavi (Prahlad), Bhaurao Datar (Narasimha), Bachu Pawar (Hiranyakashipu), Yamuna Gole. Original length: 7447 feet, length of fragment: 566 feet. 35mm. Hindi and English titles.

Drawn from one of the great treasuries of Hindu myths, the *Bhagavata Purana, Bhakta Prahlad* tells the story of Prahlad's devotion to God Vishnu, who is the hated enemy of his father—the arrogant demon-king,

▲ **Bhakta Prahlad**

Hiranyakashipu. Chanting '*Hari*! *Hari*!' (another name for Vishnu) Prahlad remains miraculously unharmed by a series of tortures which includes being plunged in a cauldron of boiling oil, trampled by an elephant and poisoned at the hands of his own mother.

In the magnificent climax Vishnu emerges from a pillar in his Narasimha *avatar* as man-lion to vanquish the demon. With a rocking camera and superimposed streaks of lightning shooting out as the pillar bursts open to reveal the wrathful Narasimha, this is perhaps Phalke's most brilliantly executed and elaborate special effects sequence.

Initially, Gangaram Nhavi's representation of the adolescent Prahlad could seem somewhat comical because of his constant clapping and monotonous chanting of Vishnu's name. But subsequently it assumes a powerful spiritual charge and trance-like communion with the divine.

BRICK LAYING

(Production company and year unknown)

Directed by D.G. Phalke. Original length: unknown, length of fragment: 136 feet. 35 mm. Titles missing.

Only a small fragment of this documentary survives showing glimpses of rural artisanal methods of manufacturing bricks. Phalke made a number of documentaries on a wide range of subjects which included a glass works, religious festivals, sports events, important political functions and the monuments of Ellora and Bodh Gaya.

BUDDU KI AKKAL

(Production company and year unknown)

Credits unknown. Length of print: 897 feet. 35 mm. Hindi, Urdu and English titles.

A one-reel comedy about whose makers nothing is known. In their master's absence a manservant and maid think that a goat has eaten the master's prize-winning lottery ticket. But all ends well when the maid finds it while sweeping the floor. Their wildest dreams come true when the master decides to share the prize money with them as a reward.

In his updated filmography, V. Dharamsey has suggested that *Buddu Ki Akkal* could possibly be the same film as *Jamaika The Fool* produced by the hitherto unknown Poona Comedy Film Corporation in 1931.

THE CATECHIST OF KIL-ARNI

(T. Gavan Duffy, Pondicherry Mission, India, 1923)

Directed by T. Gavan Duffy and R.S. Prakash. Cast: T. Gavan Duffy. Length: 1585 feet. 16 mm. English titles.

► **The Catechist of Kil-Arni**

This Catholic propaganda film produced and written by the Irish missionary T. Gavan Duffy was made at the suggestion of Mgr. McGlinchey of Boston. Duffy had accompanied McGlinchey on a tour of Ceylon and India in December 1922 and January 1923. To supplement their resources for missionary work McGlinchey proposed the making of a film which could be used for raising funds among the faithful in the US and Ireland.

Duffy states, 'All over India Mgr. McGlinchey kept looking for an enterprising missioner who would venture into movie land but found nobody willing and able to accept. Finally I made up my mind to throw aside my regular work for a few weeks and to become the movie-star of the Far East!' His adventures and experiences during the production of the film in March and April 1923 make for amusing reading. For 'professional' help he turned to Raghupati Surya Prakash, the pioneer director and cinematographer from Madras. However, he seems to have valued the assistance of a Catholic layman, Bruce Gordon, more.

The plot is about the conversion of a one-time thief called Ram. During an epidemic he is inspired by a missionary–played by Duffy himself–to become a model Christian and a catechist. Although the film was shot in the village of Sattiamangalam, the name of a nearby village, Kil-Arni, was used because it sounded Irish. Sattiamangalam was also chosen because the village already had a population of Catholic converts who were untouchables, thus avoiding the problem of caste taboos which could have hampered the making of the film elsewhere.

The film produced the desired results abroad and some highly exaggerated reviews. It was screened in India but was criticised for showing Indians in a negative light. With its open contempt for India's 'pagan' culture, the film does have several offensive portions, and today its main interest perhaps lies in the documentary style footage of agricultural practices in the district of Velantangal.

▲ Phalke directing
Raja Harishchandra (1917)

D.G. PHALKE, 1870-1944, THE FIRST INDIAN FILM DIRECTOR

(National Film Archive of India, 1965)

Compiled and scripted by Satish Bahadur. Produced by Jagat Murari. Length: 1940 feet. 35 mm. English and French titles.

Scripted and compiled by Professor Satish Bahadur in 1965 for the newly founded National Film Archive of India, the film gives an account of the career of Dhundiraj Govind Phalke, the founder of the Indian film industry. It was specially produced for the 1965 FIAF Congress which had sent out enquiries about recently discovered film pioneers in different countries. Because it was hastily made, a soundtrack could not be prepared; instead titles in English and French were used.

The film comments on the relation of Phalke's work with the Indian popular arts of that time–Ravi Varma's paintings and oleographs, Parsi theatre, folk theatre etc.–and the reasons for the success of the mythological genre with Indian audiences.

Extracts from the newly discovered Phalke films are skillfully arranged and include the entire first reel of *Raja Harishchandra* and several remarkable shots from his last silent film *Setu Bandhan* (1932-33)—which Phalke subsequently synchronised at the Imperial Studio and released in 1934. But the true highlight of the film is the extraordinary footage showing Phalke at work on the 1917 version of *Raja Harishchandra.* These shots are from the lost *How Films are Made* released in the same year in which Phalke attempted to explain the medium of cinema to his early audience.

DILER JIGAR

aka Gallant Hearts

(Agarwal Film Co., 1931)

Directed and scripted by G.P. Pawar.

Produced and photographed by Shyam Sundar Agarwal.

Cast: Amboo (Saranga), Hamir (Hameer), Daniel (Kalsen), Gopinath.

Original length: 9632 feet,

length of print: 8672 feet. 35 mm. Hindi, Urdu, Gujarati and English titles.

The phenomenal success of Douglas Fairbanks' *The Thief of Baghdad* in 1925 launched the vogue for the stunt film genre that featured acrobatic heroes who took up the cause of downtrodden people against wicked royal usurpers. Another source of these stories was provided by the heroic Rajput tales of valour of western India, but the direct inspiration of the genre was certainly Hollywood.

Kalsen is the libertine and tyrannical king who poisons his brother and rules over 'the kingdom of horror'. A loyal courtier Satyapal saves the prince but the child is lost. Years later he reappears as Hameer a circus acrobat, in the company of Saranga his ladylove, and her brother, Balbheem. The trio falls foul of the authorities. Saranga is abducted by Kalsen who offers to make her his queen. Tempted by visions of luxury, Saranga almost succumbs when Hameer arrives and is disillusioned by what he sees. But encouraged by Balbheem he vows to avenge himself

▲ Daniel in **Diler Jigar** aka **Gallant Hearts**

and is thereafter secretly helped by Saranga who appears as a masked avenger. The happy ending is inevitable.

Hitherto considered to be a minor film with some good camerawork, a revaluation has long been overdue. With its remarkable opening shots of the benevolent king's hand distributing charity among his people, the extensive and eloquent use of dissolves and fades and the energetic staging of swordfights along huge staircases, ornate corridors and outdoor locations, the film exhibits exceptional élan. As the leering and debauched Kalsen, Daniel gives one of the great portrayals of a villain in Indian cinema. One almost enjoys watching him going about his unmitigated path of evil and self-destruction. The gamine Amboo retired from films after an accident. She returned in the era of the talkies as the legendary Lalita Pawar and went on to become the arch villainess and scheming mother-in-law of countless sagas in the next four decades.

GULAMI NU PATAN

aka Fall of Slavery

(Agarwal Film Co., 1931)

Directed, produced, scripted and photographed by Shyam Sundar Agarwal. Cast: Daniel (Umedhsingh), Vatsala (Kamalbala). Original length: 10627 feet, length of print: 9545 feet. 35 mm. Hindi, Urdu, Gujarati and English titles.

This costume and stunt adventure film is about the *gola* form of slavery prevailing in feudal Marwar (in Rajasthan) and a good king's crusade against it with the help of the oppressed peasantry. Besides imposing ruinous taxation, the unquestioned assumption of the system was that the royals have complete rights over the womenfolk—a privilege exercised with nauseating frequency by the villainous king and his son.

Gulami Nu Patan lacks the verve, expert framing and coherent script and direction of *Diler Jigar*, its companion film made by Agarwal Film Co. in the same year. Even Daniel–memorable as Kalsen in the earlier film–is here reduced to a mere caricature.

▼ Gulami Nu Patan

But the sequence in the early part of the film depicting poor peasants chained to a plough and whipped and prodded with spears stands apart from the rest. Even though the film as a whole is repetitious and undistinguished, these images are exceptionally powerful and imbued with a pathos and raw realism not found in the other surviving silents. Sadly, Shyam Sundar Agarwal and his company faded out from the Indian cinema immediately thereafter.

JAMAI BABU

(Hira Film Co., 1931)

Directed and scripted by Kalipada Das. Photographed and edited by D.R. Barodkar. Cast: Kalipada Das (Gobardhan), Parvat Coomar (Amal), Shibapada Bhowmik (Upen Babu), Amulya Bandyo (Doctor), Rajen Borooah (Amal's friend), Radha Rani (Niva), Sadhana Devi (Chaya). Original length: 3000 feet, length of print: 2110 feet. 35 mm. Hindi, Bengali and English titles.

Many more short films than before were made in the late silent era as supporting programmes for the full-length feature attractions. However,

▼ A comic scene from **Jamai Babu**–
the only surviving Bengali silent film

the main contributors to this trend were small production companies which made films very quickly and with an erratic technique. The archive has three such films—all comedies.

The only surviving Bengali silent film, *Jamai Babu* is about a country bumpkin Gobardhan (Das) who comes to visit his wife and in-laws in Calcutta. Hilariously he mistakes a 'No Nuisance' sign for an address and is lost in the teeming streets of Calcutta. Reunited with his friend Amal, the two visit the famous sights of Calcutta including the Howrah Bridge, the Victoria Memorial and the Maidan. In the somewhat salacious second half Gobardhan feigns illness to prolong his stay in Calcutta and be close to his wife. When he tries to sneak into her room in the dark of night he is mistaken for a thief and beaten up—unexpected treatment for the esteemed son-in-law in his wife's maternal home! Das' conception of comic acting is limited to stumbling and falling in different ways, but the film does have flashes of genuine wit. The best part of the film is the way Calcutta is woven into the action, reminding one of the urban landscapes of distant California in early American slapstick.

KALIYA MARDAN

(Hindustan Cinema Film Co., 1919)

Directed, photographed and scripted by D.G. Phalke. Cast: Mandakini Phalke (Krishna), Anna Salunke (Yashoda), Neelkanth, Sahadevrao Tapkire, Baburao Patil. Original length: 6000 feet, length of print: 4441 feet. 35 mm. Hindi and English titles.

Kaliya Mardan is a celebration of the *lila* or divine play of the child Krishna. It begins with a marvellous prologue in which the child actress enacting Krishna (Phalke's daughter Mandakini who had earlier essayed this role in *Shri Krishna Janma*) is shown in her everyday clothes before she is dissolved into the character she is playing. After an inter-title–'Study in facial expressions by a little girl of seven'–she enacts a few of the nine

▼ **Kaliya Mardan**

rasas or aesthetic sentiments of the Indian classical arts—humour, anger, wonder etc.

The narrative of Krishna's childhood then unfolds through a juxtaposition of static tableaux with complex sequences of parallel cutting from one location or group of characters to another. Towards the end of the film, the great underwater sequence shows Krishna quelling the serpent-king Kaliya. This is followed by the ritual of *aarti* in a *tableau vivant* which reproduces the high point in Hindu temple ritual. According to the veteran exhibitor and film historian B.V. Dharap, this was the signal for audiences to break into spontaneous *kirtan* (singing of devotional songs) and shouting nationalist slogans. Kaliya thus symbolised to them not only the traditional concept of *adharma* or evil in Hindu mythology but colonial rule as well.

With its characteristic blending of the real and the imaginary and the use of Western film techniques with a distinct Indian ethos, *Kaliya Mardan* is the first definitive masterpiece of Indian cinema.

KAYA PALAT

(Shree Vithal Films, 1929)

Directed by Vithaldas Panchotia. Cast: Vithaldas Panchotia. Original length: 992 feet, length of print: 619 feet. 35 mm. Hindi, Gujarati, Urdu and English titles.

Continuing *Jamai Babu's* association of the city with sexual exploits and licence, this one-reel comedy is about 'a gentleman recently turned a loafer' or a would-be Lothario at large. On the look-out for a female companion in a park, he is involved in various clumsily executed gags. In one of them a dog rips out the seat of his new trousers. But ever resourceful, he gets the patch painted by a man who is nonchalantly painting a nearby fence. Pursuing the damsel he fancies, he manages to kidnap the wrong woman who is also dressed in a black veil. The shotgun marriage ends mortifyingly for the hero—he has married an ugly hag.

Starting as a theatre actor and film storywriter in the silent era, Panchotia had a long career as a director in the sound period.

KHEDDA OPERATIONS IN MYSORE

(Government of India, Railway Department, Central Publicity Bureau, year unknown)
Length: 621 feet. 35 mm. English titles.

Aside from the fact that it is produced by the Indian Railways, nothing is known about this beautiful little film or its director. It simply and directly shows *khedda* or the capture of wild elephants in one of the great forests of southern India. But he must have been an experienced and sensitive filmmaker for he trusts the images to speak for themselves. The grandeur of the *khedda* operations and the pathos of the capture of the majestic wild animals are observed in a discreet and symPathétic manner. Probably made in the early 1930s, the influence of British documentary can be strongly felt in this film.

LANKA DAHAN

aka Lanka Aflame

(Phalke's Films, 1917)
Produced, directed, photographed and scripted by D.G. Phalke. Cast: Anna Salunke (Sita and Rama), Ganpat Shinde (Hanuman), D.D. Dabke (Ravana). Original length: 3000 feet, length of fragment: 484 feet. 35 mm. Hindi and English titles.

A lively re-telling of an episode from the great epic *Ramayana, Lanka Dahan* is about the gentle Sita's abduction and incarceration by the arrogant demon-king Ravana, and the ultimate triumph of her husband Rama (the God Vishnu in one of his *avatars*) with the help of an army of men and monkeys.

In the extant fragment Hanuman, the monkey god, arrives in Lanka to witness Sita being tormented by Ravana and his demonic female attendants. Finding her to be a virtuous and loyal wife he delivers Rama's

► **Lanka Dahan**

► Facing page:
Marthanda Varma

ring to her—a token of his vow to rescue her. At this point, for a fleeting instant she envisions Rama in front of her. In an extraordinary piece of casting, Rama is also played by Anna Salunke which makes this the first instance of a double role in Indian cinema.

In contrast to the more static tableau-dominated *Raja Harishchandra*, Phalke varies his camera set-ups, adroitly cuts between the different spaces in Ravana's garden and elicits theatrically inspired but more convincing performances from the actors.

The film was a huge success and is often referred to as India's first big box-office hit. Phalke could now command additional finance and facilities to make more ambitious films under his new production company and studio, Hindustan Cinema Film Co.

MARTHANDA VARMA

(Shri Rajeshwari Films, 1931)

Directed and scripted by P.V. Rao. Produced by R. Sunder Raj. Based on the novel by C.V. Raman Pillai. Cast: Jaidev (Marthanda Varma), A.V.P. Menon

(Anantha Padmanabhan), V. Naick (Padmanabhan Thampi), V.C. Kutty (Velu Kurup), S.V. Nath (Sundaram Aiyer), Miss Devaki (Subhadra), Miss Padmini (Parukutty). Original length: 11905 feet, length of print: 7915. 35 mm. Malayalam and English titles.

Based on the novel by the celebrated Malayalam writer C.V. Raman Pillai, the film recounts the life of Marthanda Varma (1706-1758), the legendary founder of Travancore state. While an important sub-plot deals with a love story set in the royal court, the focus is on the conspiracies against the crown prince and how he defeats his enemies to become the unquestioned ruler.

Marthanda Varma begins with rare newsreel footage of the grand *aarathu* procession of the Travancore Maharaja Sri Chitra Tirunal with caparisoned elephants, cavalry and the famous Nair brigade. The Maharaja himself–a direct descendent of Marthanda Varma–is carried in a decorated palanquin to receive the greetings of his people. With only some portions missing, *Marthanda Varma* is the lone survivor of the relatively small but significant south Indian film industry. However, the film was never released because

the producer R. Sunder Raj had not acquired the rights to film the novel—an oversight which, according to one account, was to cause his subsequent bankruptcy. And had it been submitted for censorship, some of the titles with their indirect reference to the national movement would probably have led to difficulties as well. For instance, 'Enough of this age-long tyranny. Ye! Freedom-loving sons of the soil! Gird up your loins and fight for your birthright. Rise up from your slumber. Awake, arise and stop not, till the goal is reached.'

To add to the film's somewhat unhappy history, the picture quality of the print preserved by the NFAI is very poor due to emulsion damage in the only surviving nitrate copy found in the godowns of a publishing house in Trivandrum.

This is a great pity because the title card designs are excellent and among the better preserved sequences is a beautiful romantic scene set in a tiered garden with an artificial waterfall. Only the newsreel prologue, the scenes introducing Marthanda Varma's character and this sequence were screened at Pordenone in 1994.

PITHACHE PANJE

aka Hand Prints
or KHOD MODALI
aka Habit Crushed

(Phalke's Films, year unknown)

Length of fragment: 149 feet. 35mm. Titles missing.

This one-minute fragment of a 'social' or a film with a modern setting attributed to Phalke's Films was shown at Pordenone with the director, length and year of production given as unknown. However, in his updated filmography in this book, the film historian V. Dharamsey has established beyond doubt that *Pithache Panje* was a 500 ft. comedy sketch made by Phalke in 1913. Moreover, he has also found that Phalke later directed a feature-length film based on the same subject called *Khod Modali* for Hindustan Cinema Film Co. in 1925.

◀ **Pithache Panje**

At present, there is no clear-cut way of determining to which version this fragment belongs. However, with very few exceptions most of the earlier Phalke films featured only men in female roles while all the female characters in this fragment appear to be played by women. Therefore, it is here suggested that this fragment is more likely to be from the later film, viz., *Khod Modali* made in 1925. One may also add that the social genre was firmly established only in the mid-1920s, and this, along with the more subtle atmospheric lighting in a few shots, further suggests that it was probably made at the later date.

PITRU PREM

aka A Father's Love

(Mahavir Photoplays, 1929)

Directed and scripted by Harilal M. Bhatt. Cast: Miss Mani (Annapurna), Gaby Hill (Nurjahan), Maganlal Dave (Madhumal), Yusuf (Shashibhushan), Y.L. Chinchunkar (Madhava), S.P. Niphadkar (Rokadchand), Master Madanlal (Kishor). Original length: 9868 feet, length of fragment: 1262 feet. 35 mm. Hindi, Urdu, Gujarati and English titles.

Only the first reel of this social melodrama has survived, but because of its formal consistency it seems to be a typical example of the genre in its maturity.

After a solemn and lengthy text about filial sons and bad ones who 'convert the bliss of the domestic hearth into the torments of Hell' the main characters are introduced—Madhumal, the benevolent patriarch and city father, Mahamaya, his dutiful wife, Shashibhushan, his beloved son, Annapurna, the loving daughter-in-law and Madhava, the adopted son. Madhumal is distributing money to a crowd of people–presumably his tenants–outside his palatial mansion. When a child is hurt in the crush, Madhumal compassionately lifts him and takes him inside. The first villain Rokadchand, 'A Marwari Shylock', arrives and upbraids Madhumal for helping a child who may not be of his own faith. Madhumal declares his secular ideals by sending cheques of an equal amount to the Benares Hindu and Aligarh Muslim universities and Rokadchand predicts that dire consequences will result from such unorthodox sentiments.

The next day Shashibhushan is visited by Gadbaddas who is introduced as a 'villain who is a teacher of music'. His erotic interpretation of a 'delicate' couplet is objected to by Annapurna who accuses him of planting impure thoughts in the future master's mind. Stinging from the insult Gadbaddas goes to Nurjahan, a dancing girl, and her wily father Karim Khan. He promises to deliver a 'wealthy fool' i.e. Shashibhushan to their clutches. The reel ends here, but there is no doubt about the direction the story will take. For in a very short time, the ground has been prepared for the weak son to be eventually redeemed by his righteous father's example and Annapurna's virtue.

With the notable exception of the films directed by the German Franz Osten, the chief stylistic trait of the other extant Indian silent films is a predominantly frontal style. In *Pitru Prem* it is revealed with a rigour which approaches the level of a fully self-conscious style. As Ashish Rajadhyaksha has argued, the Indian cinema inherited frontality and privileging of a 'public domain' from traditional painting and the company theatre forms which preceded it. Conforming to popular story telling methods, each character is introduced with a title card stating their essential qualities which discloses their function and role in the unfolding of the narrative.

Harilal M. Bhatt made a few more films in the silent era and thereafter returned to work in the theatre. There is an interesting footnote accounting for the survival of this reel. It was donated to the archive by Madan Kothari, a prominent film distributor, who had preserved the reel because he appeared in it as a child artist. How one wishes his sentimental link with the film had helped to preserve the rest of the film as well!

PRAPANCHA PASHA

aka A Throw of Dice aka Schicksalswürfel

(British Instructional Films Ltd., London/ UFA, Germany/ Himansu Rai Film, 1929)

Directed by Franz Osten. Scripted by W. Burton, based on a story by Niranjan Pal. Photographed by Emil Schünemann. Cast: Himansu Rai (Sohat), Charu Roy (Ranjit), Seeta Devi (Sunita), Sarada Gupta, Lala Bijoykishen, Tincowri Chakroborty, Modhu Bose. Original length: 7630 feet, length of print: 6694 feet. 35 mm. English titles.

Borrowing from the basic premise of the pivotal gambling episode in the *Mahabharata, Prapancha Pasha* is about two neighbouring kings addicted to gambling. King Sohat's plot to kill King Ranjit with a poisoned arrow is foiled when a hermit restores him to health. Ranjit falls in love with the hermit's daughter Sunita, but Sohat has him framed for the murder of her father. Ranjit is able to establish his innocence when the real murderer confesses his guilt on his deathbed. Before Ranjit's marriage to Sunita, Sohat challenges him to a game of dice. Ranjit loses everything but the secret of the trick dice used by Sohat is accidentally revealed and his army liberates their king. In the final shot Ranjit and Sunita embrace and kiss on a mountaintop against a splendid sunset.

▼ Seeta Devi, one of the most bewitching female stars of the time in the film **Prapancha Pasha** aka **A Throw of Dice** aka **Schicksalswürfel**

As captivating as any orientalist fantasy made in Germany, *Prapancha Pasha* was the most lavish of the three Himansu Rai-Franz Osten co-productions. Again several Maharajas freely gave their palaces, gardens and armies for this extravaganza. Incidentally, V. Dharamsey has suggested that the Seeta Devi roles in the three films are played by two different actresses—the sisters Reneé and Percy Smith. Be that as it may, the actress who appears in each of the films is worthy of being ranked among the most bewitching female stars of that period.

Later Satyajit Ray was to recall the film with the following remarks: 'How wonderful to be able to see today, fifty years after it was made, a print of *A Throw of Dice* that looks as if it was shot yesterday on the finest grained panchromatic stock! That the story is a cross between *A Thousand and One Nights* and *The Mahabharata* is beside the point. What is important is that the people involved in its making, Indian and Germans, realised the need for preservation, which makes it possible for us to see it now in its historical perspective.'

PREM SANYAS

aka The Light of Asia aka Die Leuchte Asiens

(Great Eastern Film Corporation, Delhi / Emelka Film Co., Munich, 1925) Directed by Franz Osten. Scripted by Niranjan Pal, based on Edwin Arnold's 'The Light of Asia'. Photographed by Josef Wirsching and Willi Kiermeier. Cast: Himansu Rai (Gautama), Seeta Devi (Gopa), Sarada Ukil (Suddhodhana), Rani Bala (Maya), Prafulla Roy (Devadatta). Original length: 9437 feet, length of print: 6959 feet. 35 mm. English titles.

Niranjan Pal's script is adapted from Edwin Arnold's famous long poem on the Buddha, 'The Light of Asia', and was the first of three Indo-German co-

▲ Himansu Rai in **Prem Sanyas**

productions set up by the lead actor Himansu Rai and directed by Franz Osten. Rai later founded the Bombay Talkies in 1934 where he invited Osten to be his leading director until the outbreak of World War II forced Osten to return to Germany.

The film opens with documentary style shots of some foreign tourists in Bombay, Delhi and Benares. When they reach the sacred Bodhi Temple complex in Gaya, a holy man tells them the story of Prince Gautama, who renounced his patrimony to become Lord Buddha, The Enlightened One.

The miracles and prophesies that attended his birth to King Suddhodhana and Queen Maya; the King's attempt to check Gautama's mystical inclinations by banishing all signs of old age, sickness and death from the streets of his kingdom; his marriage to the Princess Gopa; Gautama's discovery of the world of ceaseless suffering beyond the palace walls; his renunciation and enlightenment under the Bodhi tree; Gopa becoming one of his first disciples—all these episodes are narrated as the Western tourists might imagine them, and not as the Indian storyteller would. Osten's claim that he had made the first completely Indian film is throughout undercut by the all-pervasive orientalism and exoticising of India and Indians. Nevertheless, *Prem Sanyas* has an extremely appealing clarity and poise in its narration and the tone is always consistent and aptly solemn.

Significantly, the film was a success in Europe but received a lukewarm response in India. Even a contemporary German reviewer was troubled by the film's failure to deal with the spiritual theme and states—

'Pictures of indescribable beauty and splendour, magnificent processions and folk festivals are projected on the screen—a tale from *A Thousand and One Nights*. Confronted with this tropical splendour, the yearning for nirvana, the merging of the self into the One seems almost unbelievable to us Europeans'.

RAJA HARISHCHANDRA

(Phalke's Films, 1917)

Produced, directed, photographed and scripted by D.G. Phalke. Cast: D.D. Dabke (Harishchandra), Anna Salunke (Taramati), Bhalchandra Phalke (Rohidas), Gajanan Sane, Ganpat Shinde. Original length: 2944 feet, length of fragment: 1475 feet. 35 mm. Hindi and English titles.

Preceded by two lost efforts at making a narrative film in India, the first or 1913 version of Phalke's *Raja Harishchandra* is commonly reckoned as India's first true, indigenous feature film. It was made in an improvised studio in Bombay by Phalke's Films, a production company consisting mainly of Phalke's family and friends. Phalke produced, directed, scripted, designed the sets and costumes, supervised the camerawork and processing, and

▼The famous bathing scene from **Raja Harishchandra**, with female impersonators

created the special effects. The film was released at Bombay's Coronation Cinematograph on 3 May 1913 and thus launched India's film industry which, within a few decades, was to become one of the most profitable, influential and popular in the world.

However, since the Pordenone retrospective where NFAI's print of *Raja Harishchandra* was shown as made in 1913–as it had always been in India–new facts have come to light. V. Dharamsey has found conclusive evidence in contemporary sources to prove that the print actually consists of the first and last reels from Phalke's 1917 remake produced after he moved to Nasik. The main proof is that while in the 1913 version an actor called Pandurang Sane played the role of Queen Taramati, this role is played by a different and far better known actor, Anna Salunke, in the extant film. In fact, Salunke again appears prominently in two more Phalke films—*Lanka Dahan* and *Kaliya Mardan.*

Dharamsey was already convinced about this important, even momentous, finding in 1994, but it could not be included in the first edition as the book had already gone to press. I also exercised caution since more time was required to examine the evidence. Besides this, there was undoubtedly reluctance on my part–as also among several other historians and colleagues familiar with the film–to immediately accept the new dating. For to do so meant that the treasured reels one had long believed to be from the very first Indian film ever made, were, in fact, from the second version made four years later.

To return to the film itself, *Raja Harishchandra* is based on one of the most popular *Mahabharata* legends and unfolds in a series of tableaux that are typical of Phalke's style. It narrates the exemplary story of King Harishchandra's devotion to truth and duty for which he is prepared to sacrifice everything. For enthusiasts of Indian silent cinema, each surviving sequence carries tremendous nostalgia and significance, even though we now know that it was made in 1917. Among these are the opening royal hunt; Sage Vishwamitra's fire sacrifice which King Harishchandra accidentally profanes and is consequently sent into exile; his breaking of the news of their banishment from the kingdom to his queen, Taramati; their tearful departure from the palace; the tribulations and sufferings of Taramati and their son Rohidas in exile; the climax in the cremation ground where Shiva, the great God of Destruction, appears to prevent Taramati's execution; and finally the family's return to the palace which movingly brings the morality play to a happy conclusion. Each of these episodes is vividly etched in our collective imagination.

Phalke apparently made the second version to replace worn out prints and is said to have copied the original very closely. Thus what a contemporary review of the 1913 film states probably applies to the 1917 version as well—'...the result of his (Phalke's) efforts exceeds one's expectation ... Dramatically the film is admirable ... one can freely praise the beauty and ingenuity with which he has succeeded in presenting effectively the most difficult scenes ...' The latter remark obviously refers to the special effects which were to become Phalke's forté and a distinctive feature of the mythological genre he pioneered.

Besides the two versions made by Phalke, Madan's Elphinstone Bioscope Co. also released its own version *Satyawadi Raja Harishchandra* in 1917, which is the first feature film produced in Calcutta. Among the several subsequent renderings of the story is Prabhat Film Co.'s *Ayodhyacha Raja* (1932) too, directed by V. Shantaram which is the earliest surviving Indian sound film.

SHIRAZ

aka Das Grambal Einer Groszen Liebe

(British Instructional Films Ltd., London/ UFA, Germany/ Himansu Rai Film, 1928)

Directed by Franz Osten. Scripted by W. Burton, based on a story by Niranjan Pal. Photographed by Emil Schünemann, H. Harris. Cast: Himansu Rai (Shiraz), Charu Roy (Prince Khurram), Seeta Devi (Dalia), Enakshi Rama Rao (Selima), Maya Devi, Profulla Roy, Esther Ricks. Original length: 9525 feet, length of print: 7778 feet 35 mm. English titles.

◄ **Shiraz** aka **Das Grambal Einer Groszen Liebe**–depiction of the exotic orient

Osten, Rai and Pal tackle another great Indian story–the building of the Taj Mahal–and the result is a truly beautiful work of filmic atmosphere and emotion. Hassan, a potter living in the Persian desert finds Selima, a princess, and raises her along with his son, Shiraz. Under his benign gaze they mature into young sweethearts.

But Selima is abducted by slave traders and sold to the Mughal prince Khurram who falls in love with her. This upsets the wily court lady Dalia's plans of becoming empress and she arranges a secret meeting between the lovelorn Shiraz and Selima. The two are seen by Khurram, who condemns Shiraz to be trampled by an elephant.

Selima successfully pleads for mercy, and Shiraz reveals the pendant which signifies her royal descent. Selima and Khurram marry, leaving Shiraz to keep a ceaseless vigil outside the palace gate. Selima is given the title Mumtaz Mahal when Khurram succeeds to the throne as Emperor Shahjahan.

When the empress dies eighteen years later, Shahjahan orders that a monument is built in her memory such as the world has never seen. The design chosen by the emperor is that of Shiraz who is now blind but has rendered his 'memories into stone.' The film ends in the gardens of the Taj Mahal with the bereaved emperor and the blind architect consoled by the fact that the monument has immortalised the woman they both loved.

Shiraz is perhaps even more orientalist and exotic than *Prem Sanyas* and *Prapancha Pasha* and fully exploits the Mughal-style architecture and costumes in lustrous images that evoke the grandeur of the Great Mughals. This theme has been repeatedly filmed in both the silent and talkie eras, but rarely with such aplomb. The German reviewers were once again enthusiastic, but in India its thunder was stolen by quickly-made rival productions based on similar stories–Charu Roy's *Loves of a Mughal Prince* and R.C. Choudhary's *Anarkali*–both made in 1928.

▲ A trick shot from **Shri Krishna Janma**

SHRI KRISHNA JANMA

aka The Birth of Shri Krishna

(Hindustan Cinema Film Co., 1918)

Directed, photographed and scripted by D.G. Phalke. Cast: Mandakini Phalke (Krishna), D.D. Dabke (Kansa), Purshottam Vaidya, Bhagirathibai, Neelkanth, Gajanan Sane. Original length: 5500 feet, length of fragment: 534 feet. 35mm. Hindi and English titles.

Shri Krishna Janma begins with a series of religious images which are perhaps the most invocatory in all Hindu mythology—the people beseeching the gods for succour and deliverance from the tyranny of demons. Vishnu rises from the cosmic ocean on the many-hooded serpent god Shesha and pledges that he will restore the balance of creation by being born as Krishna.

The framing of the human figures at foreground bottom of the frame identifies them with the spectator. Early cinema's privileging of a 'single view point and its posture of displaying something to the audience' that Gunning and Gaudreault have discussed is here confirmed in the case of India's early films as well. Phalke then cuts 180 degrees across the axis to the supplicants—an editing pattern which he repeated with memorable effect in the climax of *Kaliya Mardan*.

Unfortunately, only fragments from the original length of 5500 ft. have survived, but these include special effects of amazing virtuosity and sophistication which can be compared with the best of Méliès. The most famous of these is of the demon-king Kamsa's hallucination. Destined to be destroyed by the child Krishna, in a vision he sees his severed head floating in a geyser of blood. It is part of Indian film lore that the blood in this trick shot was hand-tinted in red.

THE SHORTEST AND BEST ROUTE TO SOUTH INDIA

(Government of India, Railway Department, Central Publicity Bureau, year unknown)

Length: 647 feet. 35 mm. English titles.

A travelogue-cum-tourism promotion film, it lacks the subtlety and perceptive quality of *Khedda Operations in Mysore* which was commissioned by the same producers. Scripted very much like a slide show with moving pictures, the film gives an account of the train journey from Mysore to Ootacamund. On the way it takes in picturesque views of the Nilgiri hills in which the premier hill resort of southern India nestles.

SINHASTHA PARVANI

aka Sinhastha Mela

(Production company unknown, 1920-21)

Directed by D.G. Phalke. Original length: unknown, length of fragment: 381 feet. 35 mm. Titles missing.

▲ **Sinhastha Parvani** aka **Sinhastha Mela**

Fragments of actuality coverage of the great Hindu festival of the Kumbh Mela which was held in Nasik from July 1920 to August 1921. The religious significance is as follows:

In mythological times *suras* and *asuras* (gods and demons) churned the cosmic ocean for obtaining various boons that were in it. One of the boons was *amrit* (nectar), the drink of immortality. But the *suras* did not want the *asuras* to drink it and become immortal. Thus Jayant, son of Indra, the King of the Gods, took the urn containing the *amrit* to heaven. On his way he rested the urn at four places—Allahabad, Haridwar, Ujjain and Nasik. Hence during the Kumbh Mela–held during the period of Jupiter's intersection with particular signs of the zodiac–bathing at the rivers in these places is considered auspicious. At Nasik the Kumbh Mela is held when Jupiter is in the sign of Leo and the sun and moon are in the sign of Cancer.

Phalke was born at Trymbak near Nasik and it is not surprising that the Kumbh Mela received his attention. However, the footage that has survived appears to be either unedited or a rough cut.

SUKANYA SAVITRI

(Kohinoor Film Co., 1922)

Directed by Kanjibhai Rathod. Scripted by Mohanlal G. Dave. Photographed by Gajanan S. Devare. Cast: Moti (Savitri), Gangaram, Sakina. Original length: 6989 feet, length of fragment: 2313 feet. 35 mm. Hindi, Gujarati and English titles.

The only surviving film produced by the major Bombay-based studio Kohinoor Film Co. and made by one of the most important Indian silent film directors, Kanjibhai Rathod , *Sukanya Savitri* is a daring interweaving of the twin myths of Sati Sukanya and Sati Savitri who are upheld in Indian tradition as paragons of the *pativrata*—the chaste and dutiful wife and a symbol of ideal womanhood.

▼ **Sukanya Savitri**—a rediscovered masterpiece

The film begins with Sukanya's story. In the existing fragments we see the following episodes: Sukanya inadvertently blinding the old sage Chyavana who is covered by an enormous ant hill which has grown around him during his deep meditation; in atonement her father, King Sharyathi weds her to the infirm sage whom she serves faithfully; a handsome Ashwini Kumar or a demi-god is attracted by her beauty and youth but she spurns him; when he follows her to their hut her angry gaze reduces him to ashes. The episode about how she succeeds in restoring her husband Chyavana to his youth is missing.

The Savitri story has survived with the most important episodes intact: Savitri's marriage to the exiled Satyavan; her devotedly caring for him and his blind parents; Satyavan's death by snake bite in the forest; her appeasement of Yama, the God of Death, who gives her the three boons of restoring her parents-in-law's eyesight, their recall to the royal court and Satyavan's return to life.

The final sequences combine the two stories as a youthful Chyavana and Sukanya arrive at Satyavan's parents' hut and the dethroned King Dyumatsena (Satyavan's father) is called back to the court by his people and Satyavan is crowned king by Chyavana. The sage Narada arrives to bless everyone, especially the dutiful Sukanya and Savitri whose devotion and humility has brought happiness to all.

It is perhaps inevitable to compare *Sukanya Savitri* with the surviving Phalke mythologicals. Rathod's film holds its own on most counts and in some ways is even more remarkable. Even though almost all the inter-titles are missing, the narration is crisper and more fluent. The riverside and other outdoor locales are shot with more dynamic compositions, and there is a sophisticated awareness of the spatial logic of the scenes. And the bold interweaving of the two stories takes one's breath away. There is an amazing moment in the early part of the Sukanya story when in a vision she first sees a young Ashwini Kumar (symbolising carnal temptation) emerge from her old husband's sleeping body and then Savitri (from the twin story yet to unfold!) who exhorts her to remain chaste.

But above all, there is the wonderful long dialogue between Savitri and Yama suspended somewhere in the 'lightless zone' straddling heaven and earth with Satyavan's flame-like soul hovering between them. This is intercut with the developments on earth as each of Savitri's arguments bears a new reward for her family.

If one adds to all this the fact that *Sukanya Savitri* is almost certainly the first instance in Indian cinema when two stories are told in a single film, it has to be recognised that the film must now be ranked among its truly great, rediscovered masterpieces.

TUKARAM

(Hindustan Cinema Film Co., 1921)

Directed by Ganpat Shinde. Original length: 6000 feet, length of fragment: 482 feet. 35 mm. Marathi and English titles.

▼ **Tukaram**—the devotional film genre

Previously attributed to Phalke, we now know that *Tukaram* was in fact directed by Ganpat Shinde, another member of the Hindustan Cinema Film Co. team. It extolls the life of Sant Tukaram, one of medieval India's greatest and much-loved saint-poets who advocated social equality and the philosophy of *bhakti* or complete devotion to God.

Set against the gaunt landscape of rural Maharashtra, the ecstatic dancing and chanting of the *warkaris* (devotees of Lord Vithoba of Pandharpur) and the heartfelt and simple charm of Tukaram's ascension to heaven have a touching naiveté and fervour that are typical of the devotional or saint film genre. The inter-titles contain some original Marathi verses of Sant Tukaram with English translations.

The extant fragment is from the ending of the film and bears an amazing resemblance to the great Prabhat classic *Sant Tukaram* (1936).

VANTOLIO

aka Whirlwind

(Wadia Brothers, 1933)

Directed by J.B.H. Wadia. Photographed by Homi Wadia. Cast: Boman Shroff, Padma, Allawali, Adi Patel, Sayani. Original length: 9876 feet, trailer length: 418 feet. 35 mm. Hindi, Gujarati and English titles.

Only the trailer of this film has survived. It was made by J.B.H. Wadia and his younger brother Homi Wadia whose stunt films of the late 1920s and 1930s were immensely popular. J.B.H. Wadia, who went on to become one of the great leaders of the film industry, writes in his memoirs about *Vantolio's* 'daredevil' star Boman Shroff, 'I had not come across a more daring stunt puller ... in my experience of 45 years ...'

The most extraordinary clip shows a death-defying fistfight on the roof of a speeding train. The Wadias were great admirers of American action films and serials, and over the next decade made their magnum opus entitled *Diamond Thriller Series.*

These films featuring the gutsy, blond Fearless Nadia (nee Mary Evans) went against the prevalent docile heroine stereotype and also contained indirect nationalistic messages.

▲ Poster for Maharashtra Film Co.'s **Kalyan Khajina** (1924)

▼ Hand painted (oil on canvas) poster for Agarwal Film Co.'s **Diler Jigar** aka **Gallant Hearts** (1931)

▼ Publicity booklet for Young India Pictures' **Rajput Swar** aka **Rajput Cavalier** (1929)

▲ Publicity booklet for Aryan Film Co.'s **Parijatak** aka **The Flowers of Heaven** (1929)

▲ Poster for Maharashtra Film Co.'s **Sati Savitri** (1927)

► Right: Publicity booklet for Saroj Film Co.'s **Dariai Devangana** aka **Sea Goddess** (1931)

Extreme right below: Publicity booklet for Saroj Film Co.'s **Lal Panjo** aka **Fighting Blood** (1931)

Extreme right above: Publicity booklet for United Pictures Syndicate's **Khooni Taj** aka **Raktacha Rajmukut** aka **All For the Crown** (1930)

▼ Publicity booklet for **Punya Prabhav** (1929)

'रक्ताचा राजमुकुट'
"All for The Crown"
produced by UNITED PICTURES SYNDICATE, KIRKEE.

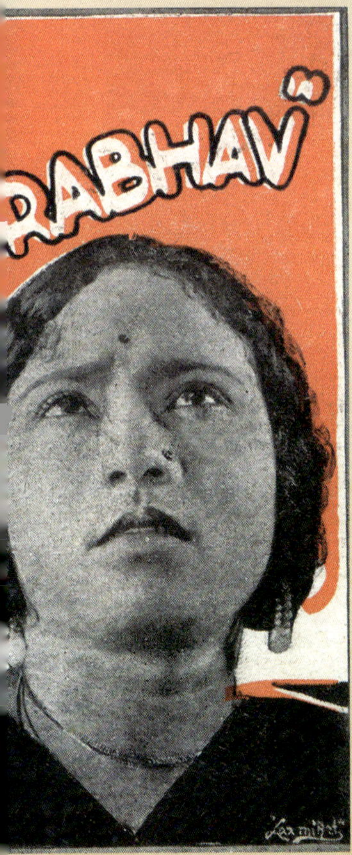
RABHAV"

SAROJ PRESENTS
CHANDRARAO,
ZEBOONISA
WITH
PRABHASHANKER &
ATTAMOHMAD
in
FIGHTING
BLOOD
Directed
By
DHIRUBHAI
B
DESAI
લાલ પંજો

▲ Publicity booklet for Paramount Film Co.'s
Mallaraj aka **The Tiger Of Rajputana** (1932)

▲ Publicity booklet for Maharashtra Film Co.'s **Nisha Sundari** aka **The Midnight Girl** (1929)

▼ Publicity booklet for Aryan Film Co.'s **Maharathi Karna** aka **Karna, The True Battler** (1928)

◀ German pubilicity booklet for Great Eastern Film Corporation and Emelka Film Co.'s **Prem Sanyas** aka **The Light of Asia** aka **Die Leuchte Aslens** (1925)

▼ Publicity booklet for Asian Film Co.'s **Radha Krishna** (1930)

▲ Publicity booklet for Aryan Film Co.'s **Patitodhar** aka **Reclamation** (1928)

▲ Publicity booklet for Imperial Film Co.'s **Vasant Bengali** aka **Bengali Bomb** (1930)

▲ Publicity booklet for Suvama Pictures'
Kusum Lata aka **Lily Of The Valley** (1929)

▲ Page from Royal Film Co.'s publicity pamphlet promoting **Badmash Ka Beta** aka **Leather Face** (1933)

Above: Publicity booklet for Royal Film Co.'s **Burkhawala** aka **White Devil** (1932)

Above: Publicity booklet for Surya Film Co.'s **Radhe Shyam** (1930)

◀ Publicity booklet for Sharda Film Co.'s **Safed Swar** aka **White Rider** (1930)

THE COBRA'S HOARD

Suresh Chabria

I joined the NFAI in 1992, beginning a stint that was to last for six eventful years. Shaped by twin enthusiasms–one born of cinephilia and the other arising out of the attraction for the mystique of the cinema's silent and nitrate years,–I naturally gave more priority to India's silent film heritage and renewed the search for silent and nitrate-based early sound films. The former came under the spotlight initially at the Pordenone Silent Film Festival (1994), where the first-ever Indian silent film retrospective was presented. This was followed by the screening of several silent classics with live music accompaniment during the Cinema Centenary celebrations in India. But the latter objective–the renewed search for nitrate films–required more patience and luck. One was chiefly following leads provided by veteran film enthusiasts and cine-club organisers who had been helping the NFAI over the years. In most cases, the 'information' was collected from myth based on youthful memories and nostalgia; in many instances, the copies had simply decomposed.

Fortunately, there was one promising lead. A business family in Kolhapur named Vankudre was known to possess a large amount of nitrate material created by the famed artist and film pioneer Baburao Painter (1890-1954). Kolhapur is a town which is 230 kilometres from Pune, where many film pioneers of western India began their careers. One of the reasons for this was the remarkable patronage received from the then Raja of Kolhapur. Legend had it that not only did the Raja extend the services of his staff and his stables of elephants and horses for film shoots, but he would also grace the sets in person with his retinue, and even offer suggestions—which usually had to be carried out immediately. To this day, Kolhapur bears traces of the fading legacy of his benevolent rule.

As one drives through the winding lanes, the crumbling *wada*s or traditional mansions are pointed out as once having housed famous film ateliers or studios. And on a monumental pedestal at a shaded intersection close to Painter's house-cum-museum stands a camera, a replica of the one he fabricated with his disciple Vishnupant Govind Damle in 1918.

Baburao Painter produced and directed numerous mythological and historical films in the 1920s and 1930s. Various histories of Indian cinema praise Painter's multifaceted career as a scenic backdrop painter, a keen technical innovator, and as the prime mover of what is referred to as the Kolhapur school of filmmaking. He influenced another well-known pioneer, Bhalji Pendharkar, and all the founders of the Prabhat Film Company—one of the most important institutions of Indian film history. Particularly talked about to this day is his 1925 film *Savkari Pash* (aka *Indian Shylock*), which was said to be an innovative realist film that tackled contemporary social issues at a time when Indian film production mostly focused on mythology and was fantasy-oriented. However, all that was known to have survived of Painter's work as a filmmaker comprised a few stills from his silent films and copies of three of his sound films. Thus, the works on which his legend rested–the films produced in the 1920s for his Maharashtra Film Company–were considered lost, unless our promising Kolhapur lead translated to anything of value. My predecessor at the NFAI–P.K. Nair–had explored this possibility but for various reasons the negotiations had failed.

▲ A still from **Sati Savitri**

It was in the hope that some of these films might still be found that I got in touch with Pune-based film critic and memorabilia collector Shashikant Kinikar and Anant Vishnu Damle. The latter had been chiefly responsible for safeguarding the legacy of the Prabhat Film Company, which was co-founded by his father in Kolhapur in Painter's heyday, before the studios were moved to Pune in 1933. With their help, contact was once again established with the Vankudre family.

The Vankudres had the material for a very good reason. In the early 1930s their grandfather, Dhandiram Gopal Vankudre, a dealer of household utensils, had attempted to diversify the traditional family business by launching a film distribution company that was to be followed by setting up a film production firm. Even as sound films began to appear on Indian screens, he bought the distribution rights and existing prints of Painter's silent films for re-issue, and at the same time initiated steps to produce talkie films under his own banner, Samrat Cinetone.

It was during the monsoon that we set out, reasoning that the cool cloudy weather would be the most favourable for returning safely with the nitrate material. As it happened, we had received excellent rainfall that year and the roads and adjoining fields were flooded for miles. Eventually, after several detours we pulled up–spirits dampened with the rain and rising anxiety–at a shop front, a rather welcoming sight with its neatly stacked and gleaming stainless steel and copper buckets, pots, pans, ladles and tumblers. We had arrived, but not quite. The four Vankudre brothers, the third generation of the family, were cordial to Damle and me, offering us hot sweet tea and agreeing on a single point—that this material should be shifted immediately. Finally, they led us to the material itself, towards the back of the shop where under a dark wooden staircase sat a row of black painted tin trunks.

As we approached someone shouted, 'Wait!' and then, 'No, it has left!'. An old shop-hand cut in, 'I saw it returning to its hole this morning'. A sigh of relief went up, and the mystery was soon explained. A cobra had apparently taken up residence among the trunks, and could occasionally be seen slithering over them before returning to its hole beneath the staircase. On this particular day it had slid away. This much is fact. The myth follows.

Folk mythology has it that the cobra guards treasures, ready to strike any intruder, but gently accedes to the surrender of its precious hoard when the true claimant comes along, full of veneration and hope.

In this case it was, undoubtedly, the spirit of film archiving. All present were suitably impressed by our credentials, even, I presume, the magnanimous cobra, for it had long guarded the trunks, preventing the most recent brood of grandchildren from pulling out strips of nitrate film to burn as fire-sparklers. One of the Vankudre brothers nostalgically recalled that these trunks had once been a ready source of fireworks for their entertainment.

But how had D.G. Vankudre–producer and founder of Samrat Cinetone–allowed this to happen? What had happened to his enthusiasm for cinema that he later turned away from it completely? His belief in the commercial viability of the re-issued Painter silents seems to have been, shall we say, somewhat misplaced. Moreover, the failure of his very first talkie, a mythological called *Naganand*a (1935)–about the legendary foes, snakes and eagles–had sealed his distaste for motion pictures. Taken together, these misadventures had constituted a great financial loss for this small merchant-cum-businessman. One of his sons informed us that after this misfortune he gathered his entire family and made them vow that they would never again have anything to do with the movie business. So disappointed was the patriarch that the customary visits to the local cinema hall or the several studio and location shootings going on in Kolhapur were strictly forbidden. Films were a taboo for the Vankudres until the demise of the disillusioned head of the family.

After some negotiations about compensation and the mode of payment, we loaded the trunks into a van and had them carefully driven back to Pune through the flooded landscape.

Was Painter's *Savkari Pash* in that hoard? One will never know. Most of the reels had decomposed and a large number could not be identified. The footage that could be salvaged by painstaking frame-by-frame printing by K.P.R. Nair, the archive's restoration consultant, was badly damaged and scratched. However, more than 4000 feet of *Muralivala* (1927)–Painter's version of Phalke's *Kaliya Mardan* (1919)–could be saved, along with portions from two of his other silent films, *Maya Bazar* (1925) and *Sati Savitri* (1927).

As I began to study the salvaged reels, they revealed a distinct and different elaboration of the mythological genre as compared to the work of the more famous D.G. Phalke. Painter's mythological films were more anecdotal, and delved into the philosophical underpinnings of the stories, thus anticipating an important feature of this genre in the early sound period. As a bonus, good copies of both the Marathi and Hindi versions of *Naganand*a were found.

While the films awaited further restoration and presentation during the 1995-96 Cinema Centenary celebrations, one reel from *Muralivala* was screened at the NFAI theatre. In the auditorium was a special invitee–Lalji Gokhale–who had acted as a nine-year-old Shri Krishna in the film. In the reel he briefly appeared in his avatar as Krishna, hovering underwater and playing the flute. A senior music teacher and *tabla* player today, it was a moving experience for the invited audience to see the child and the man reunited after nearly seventy years. Against all odds, cinema had once again bestowed upon us the miracle of crossing the barriers of space and time, past and present.

NOTE

1. An earlier version of this essay was first published in Roger Smither (ed.), *This Film is Dangerous: A Celebration of Nitrate Film*, Brussels: Fédération Internationale des Archives du Film, 2002, pp. 388-390.

THE HOARD

THREE FILMS BY BABURAO PAINTER

Suresh Chabria

The discovery and part restoration of three Baburao Painter mythologicals in the mid-nineties was one of the most important events not only during my tenure at the National Film Archive of India, but also in the whole history of its efforts to retrieve our silent cinema heritage.

It could be likened to the finding and acquisition of some of the key Phalke films in Nasik from the Phalke family residence, and, to a lesser extent, the Himansu Rai-Franz Osten films received in an archival exchange from the British Film Institute and the two virtually intact Shyam Sundar Agarwal films located in Pune during the first decade of the NFAI's existence.

The significance of this discovery lies not only in the fact that the genius and guru status of Painter can now be more fully substantiated, but also these films–particularly *Muralivala*–give us a clearer idea about the development of the silent mythological genre in its completely mature stage. The earlier stages of this growth can be seen in the simple, tableau-dominated Phalke films and in Kanjibhai Rathod's more innovative and formally adventurous approach in *Sukanya Savirti*.

Painter's mythologicals are instilled with a natural grace and a profound underlying affirmation of the ancient tradition embodied in the familiar old tales. They reveal a dignity and self-assurance in their cinematic retelling which brings to mind the deep feeling and imagination of the great 17th-and 18th-century Indian miniature and mural painters. These films were made in the still under-financed and technically primitive conditions of Indian silent cinema, but are nonetheless marked by a refined intelligence that is Painter's own. This discovery makes one more acutely aware that if the lost Bombay, Calcutta and Madras productions of that period had anything comparable in the mythological or other genres, their virtually complete destruction is an even greater loss for Indian cinema.

Thus a great silence has been partially broken by Baburao Painter's voice. These films are a testimony to his great gifts as a storyteller and craftsman and establish beyond a doubt his pre-eminent status as a master of a distinctively Indian cultural idiom of the late colonial era: the film mythological.

Maya Bazar

aka *Surekha Haran*

(Maharashtra Film Co., 1921 / 1925)

Directed by Baburao Painter. Photographed by Baburao Painter, S. Fattelal. Cast: Ganpat Bakre (Abhimanyu), Balasaheb Yadav (Ghatotkacha), V. Shantaram (Krishna), Kamladevi (Subhadra), Zunzharrao Pawar. Original length: 6,780 feet, length of fragment: 1,082 feet. 35mm. Hindi, Gujarati, Urdu and English titles.

The earliest of the three Painter mythologicals now available, *Maya Bazar* deals with episodes from the *vanvas* or exile of the Pandava brothers in the *Mahabharata*. Arjuna's wife Subhadra has obtained a promise from her brother Krishna that her son Abhimanyu will marry Vatsala, Balarama's beautiful daughter and Krishna's niece. Meanwhile, the wicked Shakuni instead plots to secure an alliance with the Yadava clan for the Kauravas through

▲ Balasaheb Yadav in **Maya Bazar**

Vatsala's marriage to Duryodhana's son Lakshmana. Keeping his promise to Subhadra, Krishna has Vatsala kidnapped by Bhima's son Ghatotkacha who then disguises himself in her external *rupa* or appearance to marry Lakshmana. Everyone is cast under his powerful spell before he finally reveals his true identity during the marriage ceremony. As the film's publicity booklet informs us, Balarama is angered by the deception, but the sage Narada pacifies him by showing him in a vision that Krishna is none other than Vishnu, the supreme god.

The surviving sequences are from three different parts of the story. Firstly, we see Abhimanyu being killed by Ghatotkacha, but Subhadra revives him with a boon that she has been granted by the goddess; her mere touch can bring back to life any two dead persons. On realising that Ghatotkacha is in fact Bhima's son, and therefore Abhimanyu's cousin, she uses the boon once again to bring him back to life after Abhimanyu has killed him. The two cousins are reconciled and the clan elder Vidur decides to go to Dwarka to remind Krishna of his promise to Subhadra. Finally, Vidur and Abhimanyu set off in a chariot for Dwarka.

The second fragment is a short comic episode in which the general populace is under Ghatotkacha's maya or magic spell. Following an announcement that a fair is being held in which old objects will be exchanged for new, a series of illusions unfolds as utensils, valuables and garments are magically transformed and appear and vanish in a bewitched manner.

The final portion is a short scene in the Kaurava court in which Balarama seems to be upset that Vatsala has disappeared and Narada shows him that she is still very much present—perhaps Ghatotkacha in his magical disguise? The young maiden is being attended to by her entourage in a beautiful vignette-like shot shaded off at the edges.

Like other early mythologicals, *Maya Bazar* is probably based on a play or folk performances and was frequently adapted in the sound era because of the free rein the subject gave for trick photography and broad comedy. Added to this appeal was perhaps also the popularity of the Hindu notion of maya according to which the sensate world is an illusion created by the gods. In any case, one regrets the film's truncated form as Painter's storytelling is sure and his visual flair is evident in each sequence. The shot of the giant Ghatotkacha (played by Balasaheb Yadav) wielding his mace is truly impressive. For the film's release in Bombay, Painter is said to have himself hand-painted a giant sized cutout—a practice which was to become common in later years.

According to Dharamsey's updated filmography, the film was already completed and released in 1921 with the title *Surekha Haran* and re-issued as *Maya Bazar* in 1925. This would place *Maya Bazar* after *Sairandhri* (1920) as the second mythological made by Painter.

Sati Savitri

(Maharashtra Film Co., 1927)

Directed by Baburao Painter. Photographed by S. Fattelal. Cast: Balasaheb Yadav (Satyavan), Sushila Devi (Savitri), V. Shantaram (Narada), Gulabbai, Zunzharrao Pawar, Nimbalkar. Original Length: 5,168 feet, length of print: 2949 feet. 35mm. Marathi, Hindi, Gujarati, Urdu and English titles.

Only the first half of *Sati Savitri* is extant. This is a great pity because Painter's style and vision are now fully expressive, and the ethos of the silent mythological genre is wholly anchored in the cultural and artistic practices of traditional Indian artists and storytellers.

Sati Savitri extols the deep-rooted Savitri myth that was frequently filmed in both the silent and sound periods. Upheld as the supreme ideal of Indian womanhood, royal-born Savitri chooses to marry Satyavan even though he is no longer a prince and she knows that he is cursed to die within a year. She is determined to have the curse lifted through divine intervention and by performing penance and acts of piety and devotion. In this archetypal resolve of a *pativrata* or devoted wife she has the blessings of the sage Narada who happens to visit her father, King Ashvapati's court. Satyavan, who is now a humble woodcutter because of the intrigues of his father's enemies, dies in the forest after a huge branch falls on him on the foretold day. Yama, the God of Death, arrives to claim his soul and Savitri pleads with him to spare her husband.

After hearing her arguments, Yama grudgingly asks her to choose any one boon which he may grant, except Satyavan's life. She therefore asks for the eyesight of her blind father-in-law, the dethroned King Dyumatsena. This wish granted Yama prepares to leave on his *vahana* or vehicle, a buffalo. The rest of the film about how she outwits Yama to restore Satyavan back to life and also the return of his rightful throne and kingdom is missing.

Painter intersperses beautifully composed, sunlit outdoor sequences with stately shots of grand interiors using the painted scenery and props that were characteristic of contemporary theatre. The narrative develops with unerring fluency and a rapid pace, taking in an account of Savitri's miraculous birth and a flashback to King Dyumatsena's downfall and blinding by his enemies—the latter in superbly executed shots of night time palace interiors, illuminated by torches. One regrets the loss of several sequences depicting the charismatic Yama because his portrayal by a massive *pehelwan* or wrestler riding a majestic buffalo is one the most impressive images in Indian silent cinema.

However, by a happy coincidence, the available reels of Kanjibhai Rathod's *Sukanya Savitri* complete the story. In the corresponding scenes of this equally great mythological, Savitri and Yama are suspended in a twilit zone between earth and sky–beautifully spattered with floating clouds–with Satyavan's flame-like soul hovering nearby. Painter's version is more earthbound but just as remarkable for its resonance and grasp of the essence of the unfolding drama. And, as an aside, the film's rare, art deco—influenced poster quoting the image of Savitri and Yama's timeless dialogue is one of the most arresting images in Indian poster design.

Muralivala

(Maharashtra Film Co., 1927)

Directed by Baburao Painter. Photographed by S. Fattelal. Cast: Madhusudan/ Lalji Gokhale (Krishna), Sushila Devi (Radha), V. Shantaram (Raman), Bal Gajbar, Ravji Mhaiskar, Padmabai, Tulsabai. Original length: 8,907 feet, length of print: 4126 feet. 35mm. Hindi, Gujarati, Urdu and English titles.

Unlike Phalke's *Kaliya Mardan* which also focuses on the subject of Krishna's childhood, *Muralivala* introduces the character of Radha in the narrative. In fact, the Radha-Krishna theme that is absent in the *Bhagavata Purana* and in Phalke's film, dominates *Muralivala*. In this it follows the later *Gita Govinda* and Vaishnavite traditions in which she figures as an older, married woman who neglects her husband and household duties to answer the 'summons' of Krishna.

Muralivala opens with the iconic sequence of the child Krishna playing the flute surrounded by cows and cowherds and is followed by his numerous pranks which torment the *gopi*s and Radha's mother-in-law. However, these sequences are brief interludes serving as the background to the larger philosophical debate about the nature of Radha's love for Krishna. Is it merely a physical attraction? Or is it the spiritual longing of a devotee to merge with the divine principle or 'incarnation of the Almighty'?

In one key episode, Krishna appears before Radha and urges her to look at him, ' ... with the eye of wisdom. You will attain me when you know me to be Omnipresent.... So unless you learn to realise me in your husband Raman, you will not attain eternal happiness'. Raman (in an exceptionally

◀ Stills from **Muralivala** with V. Shantaram (second from top) and Lalji Gokhale (third from top)

nuanced performance by V. Shantaram) and his mother are the other two participants in this theological discussion which is a core Vaishnava belief. While the child-god Krishna playfully torments the mother, Raman is torn by jealousy and all too human doubts about Radha's fidelity and love for him.

In the extraordinary climax following Radha's vision of Krishna-as-Raman and Raman-as-Krishna and Raman's realisation of Krishna's divine nature, Krishna descends in a dream like movement into Kaliya's poisoned lake and underwater palace. He then reappears triumphantly after quelling the serpent-king, and Radha, Raman, along with the entire village receive the classical theophanic vision of Krishna fluting on Kaliya's hood. These sequences are more elaborately staged than in the ending of *Kaliya Mardan* as Kaliya is shown in both his *asura* and reptilian forms, and Krishna is briefly envisioned holding the emblems of conch, discus, lotus and mace in his four arms. Finally, Raman prostrates himself before Krishna and the cosmic and human drama comes to a close.

The surviving reels were found in an advanced state of decay, but this has not completely marred the beauty of Painter's pictorial style. The pastoral landscape and the evocation of a rural paradise with its daily routine enlivened by Krishna's enchanting antics are beautifully captured by Painter's camera and seamless editing. But above all, the mystical theme of divine and physical love which is the basis of the Radha cult and *bhakti* poetry gives *Muralivala* a unique position among the surviving mythologicals of the silent period and in the history of the genre as a whole.

THE FILM RECORD

Ashish Rajadhyaksha

The perennial million-dollar question: why has research on India's silent cinema been historically so minimal.

This is a more focused version of that question. Nineteen years ago, the first edition of this book, *Light of Asia: Indian Silent Cinema 1912-1934*, was published. The book had two specific, and I think epochal, achievements. The first, following the screening of the Indian silent cinema package at the Pordenone silent film festival, was the fact that the extant silent cinema has become available to all researchers. The second was the publication of what has become, for now at least, silent cinema's definitive filmography.

Several critical essays were also published since, and workshops dedicated to silent films used the material extensively. I now ask a few focused questions. What since Suresh Chabria's collaboration with Paolo Cherchi Usai–followed by the 1994 publication of *Light of Asia: Indian Silent Cinema (1912-1934)* and the Pordenone festival–has happened in relation to *research* on the silent cinema? What did these invaluable new materials do to change the situation that existed prior to their availability? What do we now need to get serious research on the silent cinema seriously underway?

Much significant writing on the silent era has emerged since. We now have Stephen Hughes' work on very early Tamil film, Kaushik Bhaumik's magisterial PhD thesis *The Emergence of the Bombay Film Industry, 1913–1936* and Sudhir Mahadevan's *The Traffic in Technologies: Early Cinema and Visual Culture in South Asia, 1840-1920*, to name three instances. We also have the journals *BioScope* and *Journal of the Moving Image* which have

▼ Lalji Gokhale and Sushila Devi in **Muralivala**

systematically published the works of these and other writers. On its side, the surviving corpus of silent cinema since 1994 has only grown, with the spectacular addition of Baburao Painter–silent cinema's greatest silence–with particular reference to his *Muralivala* (1927). All of this, amid the standing lament of 'nothing' having remained, must count for something.

Bhaumik's diagnosis on why silent cinema studies have remained somewhat stunted in India is of particular significance.[1] The problem, he says, is to do with the curious turn the well-known labour-versus-text dichotomy (analysis of filmic texts versus analysis of industrial production conditions for example) takes in this period. That only a small number of films have survived has had a curious consequence. *It has quite unproblematically allowed this small number of films to stand in for India's silent cinema as a whole.* The overdetermination of what we can now officially dub the 'Phalke syndrome'–or the way Phalke has come to dominate the silent period as a whole–has allowed a certain kind of cinema, mostly mythologicals and historicals, to permit a 'nationalist' interpretation of Swadeshi cinema to hold sway. The argument has thence emerged that India's mythological narratives produced a way by which the cinema could 'take advantage of the wave of national awakening to forge an intimate mode of address for the people of India', and that the 'public energies of the nationalist context allowed for the absorption of a modern technological medium like cinema into Indian "tradition"'. And such an ideological stance has been unquestioningly applied to all of India's early film cultures without exception, as the cinema got wedded, deriving (as in Europe) its justification from literary movements. As a result, says Bhaumik, a vast bulk of Indian cinema has remained simply undiscussed. A very small percentage of the 1300-odd films made in India–the ones devoted to religious subjects or the kind that hinted at a 'prescribed ritualistic regime of gestures and social behaviour'–dominates all debate on the silent cinema as a whole.

What if we were to view the entire history of Indian cinema from the vantage point of the fantasy, stunt adventure and romance films that have not survived? There have been sporadic efforts, the most notable being Valentina Vitali's work on stunt stars in the 1920s and 1930s—especially the women in action films.[2]

Had they existed, would we have had a completely different starting point for Indian films? Could we then have been better equipped to take more seriously the elaborately documented testimony by the Indian Cinematograph Committee (ICC) of 1927-28, of the fact that the Indian middle class was reluctant to join the film industry? An obvious fact that the Phalke-centric nationalist interpretation either ignores or, as Paresh Mokashi's *Harishchandrachi Factory* (2009) did, resolves all too easily in its narrative? The infinitely contentious fact that the ICC Report repeatedly hammers in is that a unanimous denigration of illiterate performers, of actors from the courtesan and prostitute class led to a simplistic equation in the middle class mind between the content of fantasy and adventure romance films and the kind of bodies that essayed the tale into its cinematic variant.

> The stories and performers were all seen as rising from a disreputable quarter of popular performances, from a space that for the lack of a better word I have called the *bazaar*, serving the rude and simple desires of the unlettered folk of the subcontinent. Dirty bodies, then, in and for

▼ Mandakini Phalke in **Kaliya Mardan**

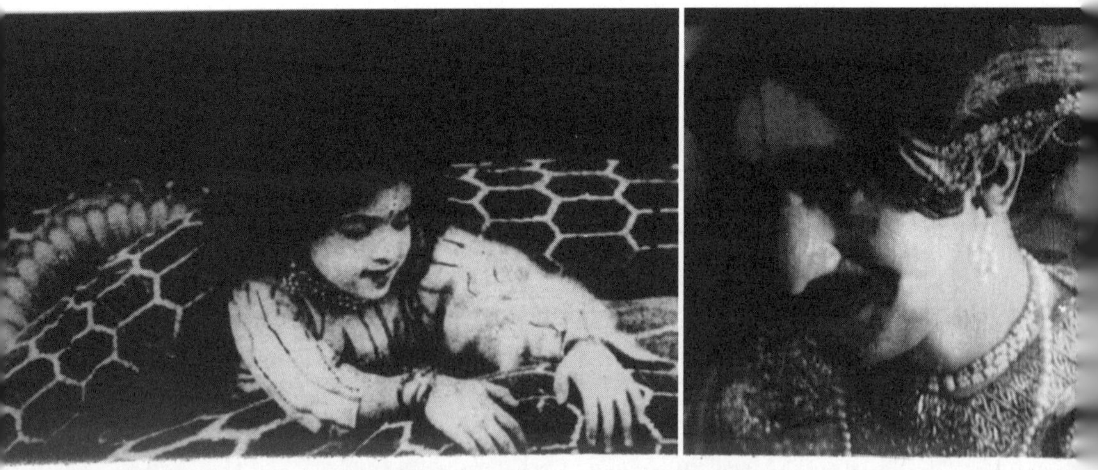

> a sordid cultural universe. The adaptations were further damned by the fact they seemed to be badly produced and were mostly thinly disguised plagiarisms of the immensely popular imported stunt film. The solution to this problem was a universally endorsed one–bring in the literate middle class and one would get a 'better' cinema (Bhaumik, 2008).

This problem becomes even more serious when Bhaumik proposes that it wasn't only that the films got ignored. The larger problem of course has been that *even the films did not survive*–just as, say, posters and calendar art from the lithograph era have substantially not survived. There are only some film stills, some booklets, and random recordings of the experiences of film personnel and cinemagoers of that generation.

Pordenone, Méliès, Phalke—Globalising Silent Film

Despite this, whatever exists is still sufficient, says Bhaumik, to complicate the consensus on the 'traditional' moorings of early Indian cinema. This allows us to now revert to our question: what has happened since 1994, given that we have now, to take just one example, the epic G.P. Pawar/ Shyam Sundar Agarwal's extraordinary *Diler Jigar* (1931) before us? What of P.V. Rao's film version of the C.V. Raman Pillai novel *Marthanda Varma*, available since Pordenone to film researchers? Finally, what of *Muralivala*?

▼ Below and centre: Amboo and Daniel in **Diler Jigar**

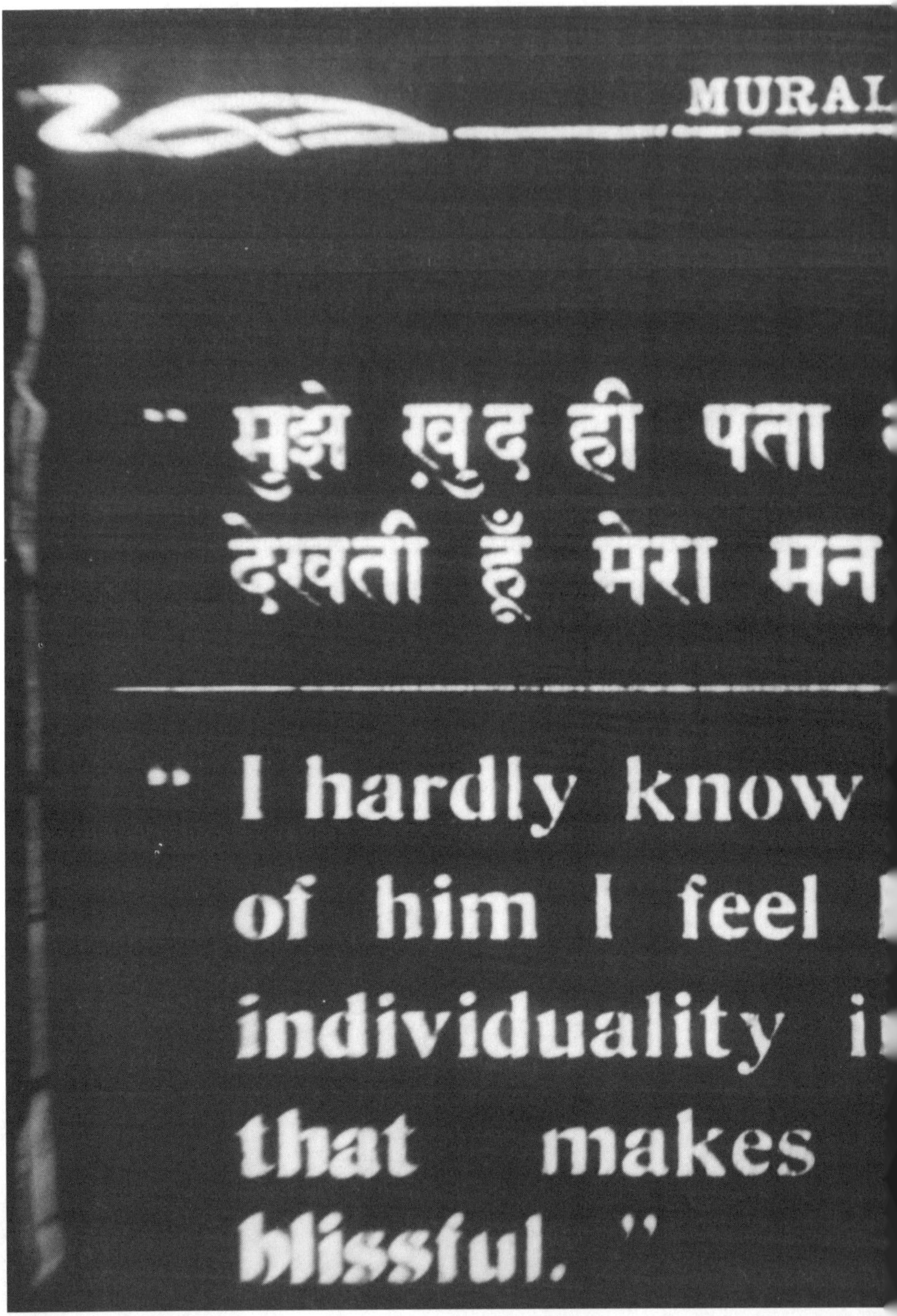

▲ A title card from **Muralivala**

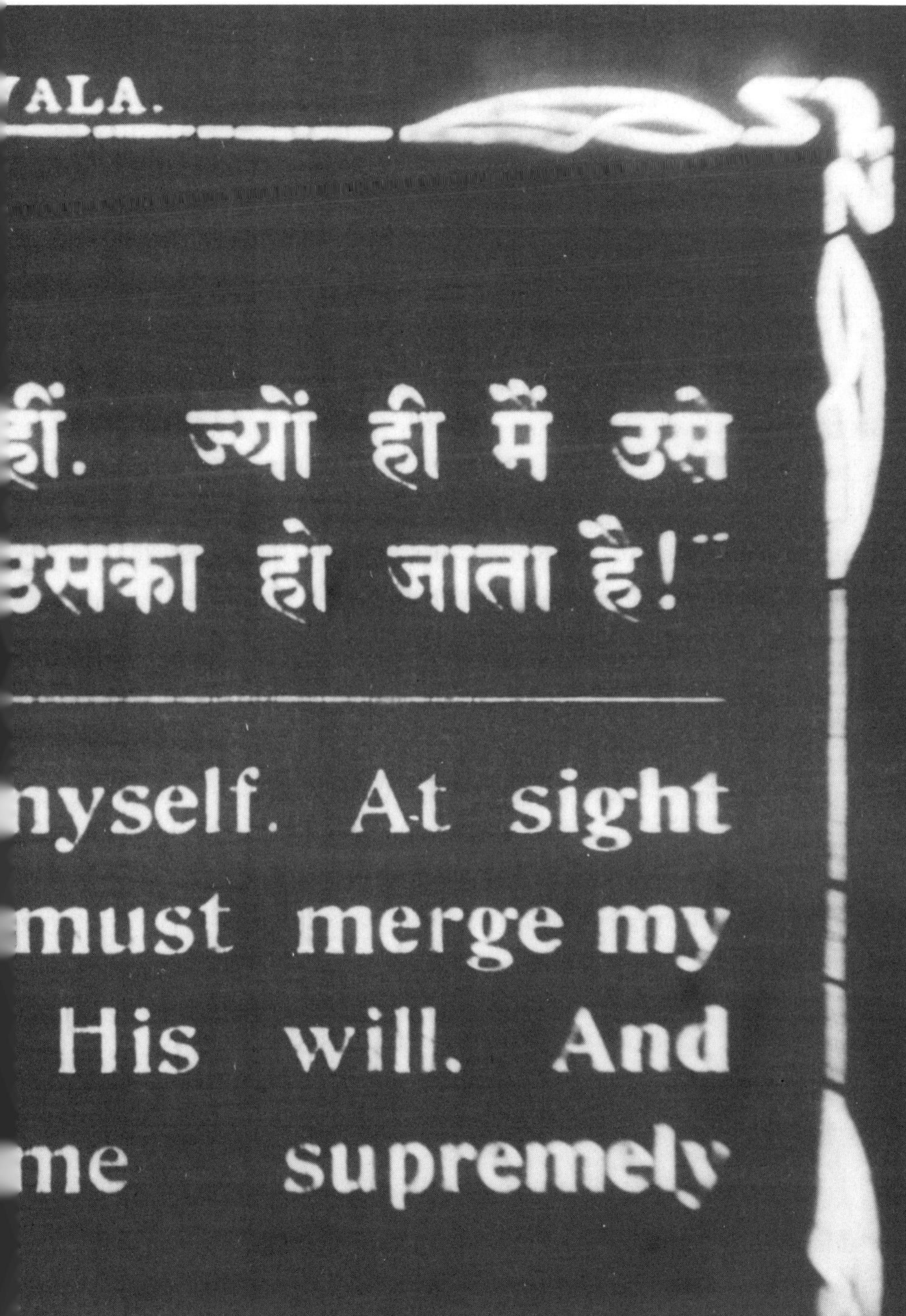
ज्यों ही मैं उसे
उसका हो जाता है!
At sight
must merge my
His will. And
supremely

The Pordenone Giornate del Cinema Muto (aka Pordenone Silent Film Festival) in 1994–of which *Light of Asia: Indian Silent Cinema (1912-1934)* was the companion text–located the Indian cinema for the first time within a world film category. It was without doubt something like the crowning glory of the National Film Archive of India (NFAI), and certainly its biggest achievement under Suresh Chabria's brief reign. Pordenone in October every year, host to thousands of film scholars sharing its dedication to the 'preservation, diffusion, and study of the first thirty years of cinema', has covered almost every aspect of the silent cinema worldwide to 'revolutionise the study of silent cinema' in the words of Kristin Thompson and David Bordwell (*Film History: An Introduction*, 1994/2010).

Inaugurated with a showcasing of French comedian Max Linder, the Giornate has also shown treasures from Moscow's Gosfilmofond archives showing pre-1917 Russian films for the first time outside the former USSR. Early European films found in the Komiya Collection were presented in 1992. Retrospectives on Italian comedians, the French company Éclair, Mack Sennett, Thomas Ince, Roscoe Arbuckle, Frank Borzage, Walt Disney, Augusto Genina, funny ladies, Feuillade, Cooper & Schoedsack, Dziga Vertov, Antoine, René Clair, Ladislas Starevich, and, since 1997, a multi-year project which continued up to 2008 involving the screening of every one of the hundreds of films made by D.W. Griffith between 1907 and 1931 have been projected. It has had exhaustive retrospectives from Australia and New Zealand (1993), China (1995 and 1997), Israel (1995), the former Yugoslavia (1988), Scandinavia (1986, 1999, 2006), Germany (1990, 2007), and Japan (2001 and 2005). In 1994, at the fourteenth Giornate, they did India.

Since Pordenone the name of at least Phalke, though as yet no one else, now surfaces in the vocabulary of the great theorists of silent film. Chabria had already made that link in 1993.[3] Tom Gunning routinely includes Phalke in his lectures at Chicago. Sean Cubitt's essay 'Phalke, Méliès, and Special Effects Today'[4] located the great man alongside Méliès, to which William

Brown made further additions, listing 'Méliès and Phalke, Lye and McLaren, and the American avant-garde' in the same breath.[5] And Brigitte Schulze perhaps outdoes them all by almost entirely uprooting Phalke from his Swadeshi milieu and giving him a solidly German ancestry, putting–this must be surely the most provocative statement on film of all time–Kracauer of all people in Phalke's footsteps.[6]

As Phalke finds himself next to Méliès and next then to the German expressionists, written thus into a European legacy of both expressionism and surrealism, one argument may well be that Pordenone has only served to reinforce, rather than destabilise the sanitised nationalist version of Indian silent film by giving it a global stage. But it is also true that such juxtaposition in turn permits, perhaps unintentionally, another purpose, namely that of permitting other phenomena, even the earliest phenomenon of Indian film to be located within larger global perspectives.

Stephen Hughes' work is exemplary in this regard, where he explores what he calls the 'lost decade' of film history and elsewhere the 'pre-Phalke' era in silent film.[7] Hughes puts the stakes on silent cinema even higher: he asks why we do not have in India, work similar to Charles Musser's multi-volume tome, *The Emergence of Cinema: The American Screen to 1907* (1990).

Hughes feels that 'paucity of sources problem' has been overrated. It has, he sternly says, become 'too easy for scholars to use the lack of sources as an alibi for justifying the lack of scholarship on this earliest period of film history in India and for avoiding the slow, patient toil of archival research'. For him, this 'unquestioned complaint about a lack of sources' betrays 'a fundamental collective lack of historical imagination on the part of films studies in India'. Far from a paucity of sources, says Hughes, the problem India's film historians actually face is that there are *too many* sources on film history in India that have not been fully considered or consulted, for example, secondary newspaper sources. The only way to address this problem is by encouraging a more determined commitment to archival research using creative approaches to what counts as a source, and a greater willingness to critically rework the corpus of ready-made historical narratives about early film history in India.

The imagination boggles at what a work on India comparable to Musser's may look like. We of course, possess nothing like it; however one could aver, nor do most other non-Western film traditions. The more interesting question is perhaps not the self-berating one but rather this: what could a film history of such incredible detail about the Indian cinema possibly look like?

Hughes provides one possible answer in his work on film exhibitors. As a pedagogic exercise in the 'Lost Decade' essay he limits his entire inquiry only to one year, 1902, and to newspaper sources, and paints an extraordinarily vivid picture of what was happening in Madras that year. Taking just one of his several examples, in just one venue, the Victoria Public Hall, and just one event there, the screenings of the Original American Biograph Company open out a new, global, imagination for silent film. That November, the Original American Biograph, rights-holders to American Mutoscope & Biograph Company (formerly Edison) patents, showcased its new high-quality 70 mm electric projection equipment. There is a flurry of extensive advertising and advance billing about the grand success of their tour through India, the highpoint of which were the special command performances before 'His Excellency the Viceroy', George Curzon at both Calcutta and Simla. The main selling point was of course technology: it was a chance for Madras to see the Biograph, and to share the same experience that the West had already had. Such showcasing of technology also went alongside numerous efforts by film exhibitors to use various kinds of innovative advertising and sales promotion to encourage the film-going habit. While ticket pricing was an important indicator of the general economic class of early film audiences, their promotional efforts suggest, he says:

> a wider range and further refinement in the constituent social differentiations amongst potential film-goers. Early exhibitors

experimented with numerous promotional tactics that reached out to a variety of niche audiences such as soldiers in uniform, Christians, women and children. Along with the content of their film and entertainment programs these promotional activities served as an important tool for exhibitors to shape their mode of public address (Hughes, 2010).

The Indian Filmographer: The 'Likelihood' Paradigm and Virchand Dharamsey's Silent Cinema Filmography

There is of course another side to Hughes' complaint about the 'fundamental collective lack of historical imagination on the part of films studies in India' or, indeed, to his sources, namely newspaper records. It is true that India has no equivalent of Charles Musser. It is also however true that India does have a long and honourable tradition of filmographers, who have used their own means to cover silent cinema fairly thoroughly on their terms, and through sources similar to the ones Hughes uses, if not always with his keen eye for historical detail. While Rangoonwala remains the figurehead, and Dharap more or less the patron saint of the Indian filmography, there have been several others who have done exemplary work on just such sources as Hughes'. But they have also produced their own problems, and the difficulties posed now by the search for the authentic detail has led to its own conundrums.

Let me illustrate the problem with a more recent, but to me classic, example. An apocryphal story has V.A.K. Ranga Rao, the irascible collector of music and authority on South Indian cinema, offering an open challenge. It seems he saw *Mother India* on his television one night and was taken aback to see Sitara Devi's name in the acting credits. The open challenge was to anyone who could spot Sitara Devi anywhere in the film. And, he asked, if she was not in the film, to answer two questions. First, what happened? Was something filmed with her and cut out? If so, when was this cut out? Almost more important: what to do with Sitara Devi's filmography? Whether *Mother India* should feature in that filmography or not?

Such a problem would cut deep among what I want to call the classic years of the assembling of an authentic Indian filmography. When we did the *Encyclopaedia of Indian Cinema*, we decided to include Sitara Devi's name in its credits, mainly because our own key source for Hindi credits before 1970 was Firoze Rangoonwala's iconic *Indian Filmography, Silent and Hindi Film: 1897-1969,* published in1970 and Har Mandir Singh Hamraaz's somewhat different, equally legendary *Hindi Film Geet Kosh* which came out with the first edition of its 1951-60 listings in 1980.[8] Like Ranga Rao, Singh and the other *Geet Kosh* editors have had their own variations of the Sitara Devi problem: Singh's focus was on songs, and he was encountering major discrepancies between film titles, their publicity material and record listings. What was he to do when songs named a particular singer in film credits and another in the record label? Was the version released on record a different, 'cover' version, or was there a deliberate cover-up?

Two years after Rangoonwala, B.V. Dharap's annual *Indian Films* compilations, begun in 1972 and later extended to the silent cinema, attempted on the face of it at least a somewhat different agenda. This agenda was to assemble, for the first time, all the material of the Indian Censor Board in one place. Although avowedly a job of the State, it was in fact a commercial venture owned by his Motion Picture Enterprises initiative housed at the Alaka Talkies theatre in Pune. Dharap managed to bring these volumes out reasonably punctually between 1972 and 1978, but couldn't sustain them. The unpublished silent film material–between 1920 and 1931 and then till 1950–the three poorly brought out volumes between 1983-85, and the four years in between (1979-82) recently acquired from his son-in-law, all present at the NFAI, show none of the attention to detail that the classic 1972-78 series possesses.

By the early 1980s, Rangoonwala and Dharap–and the focus on Hindi, or at least Mumbai-based, cinema–had been substantiated with significant regional scholarship. The very best of these was Bagishwar Jha's extraordinary *Filmography of Bengali Cinema (1897-1981)*, in his even more extraordinary *Indian Motion Picture Almanac* brought out in 1986. It is not easy to understand, or interpret in today's times, the significance or the dedication of the work of Rangoonwala, Dharap, 'Filmnews' Anandan (*1931 Mudal 1985 Varai Veliyana Padamgal*, 1986), or B. Jha. And so it is also not easy to understand their purpose: what were they working for? Such dedication also required choices to be made, as filmographers went well beyond any fidelity to the record they were reproducing, and into what I want here to call the 'likelihood' paradigm—playing a kind of curatorial role of choosing from various sources, without necessarily mentioning them, that record that they considered most likely to be the truth.

But to what was the fidelity to be? Take Dharap: the Dharap work was *meant* to be based on Censor Board records. Dharap was at the time a very privileged recipient of censorship material via the NFAI. But he too strays into what we have outlined as the Sitara Devi problem. He moves beyond scrupulous fidelity to the Censor record, which may have permitted historians to explore why they had the attributions they did, and inserts 'likely' attributions based on nothing more than personal knowledge. To take one example, all Hindustan Cinema Film Co. productions between 1920 and 1931 are attributed to Phalke's direction, and all Kohinoor scripts to Mohanlal Dave. Since the only agency that could have maintained such a record was the Censor Board, but didn't do so–partly due to its own procedural incompetence but also probably partly, I now wonder, because it was not qualified in this task mainly due to a conflict of interests (how could a Censor Board be an authentic historian and keeper of records?)–the problem did not lie in the truth of what happened to a particular film but something else that was bothering Dharap. The 'truth' itself was now and forever more to be a combination of State record with an independent record of *what must have actually happened*, at the service of a more *authorised* national historiographic record than the Censor Board could mandate, one that would happen more on a voluntary communitarian basis closer to the spirit of today's Wikipedia than anything that the State could provide at the time.

Indeed, and perhaps substantiating Hughes' point here, it was curious that the driving need among scholars to keep weeding out less reliable data and replacing it with something considered more reliable–reliability being entirely subjective, since the truth itself was unlikely to be ever known–was also accompanied by a curious reluctance to record sources from where the data was received. So Tapan Roy's *Shatattar Batsharer Bangla Chhabi* (Bapi Prakashan, 1996) updates Jha, but rarely corrects him. Likewise, Rajendra Ojha's *75 Glorious Years of Indian Cinema: 1913-1988* does nothing new with Rangoonwala, actually eliminating some of Rangoonwala's data, but updates it to 1988. Necessarily, such an organic process does not make it easy to understand gaps and omissions in the record. Were these credits not there in Jha's sources, in which case, what *were* Jha's sources? Why did he not take these details from Kalish Mukhopadhyay's *Bangla Chalacchitra Shilper Itihas 1897-1947* (Rupamancha, 1962) which had come out almost two decades earlier?

Whatever its credo, by 1970, Mukhopadhyay's generation, which included for instance A. Paul, editor of the *Kerala Film Guide* (Chitravedi, Kozhikode, 1966, in Malayalam), B.D. Garga, Rangoonwala, and Dharap himself, had firmly established the key tenets of the Indian filmography, which would rule for the next decade. Such an agenda as the filmography developed by now does not produce its purpose easily. By the 1980s, several regional film publications were routinely carrying exhaustive filmographies. Perhaps the best of these were Harish Raghuvanshi's regular lists in *G* magazine, in Mumbai, but several journals, like *Nana* in Malayalam (which did the outstanding special issue 'Malayalam Cinema from *Vigathakumaran* to *Manjil Virinja Pookkal*' (1982), or the Diwali special issue of *Roopavani* in Marathi which did D.B. Samant's *Marathi Chitrapat Samagra Suchi* in 1993, were doing great work in putting together definitive lists of regional film industries. While these included local film industries, the really popular ones were those of individual stars, composers and singers.

To this data, of varying degrees of reliability, would be added the far more unreliable data provided by personal testimony: and the new problem of dubious claims (my own personal favourite being Sarvottam

Badami, formerly of Sagar Movietone and for four years Chief Producer of Newsreels at Films Division, telling me that 'he started' Films Division because Vallabhbhai Patel asked him to) or variations of the well known Sam Goldwyn problem ('I made the film, he only directed it'). By the late 1930s, several quasi-governmental agencies had begun recording data of their own regions, with the primary purpose of putting authentic linguistic region-specific lists together. The South Indian Film Chamber of Commerce started in 1938 and launched its key *Journal of the Film Chamber* in 1955. The Andhra Film Chamber began its journal the following year, and was to carry the first definitive Telugu cinema filmography covering fifty years of Telugu film (1931-76) and twenty years of the journal itself in December 1976. In all instances, Film Chamber journals–which carry both periodic reports of censored titles, local and from elsewhere (including imported films), as well as lists of releases–straddle both industry sources as well as Censor Board data but without any particular effort to correlate the two. Equally importantly, even the South Indian Film Chamber, whose job it was to link all four southern industries, makes no attempt to address pan-regional disparities, often making both bilinguals and dubbed versions into independent productions. Film Chamber records would become definitive sources for producing regional histories, such as the Kerala Film Chamber, which started in 1956 and began its own journal in 1970, but produced the sources for M. Saraswathy (ed.), *Malayala Cinema-Aranoottandu* (1987) as well as M.G. Radhakrishnan (ed.), *Malayalam Cinema: 50 Years* (1989).

The silent cinema now poses a further problem to this practice. As a cinema that was, practically speaking, trans-regional, with production bases limited to Bombay, Madras and Calcutta and a few other places, it saw tremendous trans-regional migration that later region-driven filmographies simply could not cope with. So Raja Sandow's remarkable Mumbai career features nowhere in his Tamil work, and Gubbi Veeranna's silent productions in Mumbai (which constituted Prithviraj Kapoor's entry into the cinema, no less) do not appear anywhere in the career of the 'founder of Kannada cinema'.

I personally believe it was indeed Virchand Dharamsey's work in the 1994 publication of *Light of Asia: Indian Silent Cinema (1912-1934)* that took what I have called the 'likelihood' factor, and also trans-regionalism, to a new level: translating the organicity and evolving nature of the data into a kind of speculative filmography based on individual careers, and what was most likely, in a particular studio or production outfit. On simply names, he writes:

> Typically the title announced would not be the title completed; films produced by one company would be sold to others and reissued under new credits; stars would routinely change their names (the actress Mary became Kumudini, and was often referred to by both names even for the same film; Winnie Stewart became Manorama). Other confusions include four actresses named Gohar, two Nanubhai Desais ... and a few that remain to be solved, for example Pawar, Chavan (or Chauhan).
>
> The available information had thus to be continuously collated with separate career trajectories of who was doing what at different times, which studios started (and closed) on which dates, what happened to a studio catalogue's back-list when partnerships split up, and so on.

Dharamsey often further disentangles this by tracking the distribution patterns of a particular film, and where it was released, to separate out remakes and reissues. While Dharap too, we have seen, departs (at least in his silent and early sound listings) from his avowed purpose of recording censor data to get into the likelihood syndrome, he does this with much less attention to detail than what we have seen Dharamsey do with his main work in this book.

Dharamsey's filmography-revised and updated for the new edition- would provide the direct inspiration of the *Encyclopaedia of Indian Cinema*'s escalation of the 'likelihood factor' into a new realm, even making it a major virtue in its claim that, since most facts around Indian cinema can only be gleaned from secondary sources–given that film prints don't exist, or are not always available–the only strategy possible is to cull out from available sources the 'most reliable ones' available for each of India's cinemas. It goes on to state that:

> Given the nature of the Indian film industry, however, there were compelling reasons for drawing on this material alongside other, not always less 'reliable' sources. The editors of this book, quite deliberately and as a matter of policy, have refused to accept any single 'authoritative' source on any of India's cinemas. On the contrary, we have endeavoured to produce a book providing the 'most likely' truth on the basis of often deeply conflicting sources… ('Introduction', *Encyclopaedia of Indian Cinema).*

What the editors of the *Encyclopaedia* did not of course do was to address a question that no Indian filmographer has yet asked: namely, why do different records differ?

Why do film titles from different times give different credits? What is the reason for, say, censor records to differ from publicity material? Were titles reissued with different attributions at different times? If so, why?

As the *Encyclopaedia* went on to propose, one of its key claims then was not so much to correct the sources of its materials–although between conflicting sources, it definitely implemented the 'likelihood' system–but rather that:

> in consistently mapping India's film histories on to a national canvas, we also present several new discoveries, such as the sheer contiguity of historical processes nationwide that most Indian regions persist in viewing as unique, the influences of film-makers from one region onto another, or even the trajectories of individual careers that transgressed boundaries sometimes decades before these boundaries came to be asserted.

▲ A frame from **Muralivala**

Muralivala

Baburao Painter remains, in the overdetermination of the Phalke Era celebrating its centenary as we speak, the great silence of the silent era. Nothing of his has survived. Or so we thought, until the NFAI assembled, in-house, under the supervision of the great K.P.R. Nair, Painter's *Muralivala*.[9]

And what a film it is. At one level a fairly straightforward 'antics-of-Krishna' mythological, the film simply catapults into a new dimension unachieved by India's silent filmmakers with the entry of V. Shantaram as Radha's husband Raman, and the curiously tangled love triangle between the child, the husband and his wife. Krishna's pranks, which force villagers to consider moving out, are more viciously plausible than anything Phalke did, although the parallels with *Kaliya Mardan* are obvious. Not so obvious is the new role of Krishna, who appears before a dazed Radha and advises her on what she should do with the sage words, 'You must find me within your husband', and then matches word with act.

I am going to try and use *Muralivala* to suggest ways by which we could perhaps resolve the problem that Bhaumik outlines, discussed at the beginning of this essay. Bhaumik proposes that the nationalist distinction between indigenous mythologicals and the fantasy films effectively debars the historical inquiry into the kind of dubious and illegitimate labour that went into early cinema, forcing all historical inquiry into colluding with the nationalist sanitisation of our cinema, and thus preventing the really important questions from being asked about the vast bulk of films that were actually made in the country.

I am not entirely convinced. My sense is that the distinction between mythologicals and fantasy films is not easily made: nor does the 'Sanskritisation' of silent cinema via the Phalke process entirely exclude the fantasy genre. I think we cannot make vertical distinctions between mythologicals and fantasies, but rather see all films from this time within a horizontal divide, inside a film, between what we may call its fantasy content and which is often its base, and the realism to which the film aspires, which provides the dominant interpretative frame. That way, we will see all films, and especially our silents, as unstable condensations ceaselessly striving for their own understanding of realism, creating a dynamic that straddles their struggle for respectability, for nationalist purpose, for reform.

In one way, *Muralivala* is of course a straight mythological, and indeed the resemblance to Phalke–the Kaliya sequence being almost a direct nod to Phalke's *Kaliya Mardan* made nearly a decade earlier and, we could say, not nearly as spectacularly as its predecessor–permits Painter to be easily absorbed into the nationalist stream. But let's now pause for a moment. Painter in the first place has a social context that is certainly not Phalke's: he is not Brahmin but comes from the low-caste carpenter community, he is in the end a 'technician', as were both Damle and Fattelal after him. This is despite the fact that his artistic credentials (his visual art, where he would certainly be the equal of say M.R. Achrekar in painting, and where his Gandhi, Shivaji and Jyotiba Phule sculptures in Kolhapur were major city landmarks until recently) are certainly superior to Phalke's. Whereas Phalke's inspiration to set up his first studio, now immortalised through its domestication and providing among others a role for both Saraswatibai Phalke and little Mandakini, are very much cast into the mould of the mad scientist, Painter's Maharashtra Film Co. is based on rather sounder, if less self-glorifying, industrial lines. Importantly, Phalke has neither students nor disciples. Painter has several. His own work straddling technological skill with an aspiration towards artistic authorship moulds almost everything in the future Prabhat Film Co., moving from the concept of authorship (this mantle taken over by V. Shantaram) to technical skill (S. Fattelal).

Shantaram embodies and carries forward this Painter legacy, with all its caste and other contradictions, in a way that I have no space to explore here. Suffice it to say that the tension between fantasy–which here means special effects, dissolves, trick scenes, in turn bringing in a lower-class artisanal skill and of course thrills for a cheaper class of audience–and realism—the gesture towards thematic interpretation, the literary legacy and eventually nationalist purpose would only grow as Maharashtra Film Co. shaded into the Prabhat legacy. The distinction in the 'saint' movie for example, between the low-class thrills of a quickie like *Sant Tukaram* (1936) and the far more ponderous *Dharmatma* (1935) shunning special effects in favour of a reformist message about caste, a tension that silent cinema would be riven by, is entirely available in *Muralivala*.

Am I wrong, now, to see some of *this* self-doubt, this doubt as it stands between the mesmerising pyrotechnics of the little Krishna and the more adult responsibilities of *grihasthashrama*–the tension between fantasy and realism–in Shantaram's extraordinary performance as Raman in *Muralivala*? What does a man do, we may ask within the full-blown subjective realism that such a performance permits, when his wife is so obsessed with a child? What does it mean when the child, with a suddenly divine wisdom, tells her that she must learn to look at him with the eye of wisdom? That she can only attain eternal bliss when she knows Him to be omnipresent, and when she learns to realise Him in her husband Raman?

Let us analyse the sequence just preceding the one of the killing of Kaliya in some detail now. The children have just completed yet another of their endless pranks. A cut. Raman and Radha are together, sharing for the first time genuine conjugal happiness, Radha is also happy because she has, presumably, killed her internal demon with that message from Krishna, that she finds Him in her husband. But then the demon resurfaces again: the nightmare continues, Raman dissolves yet again into the child Krishna. The problem has not been solved. What happens thereafter we don't know (but can surely guess) for after some fairly intimate exchanges with the child, Radha falls into a dead faint. Raman reappears and he and Krishna have a confrontation. Krishna waves an accusing finger at Raman before stalking off. Raman, now helplessly standing before the unconscious Radha, keeps fantasising that Krishna is standing there, when suddenly there is a flash of lightning and thunder, Raman is blinded and falls down, as Krishna is seen descending down what seems to be a gigantic crevice. The children now find the unconscious Radha, wake her up, and they find that Raman has fallen to the ground, presumably felled by the cosmic eruptions that have broken out all round him. Krishna is now in the throes of his epic and terminal battle with the snake-demon, from which he emerges victorious—having, presumably killed the demon. Surely this is the very demon plaguing Radha's life?

However we understand this extraordinary staging of the ethical dilemmas that precede the epic battle, this is surely unprecedented in Indian cinema, and I know of little that has followed *Muralivala* that so remarkably explores the ethics of the love story between Radha and Krishna. Certainly there is very much more than an incipient realism at work here: there is, precisely, the aspiration of a cinematic form to work out of its formal location–fantasy–and to arrive at a properly realist text.

As things are, this approach is the only way I can see us overcoming the problem Bhaumik has outlined, between the low-class fantasy and the nationalist mythological. I have elsewhere argued that any industrial exploration of cinematic practices in India would need to begin, following Madhava Prasad's modification of the 'heterogeneous modes of manufacture' concept to Indian film, to see melodramatic modes as precisely straddling industrial production with textual meaning production, and that we may need innovative ways to understand both if we are to get anywhere with the silent cinema.

And these, I propose, are the possibilities that the revised and expanded *Light of Asia: Indian Silent Cinema (1912-1934)* now permits.

NOTES

1. Kaushik Bhaumik, 'Querying the 'Traditional' Roots of Silent Cinema in Asia', *Journal of the Moving Image*, no. 7, 2008.
2. Valentina Vitali, 'The 1920s' and 'Women in Action Films in the 1920s and 1930s', in her book *Hindi Action Cinema: Industries, Narratives, Bodies*, New Delhi: Oxford University Press, 2008.
3. Suresh Chabria, 'D.G. Phalke and the Méliès Tradition in Early Indian Cinema'. *KINtop 2*, Frankfurt, 1993, pp. 103-115.
4. Sean Cubitt, 'Phalke, Méliès, and Special Effects Today', *Wide Angle*, vol. 21, no. 1, Jan 1999.
5. William Brown, 'Man without a movie camera–movies without men: towards a posthumanist cinema?' in W. Buckland (ed.), *Film Theory and Contemporary Hollywood Movies*, New York: Routledge, 2009, pp. 66-85.
6. Brigitte Schulze, *Humanist and Emotional Beginnings of a Nationalist Indian Cinema in Bombay with Kracauer in the Footsteps of Phalke*, Berlin: Avinus, 2003.
7. Stephen Putnam Hughes, 'The Lost Decade of Film History in India', *Journal of the Moving Image*, no. 9, 2010.
8. The Singh *Geet Kosh* tradition would provide bulwark support both on its own but also through a series of other *Geet Koshes* by Harish Raghuvanshi on Gujarati, Murlidhar Soni on Rajasthani and many others.
9. For the always amazing saga of how the Indian silent cinema has been found, in this instance Painter's films, see Suresh Chabria's 'The Cobra's Hoard', in Roger Smither (ed.), *This Film Is Dangerous: A Celebration of Nitrate Film*, The International Fédération of Film Archives (FIAF), Brussels 2002, pp. 388-390, reprinted in this new and revised edition.

BIBLIOGRAPHICAL ESSAY

Suresh Chabria

While a number of books on Indian cinema are published each year, only a few of them deal with the silent era at any significant length. This is largely because very few silent films have survived and it requires a dedicated and patient historian to dig out new information about this period that is scattered in secondary sources in many languages in archives and libraries all over the country and abroad. Thus most of the original work done in recent years is by scholars and historians in their PhD theses, articles in academic journals or individual chapters in books that primarily focus on later Indian cinema. The upsurge in film studies in both Indian and universities outside the country has fortunately resulted in a greater, if only sporadic, interest in Indian silent cinema as well.

Before discussing some of the more important contributions, one must acknowledge the decisive role of Ashish Rajadhyaksha and Paul Willemen's *Encyclopaedia of Indian Cinema*. It was published soon after the 1994 publication of *Light of Asia: Indian Silent Cinema (1912-1934)* and along with a revised edition in 1999, has become an essential reference book for the study of every period of Indian film history. The editors marshalled the resources and talents of a number of consultants and contributors from all over India and their combined efforts have given an invaluable platform and impetus for further research. The film synopses and entries on studios, directors, actors and eminent personalities and the numerous filmographies are constantly referred to by researchers. One may not agree with all the opinions expressed in it, but as a historiographical framework, it remains a landmark achievement.

The late film historian B.D. Garga's *So Many Cinemas: The Motion Picture in India* (Eminence Designs Pvt. Ltd., Mumbai, 1996) is a thoroughly readable history of Indian cinema up to the 1990s and the opening chapters on the silent era feature an array of rare stills reproduced in an attractive and elegant manner. Among the more interesting passages in this part of the book is the brief discussion on south Indian film pioneers, especially A. Narayanan and his General Pictures Corporation (established in 1929), which produced a substantial portion of the films in the south during the last years of the silent cinema. The interaction between the film industries of Madras with those in Calcutta and Bombay is also briefly discussed and, in particular, the fascinating career of Raja Sandow who started as a major film star in Bombay and subsequently returned to Madras to establish himself as a prolific actor-director. Both these subjects would reward further attention from film historians.

Garga's posthumously published *Silent Cinema in India: A Pictorial Journey* (Collins, NOIDA, 2012) is in a similar vein. It further expands the chapters on the silent cinema in the earlier book, and includes several previously unpublished stills and publicity booklets from his personal collection that is now housed in the Indira Gandhi National Centre for the Arts, New Delhi.

A little noticed but curious book is R.K. Verma's *Filmography: Silent Cinema 1913-1934* (Dehra Dun, 2000). As convener of the research cell of the Film Federation of India (which briefly toyed with the idea of launching a national political party to contest elections in 1979), Verma single-handedly sought to compile data and statistics about the entire Indian film industry. His only publication up to now is this book which mainly consists of a filmography of silent cinema that is substantially similar to that of Dharamsey's, published six years earlier in the first edition of *Light of Asia: Indian Silent Cinema (1912-1934)*. But the book also gives useful statistics and information about the number of theatres and travelling cinemas, import of films and raw stock, regulatory laws, early film magazines and so on. A charming section–of what is evidently a labour of love–is the one with the photo albums of the 'forgotten founders of silent cinema', 'forgotten faces' and 'forgotten frames'.

Perhaps the most important original works based on archival sources such as newspaper reports, advertisements and publicity booklets are two unpublished PhD dissertations—Stephen Putnam Hughes' *Is There Anyone Out There? Exhibition and the Formation of Silent Film Audiences in South India* (University of Chicago, 1996) and Kaushik Bhaumik's *The Emergence of the Bombay Film Industry, 1913-1936* (University of Oxford, 2001). Both these historians have subsequently expanded their arguments in the journals *BioScope* and *The Journal of the Moving Image*.

Stephen Hughes' special contribution is to the documentation and understanding of the colonial context and patronage of early cinema exhibition and distribution in India. Though his main research is devoted to Madras and south India, one can extrapolate his findings to other parts of India as well. Also, in the process of reconstructing the conditions of 'When Film Came to Madras', he forcefully argues that film historians must probe deeper into the archival sources and go beyond the simplistic location of the beginnings of Indian cinema in the 1896 Lumière shows and the surviving Phalke films. His most notable essays are 'When Film Came to Madras' (*BioScope: South Asian Screen Studies*, vol. 1, no. 2, 2010) referred to above and 'The Lost Decade of Film History in India' (*Journal of the Moving Image*, no.9, 2010).

Possibly even more ambitious in scope and path breaking are Kaushik Bhaumik's PhD thesis and other writings. Combining the social history of

Bombay in the early decades of the 20th century with theoretical rigour and new insights, he argues that the earlier histories of Indian silent cinema are excessively tilted towards Phalke's self-proclaimed nationalist project and the mythological genre he worked in. Instead, he suggests that the more entertainment-oriented fantasy and stunt adventure films, or what he calls '*bazaar* cinema' , are a vital area of study and perhaps even more representative of Indian silent cinema as a whole.

Another interesting argument in Bhaumik's thesis is about how an upper class-upper caste 'Hindu ethnoscape'emerged in the films of the late 1920s and early 1930s. Comparing this shift in Indian cinema to the emergence of the 'monumental style' in pre-War Japanese cinema, he maintains that this led to a deliberate and gradual expunging of Muslim subjects and 'Islamicate idioms ' that were common at the time in popular genres like the Arabian Nights fantasies and the Rajput stunt and adventure films.

Finally, besides these important arguments, Bhaumik's PhD thesis and essays such as 'Horses in the Metropolis: Imagining the Romantic Individual in Early Bombay Cinema' (in Rachel Dwyer and Jerry Pinto (eds.), *Beyond the Boundaries of Bollywood: The Many Forms of Hindi Cinema,* OUP, New Delhi, 2011) help us to not only appreciate the variety of Indian films of the 1920s and 1930s more fully but also successfully evoke the social and cultural milieu in which they were made.

More recent is Sudhir Mahadevan's PhD thesis *The Traffic in Technologies: Early Cinema and Visual Culture in Bengal, 1840-1920* (New York University, 2009). Mahadevan examines a variety of sources to explore the pre-history and earliest days of cinema in Bengal and South Asia to highlight, 'multiple intersections between, photography and the printed image'. His subsequent essay 'Travelling Showmen, Makeshift Cinemas: The *Bioscopewallah* and Early Cinema History in India' (*BioScope*: *South Asian Screen Studies*, vol. 1, no. 1, 2010) focuses on the origin and early exhibition practices of the legendary *bioscopewallah* or travelling picture showmen in Bengal. Mahadevan writes in a vivid and urgent style and one hopes that like Hughes' and Bhaumik's theses his dissertation will also be published in the near future.

A book that deserves more notice is Richard Abel's *Encyclopedia of Early Cinema* (Routledge, London, 2005). Of direct interest are a number of entries on the earliest film companies and key pioneers of Indian silent cinema written by me. It also contains several articles by a host of early cinema specialists on technological and industrial developments, changing modes of representation and narration and early distribution and exhibition practices in different parts of the world that are relevant for the study of Indian silent cinema.

Among other published books that partially deal with Indian silent cinema is Neepa Majumdar's *Wanted Cultured Ladies Only! Female Stardom and Cinema in India, 1930s-1950s* (University of Illinois Press, Urbana and Chicago, 2009). In charting the phenomenon of female stardom in India–a combination of Hollywood discourse on film stars and a direct response to Indian cultural notions and constraints of respectability and morality–Majumdar provides a fascinating analysis of how the star profiles in film magazines combined with unofficial channels of gossip to construct the public image of a female star. Silent cinema actresses such as Manorama, Sulochana, Ermeline and even Kamalabai Gokhale (Phalke's first actress) are given as examples of how films increased the ' public circulation of women's images' and 'made women's bodies available in the public sphere'.

Valentina Vitali's *Hindi Action Cinema: Industries, Narratives, Bodies* (OUP, New Delhi, 2008) which examines the 'action ingredient' in Bombay cinema has an excellent section on the silent era's top stunt film production studio, Sharda Film Company and its main star Master Vithal, based almost entirely on magazine articles and film advertisements. Also there is a chapter on women in action films of the 1920s and 1930s where she introduces the concept of *veerangana* (warrior noblewomen) and discusses action heroines such as Ermeline, Miss Padma and the legendary Fearless Nadia who immediately followed them in the early sound cinema. Vitali highlights both the silent and sound stunt films of the Wadia Brothers by drawing on J.B.H. Wadia's unpublished memoirs and other documents in the Wadia family archive.

The focus of Sharmistha Gooptu's *Bengali Cinema: An Other Nation* (Roli Books, New Delhi, 2010) is on the sound period. It also contains a summary of some of the major developments in silent cinema in Bengal, particularly the film trade, audiences and production concerns such as Madan, Aurora and British Dominion Film Studio and the careers of leading pioneers like Hiralal Sen, Dhirendranath Ganguly and P.C. Barua.

Then there is also the offbeat work of Brigitte Schulze which I have not seen except for her essay on Phalke's *Raja Harishchandra*, 'The First Cinematic Pauranik Kathanak' (*Narrative Strategies: Essays on South Asian Literature and Film* edited by Vasudha Dalmia and Theo Damsteegt, CNWS Publications, Leiden, 1998). In her subsequent doctoral work and book *Humanist and Emotional Beginnings of a Nationalist Indian Cinema in Bombay with Kracauer in the Footsteps of Phalke* (Avinus, Berlin, 2003) she was among the first researchers to argue along with Dharamsey that the reels of *Raja Harishchandra* in the NFAI are from the 1917 version.

The only comprehensive book on Indian movie posters and publicity booklets is Rajesh Devraj and Edo Bauman's *The Art of Bollywood* (Taschen, Cologne, 2010). It deals primarily with the Bombay film industry, but the first part provides fresh insights and information about Baburao Painter and his circle's pioneering film publicity work for Maharashtra Film Co. in Kolhapur and Bombay. The authors have made a careful study of all surviving silent film posters and booklets and the publication is a visual treat.

Finally, there are two extraordinary studies of Indian visual history by the anthropologist Christopher Pinney—*Camera Indica: The Social Life of Indian Photographs* (University of Chicago Press, Chicago, 1997) and *Photos of the Gods: The Printed Image and Political Struggle in India* (OUP, New Delhi, 2004). In the former, Pinney links Phalke and the early Indian cinema to the practice of photographic portraiture and recounts fascinating anecdotes from his brief career as a photographer in Ratlam before his return to Bombay and the tryst with cinema. And in the latter, he draws a parallel between Indian silent films and the widespread medium of chromolithographs—not only are the titles, subjects and themes similar, but there is an overarching aesthetic of what he calls, 'the inter-occularity' of popular visual culture across academic painting and other new media introduced in the colonial period. In these books Pinney brilliantly demonstrates that academic painting, printed images, photographs and films make a direct appeal to traditional motifs and concerns, and by the same token, this process is always mediated by the historical context of formulating new political and visual identities in both the colonial period as well as in India today.

GULZAR
The Charming Singer &
1

PART TWO

INTRODUCTION TO REVISED AND EXPANDED EDITION

With the second edition of *Light of Asia*, we also present a revised and substantially updated Indian Silent Cinema filmography.

Although India has had a long, and venerable tradition of filmographers, the theory of the filmography has not been adequately discussed in the Indian cinema. Filmographies worldwide have existed for many reasons: they constitute a compilation of film credits (most famously *Monthly Film Bulletin/Sight & Sound* listings); they also define a compilation of national repositories, such as the Joint European Filmography assembled under the famous Project Lumière (http://www.ace-film.org/jef/), or sometimes they exist to consolidate the print/publicity records of a specific film archives (for instance, the British Film Institute's *Stills, Posters and Designs* catalogue, in itself an invaluable filmographic resource, has become even more so since its linking to the National Film Archive's catalogue). Or they may have a somewhat more specific reason relevant to India: its chronic problem of a single title redistributed under different names finds echoes in the JEF, which had also attempted to consolidate national records within Europe relating to the same film into a single, multinational entry.

Indian filmographers typically rely on secondary sources, including publicity pamphlets, advertising, and sometimes even straight hearsay, in addition where possible, to censor records. At best, this strategy has followed what we could call the 'plausibility' principle, in trying to work out what films had been completed, under what studio, and by whom. The present filmography significantly furthers that principle both by adding new methodologies to what is plausible–through casting a wider net–and through more rigorous checking with available sources.

In the first edition itself, we had encountered problems of multiple versions of a single title being shown as multiple titles. More local variants of this familiar problem in film history arise, in India, from the practices of a somewhat underdeveloped film publicity machine: films would have a release title different from the title announced at the start of production; would put out pamphlets with different credits; and repeated reissues of the same film would be under different titles. Stars would change their names, several stars would have the same name and so forth. The plausibility factor required us to know, for instance, whether a producer, director, star, cinematographer were indeed in a particular studio when the film was made, or when a studio closed, or changed hands.

Through the period between these two versions, I have kept on my work of both unearthing new sources for cross-verification, and have made several major modifications. The new filmography has been rearranged using censor certificates as reference. It also now includes the somewhat questionable category of 'short narrative films', which are defined as titles between 500 and 3200 feet. This is of interest that *Raja Harishchandra* (1917) at 2944 feet and *Lanka Dahan* (1917) at 3000 feet, fall within the category of short films. However, we have considered these full length films and categorised them as such. I have now included more names of actors/directors/cameramen etc., and carried out several changes of incorrect credits. Many names have now been identified in a more complete form (so Gurav is identified as Shankarrao Gurav, and Gade is Baburao Gade), and the problem of actors changing their names is also come fairly under control (such as the actress Nalini renaming herself as Dwarki). Several foreign films issued under Indian names have been removed as have both unreleased and incomplete films (which have been listed in Appendix C).

The present filmography therefore now identifies a total of 1338 silent films—1290 full length films and forty-eight short features.

Virchand Dharamsey

New Mumbai

28 February 2013

INTRODUCTION TO THE FIRST EDITION (1994)

The research that has culminated in this filmography began with very different concerns, around 1984, which at the time addressed specific individuals: crucially Kohinoor studio proprietor Dwarkadas N. Sampat, filmmakers Manilal Joshi and Kanjibhai Rathod, and the various studios they worked with. It became apparent even then that India's silent era–which saw the 1313 (including four re-releases) films recorded here–was a hive of frenetic activity, with individual careers intersecting those of literally hundreds of short-lived production houses surrounding the approximately ten studios that lasted through the late silent period. The experience of that research was to stand me in good stead in some unexpected ways.

The Indian Censor Board, and the process of recording completed titles, original censored footage and dates, began in 1920. In this filmography, that record, to the extent that it survives, had itself to be checked and amended—in the several instances of films re-released under different titles (and often presented as two separate films), of imported titles locally released under Indian names, with little distinction made between local production houses and importers. Orient Pictures, an import house that released a presumably foreign film under the Indian title *Salam Aleikum* (1921), has often been confused with Suchet Singh's Orient Film Manufacturing Company of the same time; likewise, *Virtuous Sinner*, a 1922 import consistently recorded as an Indian film and ascribed to a Pioneer Film Company, has occasionally been taken to be the chronologically later Pioneer studio started by S.N. Patankar, in turn causing the title to occasionally appear in Patankar's filmography. Filling in the gaps, in a context in which films routinely carried no credits except for the producer and scenarist–a practice which continued well into the 1920s–has forced silent cinema filmographers to resort to speculation, or to mechanistic attributions: for example assigning all Hindustan Cinema Film Co. films to its one-time promoter D.G. Phalke, or Madan Theatres productions to either Jyotish Bannerjee or Priyanath Ganguly.

The filmography we present introduces other sources, like film advertising in a variety of journals of the time, most importantly *Bombay Samachar, Bombay Chronicle, Times of India, Mouj Majah, Photoplay, Filmland, Chitrapat, Vismi Sadi* and *Moving Picture Monthly*. The information they provide has been substantiated by extensive research into news reports of titles announced, completed or released. There are numerous problems posed by this material, a consequence of the still underdeveloped professionalism of the 1920s film publicity machine. Typically the title announced would not be the title completed; films produced by one company would be sold to others and reissued under new credits, stars would routinely change their names (the actress Mary became Kumudini, and was often referred to by both names even for the same film; Winnie Stewart became Manorama). Other confusions include four actresses named Gohar (separated here as Gohar, Miss Gohur, Goharjaan and Gohar Jr.), two Nanubhai Desais (the Surya Film writer has been referred to with his initial as Nanubhai R. Desai) and a few that remain to be solved: for example Pawar, Chavan (or Chauhan).

The available information had thus to be continuously collated with separate career trajectories of who was doing what at different times, which studios started (and closed) on which dates, what happened to a studio's catalogue back-list when partnerships split up, and so on. On the last-mentioned problem, a valuable instance is available in the current Indian silent package: *Sukanya Savitri*, made in 1922 at Kohinoor but reissued by the studio's one-time partner Maneklal Patel and credited, in the surviving print, to the Krishna studio. There are several instances where films have been announced, for example *Satara Sarhad*, aka *Through the Khyber*, produced by the Royal Players Corporation, Peshawar and directed by J. Makhijani, advertised in 1932 but never heard of again, as well as titles like *Data Karna* (1918) and *Shiv Kumar* (undated), which have been deleted for want of information as to whether these films were ever complete. One surviving film, *Buddu Ki Akkal*, has also been omitted for want of any information as to its origins. Evidently this problem would have to be addressed only through further research

This filmography substantially adds to the number of titles included in the previous filmographies of B.V. Dharap (*Silent Filmography,* National Film Archive of India, unpublished), Firoze Rangoonwalla (*Indian Filmography: Silent and Hindi Films,* 1970), and B. Jha (*Indian Motion Picture Almanac,* 1986) while eliminating several that, we can now prove, were either re-releases or films with more than one title listed as separate productions. Re-censored or re-released versions have been indicated wherever they occur, and all the titles under which films were known have been provided. However, it may be added, that most of the English spellings of film titles (and personalities) used in this filmography, are carried over from the source materials and are by no means their only possible versions. The filmography also includes, for the first time, a substantial list of banned titles, which therefore remained either unreleased or were later distributed in partially transformed versions. While available credits have been greatly extended, there are some notable deletions: in other words, we would argue that what is *missing*–because of the doubtful nature of earlier attributions–in this filmography is arguably, at times anyway, as significant as what is there. There are also several occasions where we have changed the credits of some titles that have passed into a 'common knowledge'-type history: the major hit *Kala Nag* (1924), assumed routinely to be directed by its lead star (and future director) Homi Master, has here been credited to Kanjibhai Rathod. Another useful addition presented here for the first time is the distinction between the feature-length and the short film, in the process both correcting titles previously assumed to be feature-length, e.g. the Madan Theatres' one-reeler *Parikshit* (1922) and Angora Films' two-reel comedy *Romantic Lovers* (1931), as well as adding several others previously unrecorded.

Genre divisions have been provided under nine broad categories: the mythological, the historical, the crime movie, the literary adaptation (from classical literature), the costume movie (including fantasy, legend, folk-derived themes and 'period' movies), the comedy, the stunt movie, the devotional and the social. It is notoriously difficult to ascribe genres to Indian films in the Hollywood sense, given the fact that films routinely combine a variety of genres, and there has never been a Hollywood-type inscription of distinct budgets into genre-productions. Most of the classification heads would be self-explanatory, except perhaps the division between the mythological and the devotional: the mythological broadly adapted well-known themes from the Puranas and the two epics, *Mahabharata* and *Ramayana,* while the devotional would be a distinct sub-genre addressing medieval saint-poets, or specific local deities, creating an aura of worshipful, or even ritualistic, identification address.

Finally, no work of this kind can ever be said to be 'complete', and this compilation project, even as it builds upon earlier work, hopes to provide the basis for future investigation that will both clarify whatever ambiguities remain and add to the resources currently at the command of the Indian silent cinema researcher. I am indebted to Tatsu Dharamsey and Ashish Rajadhyaksha for help provided.

Virchand Dharamsey
Bombay/Pune
August 1994

Abbreviations

pc:	Production Company
d:	Director
c:	Camera
st:	Story
sc:	Script
lp:	Leading Players

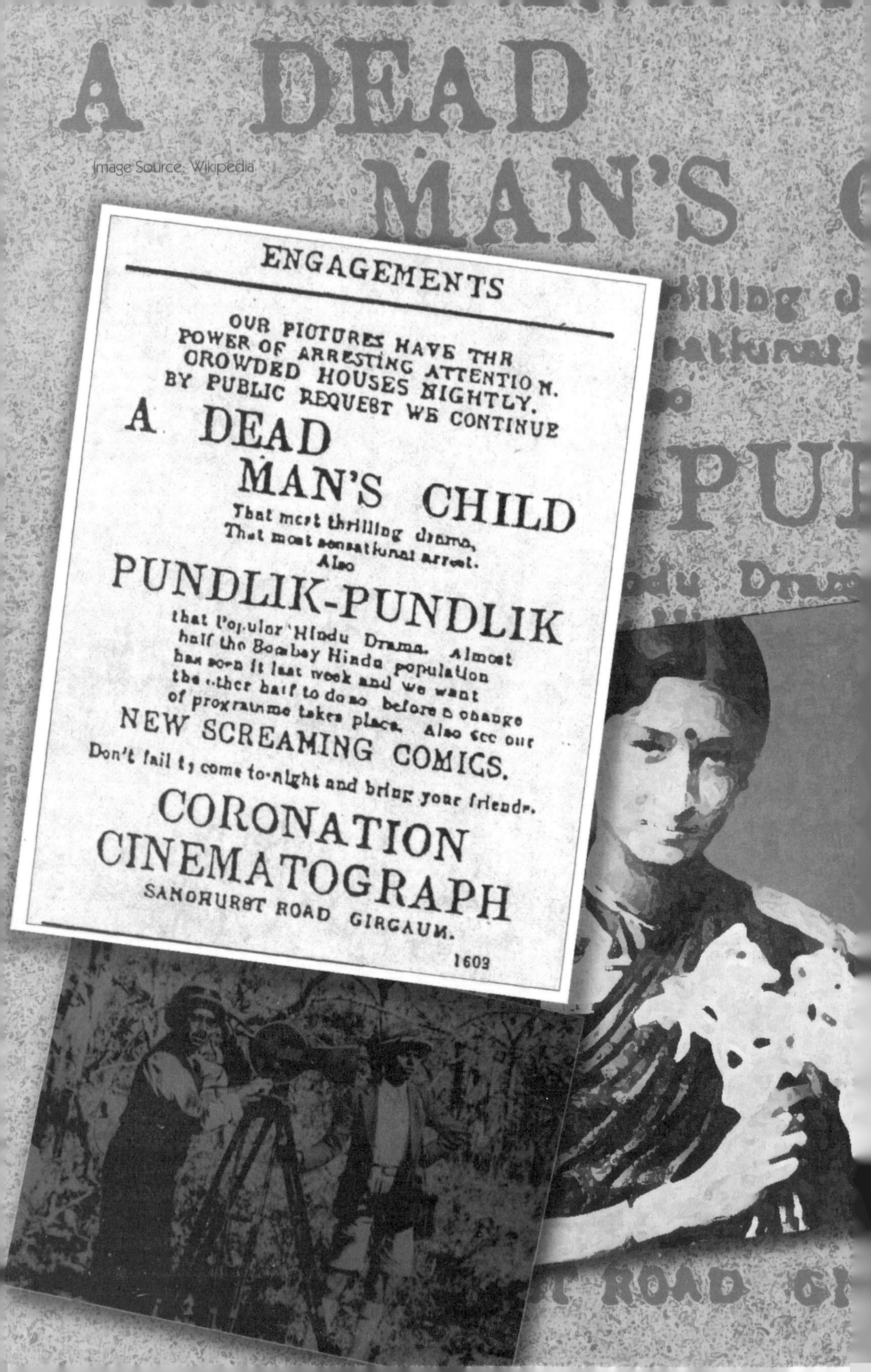

Image Source: Wikipedia

FILMOGRAPHY

INDIAN SILENT CINEMA 1912-1934

Virchand Dharamsey

1912

PUNDALIK

1000 ft. (aprox.); **genre:** Mythological

Remarks: Narayan Govind Chitre requisitioned the services of a Mr Johnson, apparently a Bourne & Shepherd cameraman, and completed it with the help of P.R. Tipnis. The film was shot at Mangaldas Gardens at Lamington Road, Bombay–that is on the grounds occupied by Naaz and Imperial Cinema. Based on Ramrao Kirtikar's Marathi play as staged by Shripad Sangeet Mandli. Released on May 18, 1912 at the Coronation Cinematograph.

1913

MOHINI

aka **Mohini Bhasmasur**, **Bhasmasur Mohini**

3600 ft.; **genre:** Mythological **pc:** Phalke's Films, Nasik **d/co-c/st/sc:** D.G. Phalke **co-c:** Trymbak B. Telang **lp:** Durgabai, Kamalabai, D.D. Dabke, Vishnu Sonar (?), Sane, D.B. Sukte (?)

Remarks: Released on December 27, 1913 at the Olympia, Bombay.

JAIMINI AND VYAS

aka **Indriya Shreshth Ki Vidya, Learning versus Passion**

1000 ft; **genre:** Mythological

pc: Patankar Union **d/c:** S.N. Patankar **co/c:** A.P. Karandikar **lp:** Narmada Mande, Vishnu Purushottam (V.P. Divekar), K.G. Gokhale

Remarks: Narmada Mande was perhaps the earliest actress to appear in films. Patankar Union's earlier film *Savitri* (1912) remained unreleased due to technical faults (see Appendix C).

Pithache Panje
aka **Hand Prints**
500 ft; **genre:** Comedy
pc: Phalke's Films, Nasik **d/co-c/st/sc:** D.G. Phalke

Raja Harishchandra
3700 ft.; **genre:** Mythological
pc: Phalke's Films, Bombay **d/co-c/st/sc:** D.G. Phalke **co-c:** Trymbak B. Telang
lp: D.D. Dabke, Pandurang Sane (as Taramati), Bhalchandra Phalke, Gajanan Sane, Dattatray Kshirsagar, Ganpat Shinde, Vishnu Hari Aundhkar, Anna Salunke, Nath Telang
Remarks: First screening for invitees on April 21, 1913 at Olympia, Bombay. First commercial screening on May 3, 1913 at the Coronation Cinematograph.

1914

Satyavan Savitri
aka **Savitri**
3680 ft.; **genre:** Mythological
pc: Phalke's Films, Nasik **d/co-c/st/sc:** D.G. Phalke **co-c:** Trymbak B. Telang

1915

Death of Narayanrao Peshwa
6000 ft.; **genre:** Historical
pc: Patankar Union
d/c: S.N. Patankar **co/c:** A.P. Karandikar
lp: Gopal Ranade, K.G. Gokhale, Damuanna Joshi, V.P. Divekar (?)

Gopal Krishna
genre: Mythological
pc: Indian Film Co., Madras **d:** Nataraja Mudaliar

1916

Dhumrapan Leela
633 ft.
Phalke's Films, Nasik **d/st/sc:** D.G. Phalke

Keechak Vatham
aka **Keechak Vadham**
5000 ft.; **genre:** Mythological
pc: Indian Film Co., Madras **d/c:** Nataraja Mudaliar
lp: Raja Mudaliar, Jeevarathnam

Prahlad Charitra
genre: Mythological
pc: Patankar Union **d/c:** S.N. Patankar **co/c:** A.P. Karandikar

Soulagnarasa
723 ft.; **genre:** Comedy
pc: Phalke's Films, Nasik **d/c/st/sc:** D.G. Phalke

Swapna Vihar
822 ft.; **genre:** Comedy
pc: Phalke's Films, Nasik **d/c/st/sc:** D.G. Phalke

1917

Dhandal Bhatji's Gangasnan
aka **Putralabh**
525 ft.; **genre:** Comedy
pc: Phalke's Films, Nasik **d/c/st/sc:** D.G. Phalke

Draupathi Vastrapaharanam
aka **Draupathi Vasthirabaharanam, Draupadi Vastraharan**
6000 ft.; **genre:** Mythological
pc: Indian Film Co, Madras **d/c:** Nataraja Mudaliar
lp: Mrs Violet Berry, Raja Mudaliar, Doraiswamy Pillai

Lanka Dahan
aka **Lanka Aflame**
3000 ft.; **genre:** Mythological
pc: Phalke's Films, Nasik **d/co-c/st/sc:** D.G. Phalke **co-c:** Trymbak B. Telang
lp: Anna Salunke (double role), Ganpat Shinde, D.D. Dabke

Raja Harishchandra
2944 ft.; **genre:** Mythological
pc: Phalke's Films, Nasik **d/co-c/st/sc:** D.G. Phalke **co-c:** Trymbak B. Telang
lp: Anna Salunke (as Taramati), D.D. Dabke, Bhalchandra Phalke, Gajanan Sane, Ganpat Shinde
Remarks: First screening on April 4, 1917 at the Aryan, Poona.

Satyawadi Raja Harischandra
7000 ft.; **genre:** Mythological
pc: Elphinstone Bioscope, Calcutta **d:** Rustomji Dotiwala
lp: Miss Savaria, Hormasji Tantara, Behramsha Tantara
Remarks: Film based on an original Gujarati play by Ranchhodbhai Udayram. Revised version by Kaikhushroo Kabaraji. Hindustani version by Vinayak Prasad Talib.

1918

Mayilravanan
aka **Mahiravana, Maruti Vijay**
5750 ft.; **genre:** Mythological
pc: Indian Film Co., Vellore **d/c:** Nataraja Mudaliar
lp: Subramanya Naidu

Raja Shriyal
aka **Sheth Sagalsha, Siruthondar Nayanar, Terrific Ordeal**
3447 ft.; **genre:** Devotional
pc: Patankar Friends & Co. **d/c:** S.N. Patankar **co/c:** A.P. Karandikar **st/sc:** Mohanlal G. Dave
lp: Kalidas Bheem, Dharap

Ram Vanvas
aka **Exile of Rama**
20000 ft.; **genre:** Mythological serial in four parts
pc: Patankar Friends & Co. **d/c:** S.N. Patankar **co/c:** A.P. Karandikar **st/sc:** Mohanlal G. Dave
lp: Dharap

Shri Krishna Janma
aka **The Birth of Shri Krishna**
5500 ft.; **genre:** Mythological
pc: Hindustan Cinema Film Co., Nasik **d/c/st/sc:** D.G. Phalke
lp: D.D. Dabke, Purshottam Vaidya, Mandakini Phalke, Bhagirathibai, Neelkanth, Gajanan Sane

1919

Ahilya Uddhar
5000 ft.; **genre:** Mythological
pc: Hindustan Cinema Film Co., Nasik **d:** Gajanan V. Sane

Bilwamangal
aka **Bhakta Surdas**
12,000 ft.; **genre:** Devotional
pc: Elphinstone Bioscope, Calcutta **d:** Rustomji Dotiwala **st:** Champsi Udeshi
lp: Miss Gohur, Dorabji Mewawala

Kabir Kamal
6746 ft.; **genre:** Devotional
pc: Patankar Friends & Co. **d/c:** S.N. Patankar **co/c:** A.P. Karandkiar
st/sc: Mohanlal G. Dave
lp: Heera Limaye, V.P. Divekar, Trymbakrao Pradhan, Baba Vyas, Damuanna Joshi, Sitaram Naik, Sitarampant Joshi

Kacha Devyani
aka **Vidya Haran**
genre: Mythological
pc: Patankar Friends & Co. **d/c:** S.N. Patankar **co/c:** A.P. Karandikar **st/sc:** Mohanlal G. Dave
lp: Damuanna Joshi, Jui, Usha, Sitarampant Joshi
Remarks: Gujarati *garaba* dance was introduced in this film.

Kaliya Mardan
6000 ft.; **genre:** Mythological
pc: Hindustan Cinema Film Co., Nasik **d/c/st/sc:** D.G.Phalke
lp: Mandakini Phalke, Anna Salunke, Neelkanth, Sahadev, Sahadevrao Tapkire, Baburao Patil

Lava Kush
4000 ft.; **genre:** Mythological
pc: Indian Film Co., Vellore **d/c:** Nataraja Mudaliar
lp: Devaki, Govindaswamy Naidu

Narasinha Avatar
5000 ft.; **genre:** Mythological
pc: Patankar Friends & Co. **d/c:** S.N. Patankar **co/c:** A.P. Karandikar **st/sc:** Mohanlal G. Dave
lp: Heera Limaye, Trymbakrao Pradhan, Vijay

Usha Swapna
aka **Okha Haran**
6025 ft.; **genre:** Mythological
pc: Hindustan Cinema Film Co., Nasik **d:** Gajanan V. Sane

Vishvamitra Menaka
aka **Shakuntala Janma**
4515 ft.; **genre:** Mythological
pc: Indian Film Mfg. Co. **d/c:** D.D. Dabke
lp: D.D. Dabke, K.P. Bhave, P.R. Joshi

1920

Dr. Pagal
aka **Three Devils**
2102 ft.; **genre:** Comedy
pc: Oriental Film Mfg. Co. **d:** Suchet Singh

Jalandhar Vrinda
6000 ft.; **genre:** Mythological
pc: Hindustan Cinema Film Co., Nasik **d:** Gajanan V. Sane

▲ **Shri Krishna Janma**

Kalingamardhanam
pc: Indian Film Co., Vellore **d/c:** Nataraja Mudaliar

Katorabhar Khoon
aka **Stinger Stung, Zaheri Saamp**

7105 ft.; **genre:** Crime

pc: Patankar Friends & Co. **d/c:** S. N. Patankar **co/c:** A.P. Karandikar **st:** based on a Bengali novel (?) **sc:** Mohanlal G. Dave

lp: Trymbakrao Pradhan, K.G. Gokhale, Baba Vyas

Madalasa
6560 ft.; **genre:** Mythological

pc: Patankar Friends & Co. **d/c:** S.N. Patankar **co/c:** A.P. Karandikar **st/sc:** Mohanlal G. Dave

lp: Trymbakrao Pradhan, K.G. Gokhale

Mahabharat
8000 ft.; **genre:** Mythological

pc: Madan Theatres Ltd. **d:** Rustomji Dotiwala

Mrichhakatik
4500 ft.; **genre:** Adaptation

pc: Oriental Film Mfg. Co. **d/sc:** Suchet Singh **c:** Gajanan S. Devare **st:** based on Shudraka's play

lp: Kanjibhai Rathod

Nala Damayanti

10,000 ft.; **genre:** Mythological

pc: Madan Theatres Ltd. **d/c:** Eugenio de Liguoro **st:** Pandit Tulsidutt Shaida

lp: Patience Cooper, Signor P. Manneli, Keki Adajania, Master Mohan, Khurshetji Bilimoria, Khurshetji Engineer, Manchersha Chapgar, Eugenio de Liguoro, Dadibhai Sarkari, Albertini (Albertina), Issac Simon, Reva Shankar

Narasinh Mehta

aka **Great Devotee of Shri Krishna**

4725 ft.; **genre:** Devotional

pc: Oriental Film Mfg. Co. **d:** Suchet Singh **c:** Gajanan S. Devare

lp: Kanjibhai Rathod

Ram Janma

6000 ft.; **genre:** Mythological

pc: Hindustan Cinema Film Co., Nasik **d:** Gajanan V. Sane

Rama or Maya

7500 ft.; **genre:** Social

pc: Oriental Film Mfg. Co. **d:** Suchet Singh **c:** Gajanan S. Devare

lp: Kanjibhai Rathod, Gohar Jaan

Sairandhri

4958 ft.; **genre:** Mythological

pc: Maharashtra Film Co., Kolhapur **d/c/st/sc:** Baburao Painter **co/c:** S. Fattelal

lp: Balasaheb Yadav, Zunzharrao Pawar, Kamaladevi (Gulab bai), Kishabapu Bakre, Sushila Devi (Anasuya bai), Baburao Pendharkar, Ravji Mhaiskar, Ganpat Bakre, Sitaram Kulkarni, Shivram Vashikar, V.G. Damle

► **Sairandhri**

Sati Parvati
aka **Dakshayagna**
4000 ft.; **genre:** Mythological
pc: Kohinoor Film Co. **d:** V.P. Divekar **c:** A.P. Karandikar
lp: Prabha, Khalil, Vaidya, Trymbakrao Pradhan

Seeta Swayamvar
6950 ft.; **genre:** Mythological
pc: S.N. Patankar **d/c:** S.N. Patankar **st/sc:** Mohanlal G. Dave
lp: Heera Limaye

Shakuntala
aka **Lost Ring**
6000 ft.; **genre:** Adaptation
pc: Oriental Film Mfg. Co. **d/sc:** Suchet Singh **st:** based on Kalidasa's play **c:** Baron von Rayvon
lp: Dorothy Kingdom, Sampson, Mrs Sutaria, Gohar Jaan, Kanjibhai Rathod

Shakuntala
aka **Fateful Ring, The Lost Ring**
6500 ft.; **genre:** Adaptation
pc: Patankar Friends & Co. **d/c:** S.N. Patankar **co/c:** A.P. Karandikar **st:** based on Kalidasa's play **sc:** Mohanlal G. Dave
lp: Tara Koregaonkar, Thatte, Baba Vyas

Shani Prabhav
5169 ft.; **genre:** Mythological
pc: Hindustan Cinema Film Co., Nasik **d:** Gajanan V. Sane

Shri Krishna Sudama
6738 ft.; **genre:** Mythological
pc: Kohinoor Film Co. **d:** Vishnupant Divekar **c:** A.P. Karandikar **st/sc:** Mohanlal G. Dave
lp: Khalil, Moti, Prabha, Kesarbai, Sakina, Alimiyan, Vaidya

Vichitra Gutika
aka **Enchanted Pills**
4500 ft.; **genre:** Comedy
pc: Patankar Friends & Co. **d/c:** S.N. Patankar **co/c:** A.P. Karandikar **st/sc:** Mohanlal G. Dave
lp: Trymbakrao Pradhan, Marathe, Sitarampant Joshi, K.G. Gokhale, Damuanna Joshi, Dighe

1921

Behula
aka **Mansha Pooja**

4000 ft.; **genre:** Devotional
pc: Madan Theatres Ltd. **d/c:** Camille de Grand (C Legrand)
lp: Patience Cooper

Bhakta Vidur
6835 ft.; **genre:** Mythological
pc: Kohinoor Film Co. **d:** Kanjibhai Rathod **c:** Gajanan S. Devare **st/sc:** Mohanlal G. Dave
lp: Dwarkadas Sampat, Maneklal Patel, Sakina, Homi Master, Prabhashankar, Gangaram
Remarks: After a successful run of four weeks in Bombay, the film was banned on political grounds. Later re-released as *Dharma Vijay* (1922).

Bhishma Pratigna
8000 ft.; **genre:** Mythological
pc: Star of the East Film Co., Madras **d/sc:** R.S. Prakash

Bilet Pherat
aka **The England Returned**
4000 ft.; **genre:** Comedy
pc: Indo-British Film Co., Calcutta **d/st/sc:** Nitish C. Lahiri **c:** Jyotish Sarkar
lp: Dhiren Ganguly, Sushiladevi, Manmath Pal, Kunjalal Chakrabarty, Usharani Dasi, Benodebala Devi

Chandrahasa
5865 ft.; **genre:** Mythological
pc: Kohinoor Film Co. **d:** Kanjibhai Rathod **st/sc:** Mohanlal G. Dave
lp: Khalil, Tara, Moti, Savita, Dhanji, Chimanlal Bhojak (Chandrahas Jr.)

Dabbur Kelenkari
2000 ft.
pc: Aurora Film Co., Calcutta **d/c:** Debi Ghosh
lp: Chani Datta

Dhruva Charitra
genre: Mythological
pc: Madan Theatres Ltd. **d/c:** Eugenio de Liguoro **st/sc:** Pandit Tulsidutt Shaida
lp: P. Mannelli, Signorina F. Mannelli, Patience Cooper, Master Mohan, Pestonji Madan, Reva Shankar, Surajram, James Mcgrath, Manilal, Dadibhai Sarkari, Aga Hashr Kashmiri, Kusum Kumari, Khurshetji Bilimoria, Jasoda Singh, Isaac Simon, Cowasjee Gotla, Mr Palwan, Miss Dorros

Govardhandhari
5940 ft.; **genre:** Mythological
pc: Hindustan Cinema Film Co., Nasik **d:** Gajanan V. Sane

Kansa Vadha
aka **End of the Tyrant King**
6157 ft.; **genre:** Mythological
pc: Hindustan Cinema Films Co., Nasik **d:** Gajanan V. Sane

Krishna Maya
5220 ft.
pc: Kohinoor Film Co. **d:** Kanjibhai Rathod **c:** Vishnu B. Joshi **st/sc:** Mohanlal G. Dave
lp: Jamuna, Alimiyan, Kesar, Rajababu

Ma Durga
aka **Jagat Janani Jagadamba**
4000 ft.; **genre:** Mythological
pc: Madan Theatres Ltd. **d/c:** Camille de Grand

Mira Bai
6942 ft.; **genre:** Devotional
pc: Kohinoor Film Co. **d:** Kanjibhai Rathod **st/sc:** Mohanlal G. Dave
lp: Tara, Khalil

Mohini
aka **Ekadashi**, **Triumph of Faith**
4000 feet; **genre:** Mythological
pc: Madan Theatres Ltd. **d:** Sisir Bhaduri **c:** Noni Gopal Sanyal
lp: Sisir Bhaduri, Albertini, Patience Cooper, Akshoy Kumar Chakrabarty, Shefalika, Kashinath Chatterji, Prova, Nipendranath Bose, Hiralal Dutt

Pradyumna
aka **Krishna Kumar, Burning of Kama**
5820 ft.; **genre:** Mythological
pc: Bharat Cinema Film Co., Poona **d:** Vishnupant Divekar **c:** A.P. Karandikar

Pundalik
5987 ft.; **genre:** Mythological
pc: Hindustan Cinema Films Co., Nasik **d:** Ganpat Shinde

Pundalik
6875 ft.; **genre:** Mythological
pc: Kohinoor Film Co. **d:** Kanjibhai Rathod **st/sc:** Mohanlal G. Dave

Raja Gopichand
5820 ft.; **genre:** Mythological
pc: Bharat Cinema Film Co., Poona **d:** Vishnupant Divekar **c:** A.P. Karandikar
lp: Mama Bhatt, Heera Limaye

Ratnakar
aka **Valmiki**
4000 ft.; **genre:** Mythological
pc: Aurora Cinema Co., Calcutta **d/st/sc:** Surendra Narayan Roy **c:** Debi Ghosh
lp: Sushiladevi, Chunilal Deb, Shashimukhi
Remarks: The film was released in Bengal as *Dasyu Ratnakar.*

Rukmini Haran
6957 ft.; **genre:** Mythological
pc: Kohinoor Film Co. **d:** Kanjibhai Rathod **c:** Vishnu B. Joshi **st/sc:** Mohanlal G. Dave
lp: Khalil, Tara, Moti, R.N. Vaidya, Sakina, Gangaram

Rukmini Kalyanam
aka **Rukmini Satyabhama**
4000 ft.; **genre:** Mythological
pc: Indian Film Co., Vellore **d:** Nataraja Mudaliar
lp: Janaki, Jeevarathnam, Natesa Naidu, Devaki

Sant Tukaram
7336 ft.; **genre:** Devotional
pc: Kalanidhi Pictures Co. **d/c:** S.N. Patankar (?)
lp: Tara Koregaonkar, K.G. Gokhale, Baba Vyas

Sati Anasuya
aka **Mahasati Anasuya, Birth of Shri Dattatreya**
6927 ft.; **genre:** Mythological
pc: Kohinoor Film Co. **d:** Kanjibhai Rathod **c:** Vishnu B. Joshi **st/sc:** Mohanlal G. Dave
lp: Sakina, Khalil, R.N. Vaidya

Sati Sulochana
5927 ft.; **genre:** Mythological
pc: Hindustan Cinema Film Co., Nasik **d:** Gajanan V. Sane
lp: Shanta Nalgunde, D.B. Sukte

Shivaratri
6000 ft.; **genre:** Mythological
pc: Madan Theatres Ltd. **d/c:** Camille de Grand **lp:** Prabodh Ch Bose, Kusum Kumari, Basanta Kumari, P. Mannelli, F. Mannelli, Gopal Bhattacharya

Shri Krishna Leela
5344 ft.; **genre:** Mythological
pc: Hindustan Cinema Film Co., Nasik **d:** Gajanan V. Sane

Subhadra Haran
6225 ft.; **genre:** Mythological
pc: Kohinoor Film Co. **d:** Kanjibhai Rathod **c:** Vishnu B. Joshi **st/sc:** Mohanlal G. Dave
lp: Tara, Khalil
Remarks: Film reissued under the banner of Krishna Film Co. in 1924.

Surekha Haran
aka **Surekha Abhimanyu, Vatsala Haran, Maya Bazar**
6780 ft.; **genre:** Mythological
pc: Maharashtra Film Co., Kolhapur **d/c:** Baburao Painter **co/c:** S. Fattelal
lp: Ranganath Khatavkar, V. Shantaram, Ravji Mhaiskar, Balasaheb Yadav, Ganpat Bakre, Kamladevi, Vishnupant Pagnis, Zunzharrao Pawar, Baburao Pendharkar, Gajrabai, Chimasaheb Ghorpade, Neelkanth Bulbule, Kishabapu Bakre, K. Dhaibar
Remarks: This film was reissued as *Maya Bazar* aka *Vatsala Haran* in 1925.

Tehmuras & Temuljee
5000 ft.; **genre:** Comedy
pc: Madan Theatres Ltd. **st:** Pijam, based on the play *Aflatoon*
lp: Master Mohan, Dadibhai Sarkari, Keki Adajania, Ratansha Sinor, Master Bhrigu, Peroj Shah

Thief Entertained
957 ft.; **genre:** Comedy
pc: Bharat Cinema Film Co., Poona

Tridandi Sanyas
6447 ft.; **genre:** Mythological
pc: Bharat Cinema Film Co., Poona **d:** V.P. Divekar **c:** A.P. Karandikar
lp: Heera Limaye, Soni, Anand Shinde

Tukaram
6000 ft.; **genre:** Devotional
pc: Hindustan Cinema Film Co., Nasik **d:** Ganpat Shinde

Urvashi
aka **Nymph Celestial**
5500 ft.; **genre:** Mythological
pc: Bharat Cinema Film Co., Poona **d:** V.P. Divekar **c:** A.P. Karandikar **st:** based on Kalidasa's play
lp: Vithabai, Heera Limaye

Valli's Wedding
aka **Valli Thirumanam**
6000 ft.; **genre:** Mythological
pc: Whittaker, Madras **d:** Whittaker

Valmiki
5608 ft.; **genre:** Mythological
pc: Hindustan Cinema Film Co., Nasik **d:** Gajanan V. Sane

Vikram Satva Pariksha
5469 ft.; **genre:** Mythological
pc: Hindustan Cinema Film Co., Nasik **d:** Gajanan V. Sane

Vikram Urvashi
5271 ft.; **genre:** Mythological
pc: Kohinoor Film Co. **d:** Kanjibhai Rathod **c:** Vishnu B. Joshi **st/sc:** Mohanlal G. Dave
lp: Lina Valentine, R.N. Vaidya, Sakina

Vishnu Avatar
4000 ft.; **genre:** Mythological
pc: Madan Theatres Ltd. **d/c:** Camille de Grand **st:** Pandit Tulsidutt Shaida
lp: Patience Cooper

Yashoda Nandan
aka **Radha Krishna**
5600 ft.; **genre:** Mythological
pc: Indo-British Film Co., Calcutta **d:** Nitish C. Lahiri **c:** Jyotish Sarkar
lp: Dhiren Ganguly, Sushiladevi, Pramoda Sundari, Kunjalal Chakrabarty

1922

Ahiravan Mahiravan Vadha
aka **Ahi-Mahi Vadha**
6950 ft.; **genre:** Mythological
pc: Hindustan Cinema Film Co., Nasik **d:** Gajanan V. Sane **c:** Anna Salunke
lp: Bhaurao Datar, Sane, Bachu Pawar, Shanta Nalgunde, Ghanshyam Singh

Ajamil
6956 ft.; **genre:** Mythological
pc: Kohinoor Film Co. **d:** Kanjibhai Rathod **st/sc:** Mohanlal G. Dave
lp: Khalil, Jamuna, Gangaram, Homi Master
Remarks: Film reissued under the banner of Krishna Film Co. in 1924.

Andhare Alo
aka **Influence of Love**
5000 ft.; **genre:** Social
pc: Taj Mahal Film Co., Calcutta **d:** Sisir Bhaduri/ Naresh Mitra **c:** Noni Gopal Sanyal
st: Saratchandra Chatterjee
lp: Sisir Bhaduri, Naresh Mitra, Jogesh Choudhury, Durga Rani

Barer Bazar
aka **Biyer Bazar, Bridegroom Market, Marriage Market**
5000 ft.; **genre:** Social Comedy
pc: Madan Theatres Ltd. **d:** Sisir Bhaduri
lp: Chittaranjan Goswami, Niroda Sundari

Bhagwata Bhakta Damaji
aka **Damaji**
5680 ft.; **genre:** Devotional
pc: Maharashtra Film Co., Kolhapur **d/c:** Baburao Painter **co/c:** S. Fattelal
lp: Ravji Mhaiskar, Kamaladevi, N.D. Sarpotdar, Baburao Pendharkar, Zunzharrao Pawar, Balasaheb Yadav

Bhakta Ambarish
6733 ft.; **genre:** Mythological
pc: Kohinoor Film Co. **d:** Kanjibhai Rathod **c:** Gajanan S. Devare **st/sc:** Mohanlal G. Dave
lp: Khalil, Tara, R.N. Vaidya

Bhakta Bodana
aka **Shri Ranchhodrai**
7925 ft.; **genre:** Devotional
pc: National Film Co. **d:** S.N. Patankar **st/sc:** Mohanlal G. Dave
lp: Raja Sandow

Bhishma
5000 ft.; **genre:** Mythological
pc: Madan Theatres Ltd.
lp: Master Mohan, Keki Adajania

Bhishma Banashayya
aka **Supreme Sacrifice of Bhishma**
5865 ft.; **genre:** Mythological
pc: Star Films Ltd. **c:** Vishnu B. Joshi
lp: Madanrai Vakil, Ermeline (?)

Bidya Sunder
aka **Lover's Trance**
5000 ft.; **genre:** Legend
pc: Aurora Film Co., Calcutta **d/st/sc:** Surendra Narayan Roy **c:** Debi Ghosh
lp: Durga Rani

Bimata
aka **Step Mother, Bijoya Basant**

5000 ft.; **genre:** Social
pc: Lotus Film Co., Hyderabad DN **d:** Dhiren Ganguly **st:** Amritlal Bose
lp: Dhiren Ganguly, Miss Bell

Bisha Briksha
aka **Poison Tree**
5000 ft.; **genre:** Social
pc: Madan Theatres Ltd. **st:** Bankimchandra Chatterjee
lp: Gopal Bhattacharya, Kusum Kumari

Boodha Boobukh
4306 ft.; **genre:** Comedy
pc: Madan Theatres Ltd. **st:** Gulfam
lp: Miss Gohur, Master Mohan, Manchersha Chapgar, Dadibhai Sarkari, Vallabh Naik

Chintamani
3836 ft.; **genre:** Devotional
pc: Lotus Film Co., Hyderabad DN **d:** Dhiren Ganguly

Devi Todi
7204 ft.; **genre:** Devotional
pc: Kohinoor Film Co. **d:** Kanjibhai Rathod **c:** Gajanan S. Devare **st:** Gopalji Delwadakar
lp: Jamuna, Moti, Khalil, Sakina
Remarks: Film reissued under the banner of Krishna Film Co. in 1924.

Draupadi Swayamwar
6918 ft.; **genre:** Mythological
pc: Bharat Cinema Film Co., Poona **d:** V.P. Divekar **c:** A.P. Karandikar
lp: Kamala

Gadhaganjravancha Swapna Vihar
aka **Mr. Sleepy's Good Luck**
1978 ft.; **genre:** Comedy
pc: Hindustan Cinema Film Co., Nasik **d/st/sc:** D.G. Phalke

Ganesh Avatar
aka **Shri Ganesh Janma**
5560 ft.; **genre:** Mythological
pc: Hindustan Cinema Films Co., Nasik **d:** Gajanan V. Sane **c:** Anna Salunke
lp: Bhaurao Datar, Madhav Malusare

Ganga Avataran
aka **Bhagirath Ganga**

6000 ft.; **genre:** Mythological
pc: Madan Theatres Ltd. **st/sc:** Pandit Tulsidutt Shaida
lp: Patience Cooper, Dadibhai Sarkari

Garudi Ke Govind
aka **Juggler or Jadunath**
ft; **genre:** Mythological
pc: National Film Co. **d/c:** S.N. Patankar
lp: Trymbakrao Pradhan, Baba Vyas, Tara Koregaonkar, K.G. Gokhale, Kelkar

Hairstorm
768 ft.
pc: Bharat Cinema Film Co., Poona

Haritalika
2295 ft.; **genre:** Mythological
pc: Hindustan Cinema Films Co., Nasik **d:** Gajanan V. Sane **c:** Anna Salunke
lp: Bhaurao Datar

Indrajit
6000 ft.
pc: Lotus Film Co., Hyderabad DN **d:** Dhiren Ganguly

Kalidas
6903 ft.; **genre:** Biographical
pc: National Film Co. **d/c:** S.N. Patankar **st/sc:** Mohanlal G. Dave
lp: Baba Vyas, Tara Koregaonkar

Kamaley Kamini
aka **Maid of the Lotus**
6000 ft.
pc: Madan Theatres Ltd. **d:** Sisir Bhaduri
lp: Sisir Bhaduri, Patience Cooper, Tulsi Banerjee (?)

Kunti Putra Karna
aka **The Deserted Son of Kunti**
7945 ft.; **genre:** Mythological
pc: National Film Co. **d/c:** S.N. Patankar
lp: Raja Sandow

Krishna Tula
6403 ft.; **genre:** Mythological
pc: Bharat Cinema Film Co., Poona **d:** V.P. Divekar **c:** A.P. Karandikar
lp: V.V. Date, Vithabai

Lady Teacher
2677 ft.; **genre:** Social
pc: Lotus Film Co., Hyderabad DN **d:** Dhiren Ganguly

Laila Majnu
6000 ft.; **genre:** Costume
pc: Madan Theatres Ltd. **d:** J.J. Madan
lp: H.B. Waring, Jeanetta Sherwin, Miss Dot Foy, Patience Cooper

Mahashweta Kadambari
aka **Shap Sambhram**
6995 ft.; **genre:** Adaptation
pc: National Film Co. **d/c:** S.N. Patankar **st:** based on Bana's *Kadambari* **sc:** Mohanlal G. Dave
lp: Tara Koregaonkar, S.N. Patankar, Thatte, Baba Vyas

Malti Madhav
6997 ft.; **genre:** Adaptation
pc: Kohinoor Film Co. **d:** Kanjibhai Rathod **c:** Gajanan S. Devare **st:** based on Bhavabhuti's play **sc:** Mohanlal G. Dave
lp: Khalil, Tara, Moti, Gangaram, R.N. Vaidya
Remarks: Film reissued under the banner of Krishna Film Co. in 1924.

Marriage Tonic
genre: Social
pc: Lotus Film Co., Hyderabad DN **d:** Dhiren Ganguly

Matri Sneh
aka **Mother's Devotion**
6000 ft.; **genre:** Social
pc: Madan Theatres Ltd. **d:** Jyotish Banerjee **st:** Aga Hashr Kashmiri
lp: Tulsi Banerjee, Amar Chaudhary, Patience Cooper, Binapani, Ezra Mir

Nartaki Tara
aka **Tara the Dancer**
6000 ft.; **genre:** Social
pc: Madan Theatres Ltd. **d:** J.J. Madan
lp: Patience Cooper, Miss Chanda, Prabodh Ch Bose, Albertini

Pandav Vanvas
aka **Pandav in Exile**
6123 ft.; **genre:** Mythological
pc: Hindustan Cinema Film Co., Nasik **d:** Gajanan V. Sane **c:** Anna Salunke
lp: Bhaurao Datar, Bachu Pawar, Sakharam Jadhav

Parashuram
6789 ft.; **genre:** Mythological
pc: Kohinoor Film Co. **d:** Kanjibhai Rathod **st/sc:** Mohanlal G. Dave
lp: Lina Valentine, Tara, Khalil

Parikshit
1000 ft.; **genre:** Mythological short
pc: Madan Theatres Ltd. **lp:** Vithaldas Panchotia

Pati Bhakti
aka **Human Emotions**
11710 ft.; **genre:** Social
pc: Madan Theatres Ltd. **d:** J.J. Madan **st:** Babu Hari Krishna Jauhar
lp: F Mannelli, Patience Cooper, Master Mohan, Manilal, Sayed Hussain
Remarks: Re-censored on Nov 16, 1923 (CC. No. 2968).

Pitroddhar
aka **Ganga the Redeemer**
6789 ft.; **genre:** Mythological
pc: Star Film Ltd. **d:** Manilal Joshi **c:** Vishnu B. Joshi **st:** Gopalji Delwadakar

Radha Vilas
5990 ft.; **genre:** Mythological
pc: Bharat Cinema Film Co., Poona **d:** V.P. Divekar **c:** A.P. Karandikar
lp: Soni, V.V. Date

Raja Bhartrahari
7487 ft.; **genre:** Devotional
pc: National Film Co. **d/c:** S.N. Patankar **st/sc:** Mohanlal G. Dave
lp: Thatte, Tara Koregaonkar

Raja Bhoj
6000 ft.; **genre:** Costume
pc: Madan Theatres Ltd.
lp: Patience Cooper, Albertina

Raja Parikshit
6427 ft.; **genre:** Mythological
pc: Star Films Ltd. **d/sc:** Manilal Joshi **c:** Vishnu B. Joshi **st:** Kanji Kalidas Joshi
lp: Yakbal

Rajarshi Ambarish
5780 ft.; **genre:** Mythological
pc: Hindustan Cinema Film Co., Nasik

Rajkumari Budur
aka **Kamar-al-Zaman**

5000 ft.; **genre:** Costume
pc: Madan Theatres Ltd. **d/st/sc:** J.J. Madan
lp: Edna Dalies, Patience Cooper, Dadibhai Sarkari, Mancharsha Chapgar, E. de Liguoro, Dorothy Dayley and her troupe of dancers—M. Staries, W. Beecroft, H. Taylor, C.L. Ancell, Dorris Pratt, Marjorie Jardine, Olga Bradlaugh, Elliot, Morley, Hamer, Teska Hodson, Patty Girling

Ramayan
22000 ft.; **genre:** Mythological serial in four parts
pc: Madan Theatres Ltd. **d/c:** Eugenio de Liguoro
lp: F. Mannelli, Patience Cooper

Ratnavali
6556 ft.; **genre:** Adaptation
pc: Star Films Ltd. **d/sc:** Manilal Joshi; **c:** Vishnu B. Joshi **st:** based on Harsha's play
lp: Yakbal, Elizer

Ratnavali
7898 ft.; **genre:** Adaptation
pc: Madan Theatres Ltd. **d/c:** Camille de Grand **st:** based on Harsha's play
lp: Miss Gohur, Patience Cooper, C de Grand, Pandit Tulsidutt Shaida

Sadhu Ki Shaitan
5000 ft.; **genre:** Social
pc: Indo-British Film Co., Calcutta **d:** Nitish C. Lahiri
lp: Lina Valentine, Sushiladevi, Dhiren Ganguly

Samrat Ashoka
5000 ft.; **genre:** Historical
pc: Madan Theatres Ltd.

Sant Namdev
6655 ft.; **genre:** Devotional
pc: Hindustan Cinema Film Co., Nasik **d/st/sc:** D.G. Phalke

Sant Sakhubai
5987 ft.; **genre:** Devotional
pc: Hindustan Cinema Film Co., Nasik **d:** Gajanan V. Sane **c:** Trymbak B. Telang **st:** H.N. Apte
lp: Shanta Nalgunde, V.S. Nirantar

Sati
aka **Daksha Yagna**

6000 ft.; **genre:** Mythological
pc: Madan Theatres Ltd. **lp:** Patience Cooper

Sati Anjani
aka **Birth of Hanuman**
7745 ft.; **genre:** Devotional
pc: National Film Co. **d/c:** S.N. Patankar
lp: Tara Koregaonkar, C.C. Shah

Sati Toral
6897 ft.; **genre:** Devotional
pc: Kohinoor Film Co. **d:** Kanjibhai Rathod **c:** Gajanan S. Devare **st/sc:** Mohanlal G. Dave
lp: Moti, Khalil, Ganibabu, Jamuna, Sakina

Satyanarayan
5962 ft.; **genre:** Mythological
pc: Hindustan Cinema Films Co., Nasik **d:** V.S. Nirantar
lp: Anna Salunke, Ganpat Shinde

Sharmishtha Devyani
5350 ft.; **genre:** Mythological
pc: Bharat Cinema Film Co., Poona **d:** V.P. Divekar **c:** A.P. Karandikar
lp: Vithabai

Shishupal Vadha
aka **Rajasooya Yagna**
6642 ft.; **genre:** Mythological
pc: Hindustan Cinema Films Co., Nasik **d:** Gajanan V. Sane **c:** Anna Salunke
lp: Bhaurao Datar, Sane, Bachu Pawar, Sonubai

Shree Markandeya Avatar
aka **Shiva Mahima**
7875 ft.; **genre:** Mythological
pc: National Film Co. **d/c:** S.N. Patankar
lp: Baba Vyas, Damle, C.C. Shah

Shri Satyanarayan
6120 ft.; **genre:** Mythological
pc: Kohinoor Film Co. **d:** Kanjibhai Rathod **st/sc:** Mohanlal G. Dave
lp: Tara, Khalil, Moti, R.N. Vaidya, Rajababu, Ganibabu, Sakina

Sukanya Savitri
6989 ft.; **genre:** Mythological

pc: Kohinoor Film Co. **d:** Kanjibhai Rathod **c:** Gajanan S. Devare **st/sc:** Mohanlal G. Dave
lp: Moti, Gangaram, Jamuna (?), Sakina
Remarks: Double-bill with short *Shri Krishna Raas Leela* (285 ft.). *Sukanya Savitri* was reissued under the banner of Krishna Film Co. in 1924.

Surya Kumari
7856 ft.; **genre:** Costume
pc: Kohinoor Film Co. **d:** Kanjibhai Rathod **st/sc:** Mohanlal G. Dave **c:** Gajanan S. Devare
lp: Raja Sandow, Khalil, Moti, Daduji
Remarks: Film reissued under the banner of Krishna Film Co. in 1924.

Veer Abhimanyu
6500 ft.; **genre:** Mythological
pc: Star Films Ltd. **d:** Manilal Joshi **c:** Vishnu B. Joshi **st/sc:** Mohanlal G. Dave
lp: Sultana, Fatma Begum, Joshi, Madanrai Vakil

Veni Bandhan
aka **The Fall of Kauravas**
5597 ft.; **genre:** Mythological
pc: Bharat Cinema Film Co., Poona **d:** V.P. Divekar **c:** A.P. Karandikar
lp: Patankar, Soni, Damle

Virat Parva
6113 ft.; **genre:** Mythological
pc: Bharat Cinema Film Co., Poona **d:** V.P. Divekar **c:** A.P. Karandikar

Yadav Vinash
aka **Doom of Yadavas**
6655 ft.; **genre:** Mythological
pc: Star Films Ltd. **c:** Vishnu B. Joshi

1923

Aswathama
5953 ft.; **genre:** Mythological
pc: Hindustan Cinema Film Co., Nasik **d/st/sc:** D.G. Phalke **c:** Anna Salunke/P.B. Chavan
lp: Bhaurao Datar, Gotiram, Dada Pendse, Madhav Malusare

Babruwahan
6207 ft.; **genre:** Mythological
pc: Hindustan Cinema Film Co., Nasik **d/st/sc:** D.G. Phalke **c:** Anna Salunke/P.B. Chavan
lp: Bhaurao Datar, Sakharam Jadhav, Dada Pendse

Bhakta Sudhanva
6448 ft.; **genre:** Devotional
pc: Star Films Ltd. **c:** V.B. Joshi (?)

Buddha Dev
6973 ft.; **genre:** Biographical
pc: Hindustan Cinema Film Co., Nasik **d/st/sc:** D.G. Phalke **c:** Anna Salunke
lp: Anna Salunke, Bhaurao Datar

Catechist of Kil-Arni, The
1585 ft. (16 mm)
pc: T. Gavan Duffy, Pondicherry Mission **d:** R.S. Prakash **co-d:** T. Gavan Duffy
lp: T. Gavan Duffy

Champraj Hado
6527ft.; **genre:** Historical
pc: Star Films Ltd. **d/sc:** Nanubhai Desai **c:** V.B. Joshi (?) **st:** Vinodkant
lp: Tara, Jilloo, Asooji, Elizer, Madanrai Vakil

Chandragupta Chanakya
aka **Mahatma Chanakya**
7652 ft.; **genre:** Historical
pc: Star Films Ltd. **c:** V.B. Joshi (?) **st/sc:** Mohanlal G. Dave
lp: Jilloo, Asooji
Remarks: Film was reissued by Royal Art Studio in 1926 as *Mahatma Chanakya*.

Durvasa Shap
aka **Curse of Durvasa**
6783 ft.; **genre:** Mythological
pc: National Film Co. **d/c:** S.N. Patankar
lp: Tara Koregaonkar, Thatte

Gajendra Moksham
5389 ft.; **genre:** Mythological
pc: Star of the East Film Co., Madras **d/sc:** R.S. Prakash

Gayatri Mahatmya
aka **Venukumar**
6588 ft.; **genre:** Mythological
pc: Star Films Ltd. **c:** V.B. Joshi
lp: Madanrai Vakil

Light of Asia: Indian S

Gora Kumbhar
6013 ft.; **genre:** Devotional
pc: Hindustan Cinema Film Co., Nasik **d:** Gajanan V. Sane **c:** Anna Salunke/P.B. Chavan
lp: Bhaurao Datar, Bhonsle

Goswami Tulsidas
7657 ft.; **genre:** Devotional
pc: Kohinoor Film Co. **d:** Kanjibhai Rathod **st/sc:** Mohanlal G. Dave
Remarks: Film reissued under the banner of Krishna Film Co. in 1924.

Guru Dronacharya
6282 ft.; **genre:** Mythological
pc: Hindustan Cinema Film Co., Nasik **d/st/sc:** D.G. Phalke **c:** Anna Salunke
lp: Bhaurao Datar, Dada Pendse, Charubai

Guru Machhindranath
aka **Treeyaraj**
7743 ft.; **genre:** Mythological
pc: National Film Co. **d/c:** S.N. Patankar
lp: Trymbakrao Pradhan

Haragouri
4998 ft.; **genre:** Mythological
pc: Lotus Film Co., Hyderabad DN **d:** Dhiren Ganguly

Indrakumari
6459 ft.; **genre:** Costume
pc: Star Films Ltd. **c:** V.B. Joshi (?) **st:** Gopalji Delwadakar
lp: Jilloo

Jarasandha Vadha
5496 ft.; **genre:** Mythological
pc: Hindustan Cinema Film Co., Nasik **d/st/sc:** D.G. Phalke **c:** Anna Salunke/P.B. Chavan
lp: Bhaurao Datar, Bachu Pawar, Ghanshyam Singh

Kalicha Narad
aka **Ram Maruti Yuddha, Quarrel Game of Narada**
5848 ft.; **genre:** Mythological
pc: Hindustan Cinema Film Co., Nasik **d:** Ganpat Shinde
lp: Bhaurao Datar, Sakharam Jadhav

Kanyavikraya
aka **Sharada**

6056 ft.; **genre:** Social

pc: Hindustan Cinema Film Co., Nasik **d:** V.S. Nirantar **c:** Anna Salunke/P.B. Chavan

lp: Bhaurao Datar, Krishna Chavan

Karmadevi
aka **Destiny**

8891 ft.; **genre:** Costume

pc: Kohinoor Film Co. **d:** Kanjibhai Rathod **c:** D.D. Dabke **st/sc:** Mohanlal G. Dave

lp: Jamuna, Khalil, R.N. Vaidya

Khoka Babu
aka **Old Infant**

genre: Comedy

pc: Taj Mahal Film Co., Calcutta **d:** Sisir Bhaduri **c:** Noni Gopal Sanyal **st:** Raj Krishna Roy

lp: Chittaranjan Goswami

Kirat Arjun
5887 ft.; **genre:** Mythological

pc: Kohinoor Film Co. **d:** Manilal Joshi **c:** V.B. Joshi **st/sc:** Mohanlal G. Dave

Krishna Arjun Yuddha
6878 ft.; **genre:** Mythological

pc: Star Films Ltd. **c:** V.B. Joshi (?)

lp: Madanrai Vakil, Asooji

Krishna Satyabhama
aka **Syamantak Mani**

7748 ft.; **genre:** Mythological

pc: National Film Co. **d/c:** S.N. Patankar

lp: Tara Koregaonkar, Thatte

Life of Lord Buddha
6000 ft.; **genre:** Biographical

pc: Madan Theatres Ltd.

Remarks: In 1926 a revised version titled *Life of the Enlightened One* (1926) was released in competition with *Prem Sanyas/The Light of Asia*.

Mahananda
6786 ft.; **genre:** Devotional

pc: Hindustan Cinema Film Co., Nasik **d/st/sc:** D.G. Phalke **c:** Anna Salunke

lp: Bachu Pawar, Dada Pendse, Bhaurao Datar

Manbhanjan
6000 ft.; **genre:** Social
pc: Taj Mahal Film Co., Calcutta **d:** Naresh Mitra **c:** Noni Gopal Sanyal **st:** Rabindranath Tagore
lp: Durgadas Banerjee, Naresh Mitra, Indu Mukherjee, Tinkowri Chakraborty, Nilam Rani

Markandeya
aka **Shivleela**
5650 ft.; **genre:** Mythological
pc: Indian Film Co., Vellore **d:** Nataraja Mudaliar
lp: Subramanya Naidu

Matsya and Varah Avatar
5912 ft.; **genre:** Mythological
pc: Star Films Ltd. **c:** V.B. Joshi (?)
lp: Madanrai Vakil

Minaldevi
7647 ft.; **genre:** Historical
pc: Kohinoor Film Co. **d:** Kanjibhai Rathod **c:** D.D. Dabke **st/sc:** Mohanlal G. Dave
lp: Tara, Moti, Khalil

Nandanar
aka **Bhaktha Nandan**
6000 ft.; **genre:** Devotional
pc: Star of the East Film Co., Madras **d/sc:** R.S. Prakash

Nurjehan
6000 ft.; **genre:** Historical
pc: Madan Theatres Ltd. **d:** J.J. Madan **c:** Charles Creed
lp: Patience Cooper, Dadibhai Sarkari, Manchersha Chapgar, Ezra Mir, Albertini, Charles Creed

Patni Pratap
16420 ft.; **genre:** Social serial in two parts
pc: Madan Theatres Ltd. **d:** J.J. Madan
lp: Patience Cooper (double role)

Raja Mayurdwaj
6500 ft.; **genre:** Mythological
pc: Star Films Ltd. **c:** V.B. Joshi **st:** Krishnakant **sc:** Asooji
lp: Madanrai Vakil, Asooji

Ranakdevi Ra Khengar
6756 ft.; **genre:** Historical
pc: National Film Co. **d/c:** S.N. Patankar **st/sc:** Mohanlal G. Dave
lp: Tara Koregaonkar, C.C. Shah

Samudra Madanam
aka **Samudra Manthan**
6000 feet; **genre:** Mythological
pc: Star of the East Film Co., Madras **d/sc:** R.S. Prakash

Sati Narmada
9915 ft.; **genre:** Mythological
pc: Kohinoor Film Co. **d:** Kanjibhai Rathod **st/sc:** Mohanlal G. Dave
lp: Kanjibhai Rathod, Sakina, Baby Anwari, Khalil

Sati Virmati
aka **Jagdeo Parmar**
7723 ft.; **genre:** Historical
pc: National Film Co. **d/c:** S.N. Patankar **st:** Thakorlal H. Vakil
lp: Tara Koregaonkar, C.C. Shah, Thatte

Sati Ka Shap
aka **Satino Shap, Silent Curse**
6086 ft.; **genre:** Historical
pc: Swastik Pictures **d/sc:** Manilal Joshi **st:** adapted from Col. Tod's *Annals and Antiquities of Rajasthan*
lp: Sultana, Begum Fatma
Remarks: First independently produced film by an Indian filmmaker.

Shaitan Pujari
6000 ft.; **genre:** Social
pc: Punjab Film Mfg. Co., Punjab

Shree Bal Krishna
7885 ft.; **genre:** Mythological
pc: Kohinoor Film Co. **d:** Kanjibhai Rathod **c:** Gajanan S. Devare **st/sc:** Mohanlal G. Dave

Shree Krishna Avatar
4483 ft.; **genre:** Mythological
pc: Maharashtra Film Co., Kolhapur **d/c:** Baburao Painter **co/c:** S. Fattelal
lp: V. Shantaram, Kamaladevi, Zunzharrao Pawar, Ganpat Bakre

Shri Dnyaneshwar
6860 ft.; **genre:** Devotional

pc: National Film Co. **d/c:** S.N. Patankar
lp: Kelkar

Shri Krishna Bhakta Pipaji

6432 ft.; **genre:** Devotional
pc: National Film Co. **d/c:** S.N. Patankar **st/sc:** Mohanlal G. Dave

Shukdeo

aka **Shuk Rambha**
7575 ft.; **genre:** Mythological
pc: Kohinoor Film Co. **d:** Kanjibhai Rathod **st/sc:** Mohanlal G. Dave
lp: Khalil, Tara

Sinhagad

6880 ft.; **genre:** Historical
pc: Maharashtra Film Co., Kolhapur **d:** Baburao Painter **c:** S. Fattelal **st:** Hari Narayan Apte
lp: Balasaheb Yadav (double role), Kamaladevi, V. Shantaram, Baburao Painter, Zunzharrao Pawar, G.R. Mane, Nalini (Dwarki), K.P. Bhave

Soul of The Slave

7000 ft.; **genre:** Costume
pc: Photoplay Syndicate of India, Calcutta **d:** Hemchandra Mukherjee **c:** Charles Creed
st/sc: Rakhaldas Bannerjee
lp: Ahindra Choudhury, Gokul Nag, Prafulla Ghosh, Hem Mukherjee, Jane Richards, Adele Willinsonwirth
Remarks: The film was re-censored and re-released in 1929 with the additional title *Pilgrims of Love*.

Vali and Sugriv Yudh

6739 ft.; **genre:** Mythological
pc: Star Films Ltd. **c:** V.B. Joshi **st/sc:** Raja Sandow
lp: Raja Sandow, Madanrai Vakil

Vaman Avatar

aka **Raja Bali**
7472 ft.; **genre:** Mythological
pc: National Film Co. **d/c:** S.N. Patankar
lp: Trymbakrao Pradhan, Tara Koregaonkar, S.N. Patankar

Vanraj Chavda

7830 ft.; **genre:** Historical
pc: National Film Co. **d/c:** S.N. Patankar
lp: C.C. Shah, Thatte

Veer Bhimsen
7887 ft.; **genre:** Mythological
pc: Kohinoor Film Co. **d:** Kanjibhai Rathod **c:** Gajanan S. Devare
st/sc: Mohanlal G. Dave
lp: Raja Sandow, Tara, Moti, Savita, Sakina

Videhi Janak
aka **Janak Videhi**
6448 ft.; **genre:** Mythological
pc: National Film Co. **d/c:** S.N. Patankar **st:** Gopalji Delwadakar
lp: S.N. Patankar

Vratasur Vadha
aka **Indra Vijay, Indra the Victorious**
7667 ft.; **genre:** Mythological
pc: Kohinoor Film Co. **d:** Kanjibhai Rathod **c:** D.D. Dabke **st/sc:** Mohanlal G. Dave
lp: Raja Sandow, Moti, Homi Master, Savita, Sakina

Yayati
6789 ft.; **genre:** Mythological
pc: Lotus Film Co., Hyderabad DN **d:** Dhiren Ganguly

1924

Atmabal
aka **Sunder Kamdar**
7630 ft.; **genre:** Costume
pc: Majestic Film Co. **st:** A.S. Desai
lp: Elizer, Asooji

Babardeva
aka **Dare Devil**
6524 ft.; **genre:** Crime
pc: Majestic Film Co.
Remarks: The film was banned for allegedly glorifying crime.

Bal Shringi
5865 ft.; **genre:** Mythological
pc: Eastern Film Co., Baroda

Bali Yagna
6245 ft.; **genre:** Mythological
pc: Saurashtra Kinematograph Co., Rajkot **d:** Vajeshankar Pattani **c:** Champaklal Pattani
lp: Balabhai Bhat, Jatilbhai Vyas, Nanbai, Maganlal Dave

Remarks: The film was released at Majestic on March 3, 1924. The advertisement appeared on the same day stating that it was their first Supreme Art Productions.

Basant Prabha
7500 ft.; **genre:** Costume
pc: Madan Theatres Ltd.
lp: Kusum Kumari, Prova, Prabodh Ch Bose, Mohamed Hussein

Chandan Malayagiri
7315 ft.; **genre:** Costume
pc: Majestic Film Co. **d:** Naval Gandhi

Chandranath
5000 ft.; **genre:** Social
pc: Taj Mahal Film Co., Calcutta **d:** Naresh Mitra **c:** Noni Gopal Sanyal **st:** Saratchandra Chatterjee
lp: Durgadas Banerjee, Naresh Mitra, Jogesh Choudhary, Nirmal Bala, Shishubala
Remarks: Film reissued with additional footage under the banner of Madan Theatres Ltd. in 1926.

Datta Janma
aka **Sati Anasuya**
6495 ft.; **genre:** Mythological
pc: Hindustan Cinema Film Co., Nasik **d:** Gajanan V. Sane **c:** Anna Salunke/P.B. Chavan
lp: Bhaurao Datar, Bachu Pawar, Motiram, Ashrabai

Draupathi Bhagya
aka **Draupadi's Fate, A Game of Krishna**
5435 ft.; **genre:** Mythological
pc: Hindustan Cinema Film Co., Nasik /for Indian Art Craft Co., Madras

Go Mata
aka **Sacred Cow**
genre: Mythological
pc: Madan Theatres Ltd.

Gul-e-Bakavali
7997 ft.; **genre:** Legend
pc: Kohinoor Film Co. **d:** Kanjibhai Rathod **st/sc:** Mohanlal G. Dave
lp: Zubeida, Sultana, Khalil, Jamuna, Nur Mohamed, Abbdul Gafur, Usharani, Savita, Siddimiyan, Rajababu, Mani, Malvankar, Ramappa, Homi Master, Lakshmanrao
Remarks: First film with an 'Oriental' background.

Ishq No Umedvar
2222 ft.; **genre:** Comedy
pc: Saurastra Kinematograph Co., Rajkot

Jayadratha Vadha
6313 ft.; **genre:** Mythological
pc: Hindustan Cinema Film Co., Nasik **d:** Gajanan V. Sane **c:** Anna Salunke/P.B. Chavan
lp: Bachu Pawar, Bhaurao Datar

Kala Nag
aka **Kaliyug Ki Sati, Triumph of Justice**
8200 ft.; **genre:** Crime Social
pc: Kohinoor Film Co. **d:** Kanjibhai Rathod **c:** D.D. Dabke/Gajanan S. Devare **st/sc:** Mohanlal G. Dave
lp: Sultana, Khalil, Homi Master, Moti, Fatma Begum, Savita, Ebrahim, Behram Vasania, R.N. Vaidya

Kalyan Khajina
aka **Treasure of Kalyan**
9440 ft.; **genre:** Historical
pc: Maharashtra Film Co., Kolhapur **d:** Baburao Painter **c:** S. Fattelal
lp: Sultana, Nalini (Dwarki), Chimasaheb Bhosle, Vedi, K.P. Bhave
Master Vithal (minor role)

Kanya Vikrya
aka **Navi Shethani**
9300 ft.; **genre:** Social
pc: Kohinoor Film Co. **d:** Homi Master **st/sc:** Mohanlal G. Dave
lp: Jamuna

Karan ghelo
aka **Karan Waghela**
7460 ft.; **genre:** Historical
pc: National Film Co. **d/c** S.N. Patankar **st/sc:** Mohanlal G. Dave

Kismat Ka Shikar
aka **Victims of Fate**
5000 ft.; **genre:** Social
pc: Madan Theatres Ltd.

Krishna Kumari
aka **Daughter of Shripur**
6995 ft.; **genre:** Costume
pc: Kohinoor Film Co. **d/c:** Gajanan S. Devare **st/sc:** Mohanlal G. Dave

Manorama
aka **Hridaya Triputi**
7785 ft.; **genre:** Social
pc: Kohinoor Film Co. **d:** Homi Master **sc:** Mohanlal G. Dave
lp: Khalil, Zubeida, Sultana
Remarks: Based on Kalapi's poem *Hridaya Triputi.*

Mishar Rani
7326 ft.; **genre:** Costume
pc: Madan Theatres Ltd. **d:** Jyotish Banerjee **st/sc:** Aparesh Mukherjee
lp: Durgadas Banerjee, Ahindra Choudhary, Nihar Bala

Mumbai Ni Shethani
aka **Shethanino Sapno, Call of Satan**
6827 ft.; **genre:** Social
pc: Majestic Film Co. **d:** Ardeshir Irani/Naval Gandhi **st/sc:** Mohanlal G. Dave
lp: Jilloo, B.P. Mishra

Municipal Nivadnuk
aka **Municipal Election**
2892 ft.; **genre:** Social
pc: Hindustan Cinema Film Co., Nasik **d:** D.G. Phalke
lp: Bachu Pawar, Sakharam Jadhav (female role), Ganpat Shinde, Bhaurao Datar

Nabin Bharat
7000 ft.; **genre:** Social
pc: Madan Theatres Ltd. **d:** Kashinath Chatterjee

Nand batrishi
6500 ft.; **genre:** Costume
pc: Majestic Film Co. **st:** Shamal Bhat
lp: Miss Dolores Berry, Asooji

Narasinha Mehta
7995 ft.; **genre:** Devotional
pc: Kohinoor Film Co. **d/c:** Gajanan S. Devare **st/sc:** Mohanlal G. Dave
lp: Ghanshyam

Paper Parinam
aka **Crime and its Punishment**
8000 ft.; **genre:** Costume
pc: Madan Theatres Ltd. **st:** Aga Hashr Kashmiri
lp: Nirmalendu Lahiri, Prabhadevi, Prabodh Ch Bose

Pap No Fej
aka **Debt of Sin**
6782 ft.; **genre:** Crime Social
pc: Majestic Film Co. **d:** Ardeshir Irani/Naval Gandhi **c:** Bhogilal Dave **st/sc:** Naval Gandhi
lp: Tara, Asooji, Elizer, B.P. Mishra

Pap No Paschatap
aka **Repentance**
5210 ft.; **genre:** Social
pc: Majestic Film Co. **d/st/sc:** Naval Gandhi
lp: Tara

Poona Par Hallo
aka **Poona Raided**
7453 ft.; **genre:** Historical
pc: Deccan Pictures Corporation **d/st/sc:** Mama Varerkar **c:** Ramarao Anandkar
co/c: Pandurang Talegiri
lp: Miss Kaisar, Krishnarao Ketkar, Miss Bhavani, N.D. Sarpotdar, Dulari, Baburao Sansare, Vishnupant Pagnis , Datta Varne, Shulpani Mukherjee, Ratansha Vakil, Shankarrao Shinde, Laxmanrao Rane, Mohamed Arab, Pandrinath Kale, Haripant Kulkarni, Narayanrao Phaterphaker, Shankarrao Moghe, Sunderrao Nadkarni
Remarks: Prohibited on religious grounds in some Provinces.

Prithvi Vallabh
aka **The Lord of Love and Power**
7456 ft.; **genre:** Historical
pc: Ashoka Pictures **d:** Manilal Joshi **c:** Vishnu B. Joshi **st:** K.M. Munshi **sc:** D.S. Shirur
lp: Zubeida, Wagle Sandow, Fatma Begum, Sultana, P.Y. Altekar, Miss Jaina, Bhalji Pendharkar (?)

Prithviraj Chauhan
5947 ft.; **genre:** Historical
pc: Eastern Film Co., Baroda

Ra Mandlik
7200 ft.; **genre:** Historical
pc: Kohinoor Film Co. **d:** Homi Master **c:** Gajanan S. Devare **st/sc:** Mohanlal G. Dave
lp: Raja Sandow, Yakbal, Ganibabu, Rajababu

Raja Harishchandra
8521 ft.; **genre:** Mythological
pc: Kohinoor Film Co. (Imperial Production) **d/c:** D.D. Dabke **st/sc:** Mohanlal G. Dave
lp: D.D. Dabke, Khalil, Ghanshyam, Fatma Begum, Jamuna

Ram Ravan Yuddha
aka **Sita Shuddhi**
5145 ft.; **genre:** Mythological
pc: Hindustan Cinema Film Co., Nasik **d:** Gajanan V. Sane **c:** Anna Salunke
lp: Vasant Shinde, Krishna Chavan

Razia Begum
7568 ft.; **genre:** Historical
pc: Majestic Film Co. **co-d/st/sc:** Nanubhai Desai/B.P. Mishra
lp: Raja Sandow, Jilloo
Remarks: Nanubhai Desai left midway and the film was completed by B.P. Mishra. Banned in several Provinces on religious grounds.

Sadevant Savlinga
7630 ft.; **genre:** Legend
pc: Majestic Film Co./Imperial Production **st/sc:** Mohanlal G. Dave
lp: Jilloo, Putli

Sadguni Sushila
aka **Sushila the Virtuous, Triumph of Truth**
7997 ft.; **genre:** Social
pc: Kohinoor Film Co. **d:** Kanjibhai Rathod **st/sc:** Mohanlal G. Dave
lp: Raja Sandow

Samudra Manthan
aka **Ahankar Vilay, The Churning of the Ocean**
7235 ft.; **genre:** Mythological
pc: Saurashtra Kinematograph Co., Rajkot **d:** Vajeshankar Pattani **c:** Champaklal Pattani
lp: Balabhai Bhat, Jatilbhai Vyas, Nanbai
Remarks: This film was released at Novelty on 12-4-1924. The advertisement states 'A religious photoplay in six reels'. This film was granted CC. No. 3282, dt. 16-5-24. It seems that after its release a revised version was prepared that included scenes from the company's earlier film *Bali Yagna*.

Sanyasi
5800 ft.; **genre:** Social
pc: Majestic Film Co. **d:** Naval Gandhi **st:** Narayan Hemchandra
sc: Naval Gandhi

Sati Padmini
aka **Siege of Chittor, Beauty of Rajasthan**
5990 ft.; **genre:** Historical
pc: Maharashtra Film Co., Kolhapur **d:** Baburao Painter **c:** S. Fattelal
lp: Nalini (Dwarki), Ganpat Bakre, Balasaheb Yadav, V. Shantaram, Vedi

Sati Sardarba

8747 ft.; **genre:** Costume
pc: Saraswati Film Co. **d/st/sc:** Nanubhai Desai
c: Bhogilal Dave
lp: Zubeida, Sultana, Mohanlala, Fatma Begum, Sakhu, Chimanlal Bhojak

Sati Sita

7551 ft.; **genre:** Mythological
pc: Kohinoor Film Co. **d:** Kanjibhai Rathod
c: Gajanan S. Devare
st/sc: Mohanlal G. Dave

Sati Sona

aka **Halaman Jethvo**
7925 ft.; **genre:** Legend
pc: Kohinoor Film Co. **d:** Homi Master **st/sc:** Mohanlal G. Dave
lp: Raja Sandow, Khalil, Moti, Jamuna, Rajababu, Ganibabu

Savitri

aka **Savitri Satyavan, Sati Savitri**
7000 ft.; **genre:** Mythological
pc: Madan Theatres Ltd./Cines, Rome **co-d/sc:** Giorgio Mannini **co-d:** J.J. Madan
lp: Rina de Liguoro, Angelo Ferrari, Gianna Terribili-Gonzales, Bruto Castellani, Lydianne
Remarks: Original story by A. De Gubernatis. As per Madan Theatres: Indo-Italian co-production. Production supervisors-Arturo Ambrosio and Bruno Castellanis.
According to Italian sources: this film was not a joint venture with Madan Theatres and J.J. Madan was not credited as co-director. The production supervisors were not mentioned either. The credits given are: **pc:** Cines, Roma **d/sc:** Giorgio Mannini **c:** Gioacchino Gengarelli **st:** Ferdinando Paolieri/Aldo de Benedetti.
The film was released in Italy in 1923 (5361 ft.).

▶ Advertisement for Madan Theatres' **Savitri**

Shahjahan
8420 ft.; **genre:** Historical
pc: Majestic Film Co. **co-d/st/sc:** Naval Gandhi **co-d:** Ardeshir Irani
lp: Elizer, Jilloo, B.P. Mishra
Remarks: Banned in several Provinces on religious grounds.

Sharif Badmash
aka **Society Scoundrel**
1650 ft.; **genre:** Social
pc: Saurashtra Kinematograph Co., Rajkot
d: Vajeshankar Pattani(?) **c:** Champaklal Pattani(?) **st:** Manilal M. Vaidya
lp: Madanrai Vakil, Ermeline

Shivaji The Social Reformer
6320 ft.; **genre:** Historical
pc: Hindustan Cinema Film Co., Nasik
Remarks: The film was refused a censor certificate on the grounds that it was 'likely to promote ill-feeling'.

Shivajichi Agryahun Sutaka
aka **Shivaji's Escape from Moghul Court at Agra**
7567 ft.; **genre:** Historical
pc: Hindustan Cinema Film Co., Nasik **d/sc:** D.G. Phalke **c:** Anna Salunke
lp: Bhaurao Datar, Jardos, Laxman Malusare

Sita Vanvas
aka **Uttar Ram Charita**
6582 ft.; **genre:** Mythological
pc: Hindustan Cinema Film Co., Nasik **d:** V.S. Nirantar, Vasant Shinde (Maruti)

Sundopasunda
6013 ft.; **genre:** Mythological
pc: Hindustan Cinema Film Co., Nasik **d:** Gajanan V. Sane **c:** Trymbak B. Telang/Anna Salunke/P.B. Chavan
lp: Bhaurao Datar, Bachu Pawar, Sane, Krishna Chavan

Toorkey Hoor
14355 ft.; **genre:** Costume
pc: Madan Theatres Ltd. **d:** J.J. Madan **st:** Aga Hashr Kashmiri
lp: Master Narmada Shankar (as Toorkey Hoor), Patience Cooper, Master Mohan, Surajram, Sarifa, Manilal, Dadibhai Sarkari, Sayed Hussein, Miss Williams, Lilian Fox
Remarks: Banned in several Provinces on the grounds that it depicted a scantily clad European girl. Revised version cleared later.

Veer Ahir
8505 ft.; **genre:** Social
pc: Kohinoor Film Co. **d:** Homi Master **st/sc:** Mohanlal G. Dave
lp: K.B. Athavale, Jamuna

Veer Durgadas
6530 ft.; **genre:** Historical
pc: Majestic Film Co. **d:** B.P. Mishra
lp: Jilloo, B.P. Mishra, Asooji
Remarks: The film was prohibited on 10 June 1924 on religious grounds in several Provinces. Revised and re-censored version cleared later.

Vijaya
aka **Conquest of Ceylon**
6727 ft.; **genre:** Costume
pc: Star Films Ltd. **d:** B.P. Mishra **c:** Vishnu B. Joshi **st/sc:** B.P. Mishra
lp: B.P. Mishra, Madanrai Vakil (?)

Vikram Charitra
aka **Buddhi Bala**
7568 ft.; **genre:** Legend
pc: Saraswati Film Co. **d:** Nanubhai Desai/Darab Shah Kohla **c:** Bhogilal Dave **sc:** Vinodkant
lp: Tara, Asooji, Gangaram, Sakhu, Gopalji

Vinchucha Dansh
aka **Scorpion Bite**
2633 ft.; **genre:** Social
pc: Hindustan Cinema Film Co., Nasik **d:** D.G. Phalke

Vir Bharat
5000 ft.; **genre:** Social
pc: Madan Theatres Ltd. **d:** Jyotish Banerjee

Vismi Sadi
aka **Bismi Sadi, Twentieth Century**
9170 ft.; **genre:** Social
pc: Kohinoor Film Co. **d:** Homi Master **c:** D.D. Dabke **st/sc:** Mohanlal G. Dave
lp: Raja Sandow, Moti, Nur Mohamed, Gangaram

1925

Adooray Chele
aka **Pampered Youth**
8000 ft., **genre:** Social

pc: Madan Theatres Ltd. **d:** J.J. Madan
lp: Patience Cooper, Surajram, Sarifa, Modhu Bose (?)

Ahalyabai
8896 ft.; **genre:** Historical
pc: Royal Art Studio **d:** B.P. Mishra
lp: Dwarki, Madanrai Vakil

Amarsingh Daggar
aka **Marwadnun Moti**
8969 ft.; **genre:** Historical
pc: Royal Art Studio **d:** B.P. Mishra
lp: Madanrai Vakil
Remarks: Revised version titled *Veer Ramani* was released by the Alexandria Film Co. (CC. No. 3642, dt. Dec 12, 1927).

Anant Vrata
6987 ft.; **genre:** Mythological
pc: Hindustan Cinema Film Co., Nasik **d:** Gajanan V. Sane **c:** Anna Salunke
lp: Bhaurao Datar, Krishna Chavan

Anath Abala
aka **Charkha, Spinning Wheel, Unprotected Woman**
7500 ft.; **genre:** Social
pc: Saurashtra Kinematograph Co., Rajkot **d:** Kanjibhai Rathod **c:** Chimanlal Luhar
lp: Ermeline, Madanrai Vakil, Miss Moti, Master Hemant Vaidya

Baap Kamai
aka **Fortune and Fools**
8927 ft.; **genre:** Social
pc: Krishna Film Co. **d:** Kanjibhai Rathod **c:** Chimanlal Luhar **st:** Shaida
lp: Gulab, Gohar, Gangaram, Nandram, Putlibai

Bajirao Mastani
7679 ft.; **genre:** Historical
pc: Sharda Film Co. **d:** Nanubhai Desai **st/sc/co-d:** Bhalji Pendharkar **c:** Bhogilal Dave
lp: Nanasaheb Phatak, Miss Jones, Sayani, Master Vithal (minor role)

Bal Vidhva
aka **Child Widow**
7526 ft.; **genre:** Social
pc: Kohinoor Film Co. **d:** Behram Vasania **c:** Vishnu B. Joshi **st/sc:** Mohanlal G. Dave
lp: Harihar Diwana, Heera, Khalil

Bhadra Bhamini
aka **Taste of Chastity**
7289 ft.; **genre:** Costume
pc: Krishna Film Co. **d:** Nanubhai Desai **c:** Chaturbhai Patel **st:** Shamal Bhat **sc:** Premkumar
lp: Gulab, Nandram, Prabhudas, P.R. Joshi
Remarks: Banned on 24-1-1927 on grounds of indecency. Revised version cleared later.

Chalu Jamana
aka **Chalti Duniya**
6637 ft.; **genre:** Social
pc: Majestic Film Co. (Krishna Production)
lp: Tara (?)

Chandrakant
aka **Filial Duty**
7659 ft.; **genre:** Costume
pc: Krishna Film Co. **d:** Harshadrai Mehta **c:** Chaturbhai Patel **st/sc:** Mohanlal G. Dave
lp: Gulab, Ermeline, Nandram, Haridas, Malka, Hyder Shah, Gangaram

Chandrarao More
7258 ft.; **genre:** Historical
pc: United Pictures Syndicate **d/st/sc:** N.D. Sarpotdar **c:** Pandurang Talegiri
lp: P.Y. Altekar, Elizer, Dwarki, Sunderrao Nadkarni, Madanrai Vakil

Chaturthicha Chandra
aka **Moon Cursed by Ganpati**
4029 ft.; **genre:** Mythological
pc: Hindustan Cinema Film Co., Nasik **d/st/sc:** D.G. Phalke **c:** Trymbak B. Telang
lp: Bhaurao Datar, Vasant Shinde

Chhatrapati Sambhaji
8745 ft.; **genre:** Historical
pc: United Pictures Syndicate **d:** N.D. Sarpotdar **c:** Pandurang Talegiri
lp: P.Y. Altekar, Vedi, Jilloo, Elizer, D. Bilimoria, Sunderrao Nadkarni

Cinema ni Rani
aka **Cinema Queen, Love's Sacrifice**
8550 ft.; **genre:** Social
pc: Kohinoor Film Co. **d:** Mohan Bhavnani **c:** Vishnu B. Joshi **st/sc:** Mohanlal G. Dave
lp: Sulochana (Ruby Myers), Khalil, Putlibai

Desh na Dushman
aka **Veerna Ver, Divine Punishment**

7890 ft.; **genre:** Costume
pc: Kohinoor Film Co. (Imperial Production) **d:** Manilal Joshi **c:** D.D. Dabke **st/sc:** Pessi Karani
lp: Zubeida, Yakbal, Moti, Raja Sandow, Bachubanu, R.N. Vaidya, Mani, K.B. Athavale, Nur Mohamed
Remarks: Reissued in 1929 as *Rangilo Rajavi/Passionate Prince* (CC. No. 8038, dt. August 7, 1929).

Devdasi
aka **Bride of God, Temple Maid**
7870 ft.; **genre:** Costume
pc: Laxmi Pictures **d/st/sc:** Manilal Joshi **c:** D.D. Dabke
lp: Zubeida, Raja Sandow, Dabir, Fatma Begum, Shahazadi, K.B. Athavale, Prabhakar

Fankado Fituri
aka **Handsome Blackguard**
16400 ft.; **genre:** Social serial in 2 parts
pc: Kohinoor Film Co. **d:** Homi Master **c:** D.D. Dabke/Gajanan S. Devare **st:** Pijam
sc: Mohanlal G. Dave
lp: Homi Master, Yakbal, Moti, K.B. Athavale, Behram Vasania, Faram Sethna, Thelma Wallace, Yvonne Wallace

Gaud Bangal
aka **Magician of Bengal**
8396 ft.; **genre:** Costume
pc: Royal Art Studio **d:** K.P. Bhave **c:** Rustom Irani **st/sc:** K.P. Bhave
lp: Jilloo, Fatma Begum, Madanrai Vakil, Elizer

Ghar Jamai
aka **Henpecked Husband**
7997 ft.; **genre:** Comedy
pc: Kohinoor Film Co. **d:** Homi Master **c:** D.D. Dabke **st/sc:** Mohanlal G. Dave
lp: Siddimiya, Jamuna, Moti

Hedimb Bakasur Vadh
5280 ft.; **genre:** Mythological
pc: Hindustan Cinema Film Co., Nasik **d/st/sc:** D.G. Phalke **c:** Trymbak B. Telang
lp: Bhaurao Datar, Bachu Pawar, Yamuna Gole, Baba Nachan

Hirji Kamdar
8927 ft.; **genre:** Social
pc: Kohinoor Film Co. **d:** Homi Master **st/sc:** Mohanlal G. Dave
lp: Khalil, Ganibabu, Rajababu

Hothal Padmini
7893 ft.; **genre:** Costume

pc: Krishna Film Co. **d:** Harshadrai Mehta **c:** Chaturbhai Patel **st/sc:** Mohanlal G. Dave
lp: Ermeline, Gulab, Gangaram, Nandram

Indrasabha
aka **Sabzapari**
9087 ft.; **genre:** Costume/Fantasy
pc: Kohinoor Film Co. **d:** Manilal Joshi **c:** D.D. Dabke **st/sc:** Mohanlal G. Dave
lp: Zubeida, Sultana, Khalil, Raja Sandow, K.B. Athavale, Siddimiyan

Insaf
aka **Justice**
8592 ft.; **genre:** Crime
pc: Premier Photo Plays Co. **d:** Vedi **c:** Pandurang Talegiri
lp: P.Y. Altekar

Jal Kumari
aka **Hur-al-Bahar**
7887 ft.; **genre:** Costume
pc: Krishna Film Co. **d:** Harshadrai Mehta c/**st:** S.N. Patankar **sc:** Krishna Kumar
lp: Gulab, Gangaram, Vishnu, Jehangir, Hyder Shah

Jaler Meye
aka **Fisher Girl**
7000 ft.; **genre:** Social
pc: Madan Theatres Ltd. **d:** Jyotish Banerjee
lp: Durgadas Banerjee, Kalidasi, A.K. Chakraborty

Kakasahebanchya Dolyat Jhanjhanit Anjan
aka **Kakasaheb Outwitted**
7982 ft.; **genre:** Social
pc: Hindustan Cinema Film Co., Nasik **d:** D.G. Phalke **c:** Trymbak B. Telang/Anna Salunke
lp: Bachu Pawar, Sahadeva, Krishna Kumbhar

Kala Chor
aka **Black Thief**
9147 ft.; **genre:** Social
pc: Laxmi Pictures **d:** Manilal Joshi **c:** D.D. Dabke **st/sc:** Mohanlal G. Dave
lp: Raja Sandow, Zubeida, Putli, Janibabu

Kali Nagin
6985 ft.; **genre:** Social
pc: Indian Pictures Corporation **d:** B.P. Mishra
lp: Jilloo

Kamalata

7585 ft.; **genre:** Costume
pc: Krishna Film Co. **d:** Kanjibhai Rathod **c:** Chimanlal Luhar **st/sc:** Krishnakumar
lp: Ermeline

Kangal Kaidi

aka **Doomed Soul**
6969 ft.; **genre:** Costume
pc: Majestic Film Co. (Krishna Production) **d:** D.P. Mishra (?) **st:** based on Victor Hugo's *Les Miserables*
lp: P.Y. Altekar, Mohanlala, D.P. Mishra, Dorabji Mevawala, Miss Jainoo

Kashmiri Sundari

8000 ft.; **genre:** Costume
pc: Madan Theatres Ltd.
lp: Patience Cooper (double role), Mohamed Hussein

Khandani Khavis

aka **Noble Scamp**
7335 ft.; **genre:** Costume
pc: Laxmi Pictures **d:** Manilal Joshi **c:** D.D. Dabke **st/sc:** R.S.D. Chaudhary
lp: Zubeida, Baba Vyas, R.S.D. Chaudhary

Khod Modali

aka **Habit Crushed**
2967 ft.: **genre:** Comedy
pc: Hindustan Cinema Film Co., Nasik **d:** D.G. Phalke
Remarks: Probably based on the same subject as *Pithache Panje* (1913).

Krishnakumar

aka **Sacho Hakdar, Mysterious Outlaw**
7897 ft.; **genre:** Costume
pc: Krishna Film Co. **d:** Harshadrai Mehta **c:** Chaturbhai Patel **st:** S.N. Patankar
lp: Gulab, Gangaram, Hyder Shah

Kulinkanta

9144 ft.; **genre:** Social
pc: Kohinoor Film Co. **d:** Homi Master **c:** K.G. Gokhale **st/sc:** Mohanlal G. Dave
lp: Moti, Jamuna, Khalil, Yakbal, Behram Vasania, Ganibabu

Kunj Vihari

7300 ft.; **genre:** Mythological
pc: Kohinoor Film Co. **d:** Homi Master **c:** Gajanan S. Devare **st/sc:** Mohanlal G. Dave
lp: Jamuna

Lalan Vanzari

7385 ft.; **genre:** Costume
pc: Krishna Film Co. **d/sc:** Maneklal Patel (Krishnakumar) **c:** Chaturbhai Patel **st:** Gopalji Delwadakar
lp: Gulab, Gangaram, Ermeline, Hyder Shah

Lanka Ni Ladi
aka **Fairy of Ceylon**

9101 ft.; **genre:** Costume
pc: Kohinoor Film Co. **d:** Homi Master **c:** Gajanan S. Devare **st/sc:** Mohanlal G. Dave
lp: Gohar, Khalil, Jamuna

Maharachi Por
aka **Dher Ni Chhokri, Two Little Untouchables**

7986 ft.; **genre:** Social
pc: United Pictures Syndicate **d:** N.D. Sarpotdar **c:** Pandurang Talegiri
lp: P.Y. Altekar, Joshi, Miss Jones, Dattoba Rajwade

Mahashivratra
aka **Shankar Leela**

6327 ft.; **genre:** Mythological
pc: Hindustan Cinema Film Co., Nasik **d/st/sc:** V.S. Nirantar
lp: Vasant Shinde

Mahathma Kabirdas

pc: Indian Art Craft Co., Madras **c:** T.V. Rungiah Naidu

Mari Dhaniyani
aka **My Wife**

8282 ft.; **genre:** Social
pc: Kohinoor Film Co. **d:** Homi Master **c:** K.G. Gokhale **st/sc:** Mohanlal G. Dave
lp: Jamuna, Moti, Siddimiyan
Remarks: Revised CC. No. 4419, dt. November 21, 1925.

Matruprem
aka **For Mother's Sake**

8853 ft.; **genre:** Social
pc: Kohinoor Film Co. **d:** Mohan Bhavnani **st/sc:** Mohanlal G. Dave
lp: Raja Sandow, Moti, Nur Mohamed

▲ **Master Vithal**

Mewad Pati Bapa Rawal

6321 ft.; **genre:** Historical
pc: Eastern Film Co., Baroda

Mojili Mumbai

aka **Slaves of Luxury**
8220 ft.; **genre:** Social
pc: Kohinoor Film Co. **d/st/sc:** Manilal Joshi **c:** D.D. Dabke
lp: Yakbal, Raja Sandow, Jamuna, Moti, Ganibabu, Nur Mohamed, Baby Saraswati
Remarks: Censors objected to the original title *Bombay the Beautiful*.

Mularj Solanki

7546 ft.; **genre:** Historical
pc: Royal Art Studio/Patel Bros. **d:** K.P. Bhave **c:** Rustom Irani
lp: P.Y. Altekar, Jilloo, Elizer, Madanrai Vakil

Mumbai Ni Mohini

aka **Social Pirates, Night Side of Bombay**
8879 ft.; **genre:** Social
pc: Saraswati Film Co. **d/sc:** Nanubhai Desai **c:** Bhogilal Dave **st:** Thakkar Nirbhay
lp: Fatma Begum, Mohanlala, Dorabji Mewawala, Elizer

Naharsingh Daku

8324 ft.; **genre:** Costume
pc: Royal Art Studio **d:** B.P. Mishra **c:** Rustom Irani
lp: Jilloo, Elizer, Fatma Begum, Miss Jean

Navalsha Hirji

6957 ft.; **genre:** Costume
pc: Majestic Film Co. (Krishna Production) **d:** Ardeshir Irani **st/sc:** Mohanlal G. Dave
lp: Mohanlala

Noore Deccan

aka **Asare Ishq, Light of Deccan**
6900 ft.; **genre:** Historical
pc: Indian Pictures Corporation **d:** B.P. Mishra
lp: Jilloo

Paisa Ni Khumari

7869 ft.; **genre:** Social
pc: Indian Pictures Corporation **d:** B.P. Mishra
lp: Jilloo

Panchdanda
aka **Five Divine Wands**
8505 ft.; **genre:** Legend
pc: Laxmi Pictures **d:** Chandulal Shah **c:** D.D. Dabke **st/sc:** Mohanlal G. Dave
lp: Raja Sandow, Yakbal, Putli, Isdan, Ghory, Miss Fiske (Blanche Verne)

Pandav Shodh
aka **Jimut Vadha, Search for Pandavas**
4667 ft.; **genre:** Mythological
pc: Hindustan Cinema Film Co., Nasik **d:** Gajanan V. Sane

Prabhavati
6134 ft.; **genre:** Historical
pc: Deccan Pictures Corporation **d:** N.D .Sarpotdar **c:** Pandurang Talegiri
lp: P.Y. Altekar

Prem Nirasha
aka **Forsaken Love**
8800 ft.; **genre:** Social
pc: Kohinoor Film Co. **d/st/sc:** Pessi Karani
lp: Jamuna, Heera, Behram Vasania, R.N. Vaidya

Premanjali
aka **Homage of Love**
6000 ft.; **genre:** Costume
pc: Madan Theatres Ltd. **d:** Jyotish Banerjee
lp: Durgadas Banerjee, Ahindra Choudhary, Kalidasi

Ra Nawaghan
aka **Vir Pasli**
7863 ft.; **genre:** Historical
pc: Royal Art Studio **d:** B.P. Mishra
lp: Zubeida, Madanrai Vakil, Jilloo, Elizer
Remarks: Reissued as *Raj Bhakti* (1930).

Rajnagar Ni Rambha
8890 ft.; **genre:** Social
pc: Kohinoor Film Co. **d:** Homi Master **st/sc:** Mohanlal G. Dave
lp: Zubeida, Khalil, Nur Mohamed, Yakbal
Remarks: Censors objected to the original title *Amdavad ni Shethani.*

Rajyogi
aka **Prince Ascetic**

6987 ft.; **genre:** Costume
pc: Kohinoor Film Co. **d:** Manilal Joshi **c:** D.D. Dabke **st:** Dayaram Shah
lp: Yakbal, Raja Sandow, Jamuna, Moti, Nur Mohamed, Ganibabu, Baby Saraswati

Rana Hamir
6923 ft.; **genre:** Historical
pc: Maharashtra Film Co., Kolhapur **d:** Baburao Painter **c:** S. Fattelal **st:** Hari Narayan Apte
lp: Balasaheb Yadav, V. Shantaram, Kamladevi, Zunzharrao Pawar

Rana Pratap
8984 ft.; **genre:** Historical
pc: Indian Pictures Corp./Patel Bros. **d:** B.P. Mishra

Sanam Ni Shodhma
aka **Looking for Love**
7486 ft.; **genre:** Social
pc: Saurashtra Kinematograph Co., Rajkot
d: Manilal M. Vaidya **c/st:** Chimanlal Luhar
lp: Manilal M. Vaidya, Gatubhai Vaidya, Dorothy, Shanta, Maganlal Dave, Monghibai

Sansar Chakra
aka **Pahela Pyar**
7000 ft.; **genre:** Social
pc: Madan Theatres Ltd. **st:** Aga Hashr Kashmiri
lp: Patience Cooper, Sharifa, Surajram, Dadibhai Sarkari

Sansar Swapna
aka **Dream of Life**
6958 ft.; **genre:** Social
pc: Kohinoor Film Co. **d:** Homi Master **c:** Gajanan S. Devare/K.G. Gokhale **st/sc:** Bachubabu
lp: Moti, Khalil, Bachubabu, Mary (Kumudini)

Sant Janabai
6798 ft.; **genre:** Devotional
pc: Hindustan Cinema Film Co., Nasik **d:** Gajanan V. Sane
lp: Vasant Shinde, Madhav Khaire, Bhaurao Datar

Sati Laxmi
9000 ft.; **genre:** Mythological
pc: Madan Theatres Ltd. **d:** Jyotish Banerjee **c:** Jatin Das
lp: Dhiraj Bhattacharya, Patience Cooper, Manmatha Pal, Kunjalal Chakraborty, Kartik Dey, Shishubala, Manorama

▲ Seeta Devi (of Bengal)

Sati Simantini
7875 ft.; **genre:** Mythological
pc: Laxmi Pictures **d:** Manilal Joshi **c:** D.D. Dabke
lp: Zubeida, Putli

Sati Tara
aka **War Between Vali and Sugriv**
6982 ft.; **genre:** Mythological
pc: Hindustan Cinema Film Co., Nasik **d:** Shinde **c:** Trymbak B. Telang
lp: Bhaurao Datar, Shelar, Krishna Chavan

Satyabhama
6892 ft.; **genre:** Mythological
pc: Hindustan Cinema Film Co., Nasik **d/st/sc:** D.G. Phalke **c:** Anna Salunke
lp: Bhaurao Datar, Krishna Chavan

Saurashtra Vir
7892 ft.; **genre:** Legend
pc: Sharda Film Co. **d/sc:** Nanubhai Desai **c:** Bhogilal Dave **st:** Machhar
lp: P.Y. Altekar, Amir Banu, Master Vithal (minor role)

Savkari Pash
aka **Indian Shylock**
5984 ft.; **genre:** Social
pc: Maharashtra Film Co., Kolhapur **d:** Baburao Painter **c:** S. Fattelal **st:** Narayan Hari Apte
lp: V. Shantaram, Zunzharrao Pawar, Kishabapu Bakre, Kamladevi, Shankarrao Bhute, K. Dhaiber

Shahala Shaha
aka **A Check to the King**
6800 ft.; **genre:** Historical
pc: Maharashtra Film Co., Kolhapur **d:** Baburao Painter **c:** S. Fattelal **st/sc:** N.D. Sarpotdar
lp: V. Shantaram, Balasaheb Yadav, Shripatrao Mudholkar, Kishabapu Bakre, Kamladevi, Zunzharrao Pawar

Shanta
7524 ft.; **genre:** Social
pc: Madan Theatres Ltd.

Shatmukh Ravan Vadha
aka **Birth of Kalika**
6392 ft.; **genre:** Mythological
pc: Hindustan Cinema Film Co., Nasik **d:** Kashinath Bharadi **c:** Trymbak B. Telang
lp: Bhaurao Datar, Kashinath Bharadi, Vasant Shinde, Gangaram Nhavi

Sheth Shagalsha
aka **Wealth and the World**
8775 ft.; **genre:** Devotional
pc: Kohinoor Film Co. **d:** Mohan Bhavnani **st/sc:** Mohanlal G. Dave
lp: Jamuna

Shrivatsa Chinta
6872 ft.; **genre:** Mythological
pc: Indian Pictures Corporation **d:** B.P. Mishra

Suvarna
6542 ft.; **genre:** Costume/Historical
pc: Laxmi Pictures **d:** Manilal Joshi **c:** D.D. Dabke **st:** Premshankar Ojha
lp: Putli, Raja Sandow

Swapana Sundari
aka **Dream Damsel**
7589 ft.; **genre:** Costume
pc: Krishna Film Co. **d:** Kanjibhai Rathod/Harshadrai Mehta **c:** Chaturbhai Patel
st: Shamal Bhat **sc:** Krishnakumar
lp: Gulab, Nandram, Ermeline, Vishnu

Syamantaka Mani
aka **Krishna Under Charge of Theft**
6848 ft.; **genre:** Mythological
pc: Hindustan Cinema Film Co., Nasik **d/st/sc:** D.G. Phalke **c:** Anna Salunke
lp: Bhaurao Datar, Krishna Chavan, Vasant Shinde

Vachan Bhang
aka **Broken Promise**
1927 ft.; **genre:** Social
pc: Hindustan Cinema Film Co., Nasik **d:** D.G. Phalke

Ujaint Kumar
aka **Exiled Prince of Ujjain, Deshvato**
7918 ft.; **genre:** Costume
pc: Indian Pictures Corporation **d:** B.P. Mishra
lp: Jilloo

Veer Bala
8965 ft.; **genre:** Social
pc: Kohinoor Film Co. **d:** Mohan Bhavnani **c:** Vishnu B. Joshi **st/sc:** Mohanlal G. Dave
lp: Sulochana, Khalil, Nur Mohamed

Veer Kunal
aka **Son of Ashoka**
7235 ft.; **genre:** Legend/Historical
pc: Kohinoor Film Co. **d/st/sc:** Manilal Joshi **c:** D.D. Dabke
lp: Yakbal, Moti, Raja Sandow, K.B. Athavale, Bachubabu

Ver Ni Vasulat
aka **Sweet Revenge**
7963 ft.; **genre:** Social
pc: Krishna Film Co. **d:** Harshadrai Mehta
lp: Miss Bubby

Vimla
9165 ft.; **genre:** Social
pc: Laxmi Pictures **co-d:** Chandulal Shah **co-d/c:** D.D. Dabke **st/sc:** Mohanlal G. Dave
lp: Putli, Raja Sandow
Remarks: Revised version re-released as *Mother India* (CC. No. 8141, dt. Sept 18, 1929).

Yashodevi
aka **Sacrifice**
7680 ft.; **genre:** Historical
pc: Royal Art Studio **c:** Rustom Irani
lp: Madanrai Vakil, Jilloo
Remarks: Film was banned in some Provinces on religious grounds.

1926

Abola Rani
aka **Queen That Would Not Speak**
6480 ft.; **genre:** Legend
pc: Pioneer Film Co. **st:** Shamal Bhat **sc:** Manhar Vartejwala
lp: Zubeida

Ajab Kumari
8040 ft.; **genre:** Social
pc: Sharda Film Co. **d:** Manilal Joshi **c:** Naval Bhat **st:** Indulal Yagnik
lp: Mohanlala, Mary (Kumudini), Daji

Amar Asha
aka **Immortal Hope**
10205 ft.; **genre:** Costume
pc: Krishna Film Co. **d:** Harshadrai Mehta **c/st/sc:** Chimanlal Luhar
lp: Gulab, Ermeline, Nandram

Asha
aka **Andhli Phool Wali**
7275 ft.; **genre:** Social
pc: Laxmi Pictures **d/st/sc:** R.S.D. Chaudhary **c:** Pandurang S. Naik
lp: Putli, K.B. Athavale, Ghory, Baba Vyas, Nagendra Mazumdar

Babanchi Bayko
aka **Papa's Wife**
5582 ft.; **genre:** Social
pc: United Pictures Syndicate, Poona **d:** N.D. Sarpotdar **c:** Pandurang Talegiri
lp: Durga Koregaonkar, P.N. Varne, Gondhlekar, Dwarkadas Potdar

Balaji Nimbalkar
5560 ft.; **genre:** Historical
pc: Hindustan Cinema Film Co., Nasik **d:** D.G. Phalke **c:** Trymbak B. Telang **st/sc:** Saralkar
lp: Bhaurao Datar, Vasant Shinde, D.B. Sukte, Krishna Chavan

Be Dinni Badshahi
aka **Crown for Two Days**
8704 ft.; **genre:** Social
pc: Krishna Film Co. **d:** Harshadrai Mehta **c:** Chimanlal Luhar **st/sc:** Krishnakumar
lp: Gulab, Ermeline, Nandram, Vishnu, Fatma Jr., Chandra

Bhadraveshi Gunda
aka **Shethno Salo, Gentleman Loafer**
7857 ft.; **genre:** Social
pc: Royal Art Studio **st:** Machhar
lp: Gulab, Madanrai Vakil, Jilloo

Bhagva Zenda
6227 ft.; **genre:** Historical
pc: Royal Art Studio **d:** K.P. Bhave **c:** Rustom Irani **st/sc:** K.P. Bhave
lp: Madanrai Vakil, Miss Jones, Asooji, Elizer, Baburao Sansare

Bhakta Prahlad
6159 ft.; **genre:** Mythological
pc: Maharashtra Film Co., Kolhapur **d:** Baburao Painter **c:** S. Fattelal
lp: Kamladevi, Balasaheb Yadav, V. Shantaram, Bal Kelkar, Padmabai, G.R. Mane

Bhakta Prahlad
7447 ft.; **genre:** Mythological
pc: Hindustan Cinema Film Co., Nasik **d/sc:** D.G. Phalke **c:** Anna Salunke **st:** V.H. Palnitkar
lp: Gangaram Nhavi, Bhaurao Datar, Bachu Pawar, Yamuna Gole

BHAMTO BHUT
aka **Wandering Phantom**
8505 ft.; **genre:** Crime
pc: Kohinoor Film Co. **d:** Mohan Bhavnani **c:** Narayan Devare **st/sc:** Mohanlal G. Dave
lp: Sulochana, Khalil, R.N.Vaidya, Behram Vasania

BHIM SANJIVAN
aka **How Bhim Was Brought Back to Life**
6495 ft.; **genre:** Mythological
pc: Hindustan Cinema Film Co., Nasik **d:** Gajanan V. Sane **c:** Anna Salunke
lp: Bhaurao Datar, Anasuya

BHUL NO BHOG
aka **Victim**
9095 ft.; **genre:** Social
pc: Krishna Film Co. **d:** Harshadrai Mehta **c:** Chimanlal Luhar **st:** Vinay
lp: Ermeline, Nandram

BOLTUN BULBUL
aka **Wooing Nightingale**
8127 ft.; **genre:** Costume
pc: Krishna Film Co. **d:** Kanjibhai Rathod **c:** Chaturbhai Patel **st:** Ved & Vyas
sc: Krishnakumar
lp: Gulab, Ermeline, Nandram, Vishnu, Chandra

BRIEFLESS BARRISTER
8789 ft.; **genre:** Comedy
pc: Kohinoor Film Co. **d:** Homi Master **st/sc:** Mohanlal G. Dave
lp: Gohar, Siddimiya, Moti, Putlibai

BULBULE PARISTAN
9427 ft.; **genre:** Costume
pc: Fatma Film Co. **d/st/sc:** Fatma Begum **c:** Rustom Irani/Ardeshir Irani/ Pandurang S. Naik
lp: Zubeida, Sahazadi, Putli, Madam Tosca, Madanrai Vakil, K.B. Athavale, Miss Fiske (Blanche Verne)

BURKHAWALI
aka **Veiled Enemy**
8470 ft.; **genre:** Stunt
pc: Krishna Film Co. **d:** Kanjibhai Rathod **c:** Chaturbhai Patel **st:** Natwar Shyam **sc:** Krishnakumar
lp: Ermeline, Nandram, Durga, Hyder Shah, Vishnu

▲ E. Bilimoria

Chhatra Bakavali

7453 ft.; **genre:** Legend
Pioneer Film Co. **d/c:** S.N. Patankar **st/sc:** Manhar Vartejwalla
lp: Kapadia, Vithabai, Miss Rani, Nargis

Dagabaz Duniya
aka **Way of the World**

7918 ft.; **genre:** Social
pc: Sharda Film Co. **d/st/sc:** Harihar Diwana
lp: Miss Jones, Yakbal, Amirbanu

Delhi no Dodh Chhel
aka **Andher Nagari, Fearless Phantom**

10252 ft.; **genre:** Comedy
pc: Sri Vijay Film Co. **c:** Naval Bhat **st/sc:** Vijay Shankar Bhat
lp: Gangaram, Dwarki, Bapu

Delhi No Thug
aka **Thief of Delhi**

8995 ft.; **genre:** Costume
pc: Kohinoor Film Co. **d:** Homi Master **c:** Narayan Devare/K.G. Gokhale **st/sc:** Mohanlal G. Dave
lp: Gohar, Khalil

Dha Cha Ma
aka **Murder of Narayan Rao Peshwa**

7527 ft.; **genre:** Historical
pc: United Pictures Syndicate, Poona **d:** N.D. Sarpotdar **c:** Pandurang Talegiri
lp: Bandopant Sohoni, Durga Koregaonkar, Sunderrao Nadkarni, P.N. Varne, D. Bilimoria, Wamanrao Kulkarni, Jairampant Desai, Datoba Rajwade

Dharma Patni

10000 ft.; **genre:** Social
pc: Madan Theatres Ltd. **d:** Jyotish Banerjee **st:** Aga Hashr Kashmiri
lp: Durgadas Banerjee, Patience Cooper, Kartick Dey

Dharmi Dhutaro
aka **Scoundrel Monk**

7922 ft.; **genre:** Social
pc: Sharda Film Co.
Remarks: The film was refused a Censor certificate on the grounds of being offensive to religious sensibilities.

Dilaram
11449 ft.; **genre:** Costume
pc: Sharda Film Co. **d/st/sc:** Nanubhai Desai **c:** Bhogilal Dave/Naval Bhat
lp: Dwarki, Mary, Janibabu, Prabhashankar, A.P. Kapoor

Diwan Bhamasha
aka **Lion of Mewar**
9262 ft.; **genre:** Historical
pc: Imperial Film Co. **d:** Mohan Bhavnani **c:** Rustom Irani **st:** Nagendra Mazumdar
lp: Putli, Jilloo, Madanrai Vakil, Elizer

Dorangi Duniya
aka **Robes and the Rags**
6712 ft.; **genre:** Social
pc: Pioneer Film Co. **d/c:** S.N. Patankar
lp: K.B. Athavale, Thatte

Dulari
8025 ft.; **genre:** Social
pc: Saraswati Film Co. **d/st/sc:** Manilal Joshi **c:** A.P. Karandikar
lp: Putli, Jilloo, Madanrai Vakil, Yusuf, Elizer, M. Udwadia, Baburao Sansare

Gaja Gauri
6907 ft.; **genre:** Mythological
pc: Maharashtra Film Co., Kolhapur **d:** Baburao Painter **c:** S. Fattelal
lp: Balasaheb Yadav, V. Shantaram, Kamladevi, Sushila Devi, Ganpat Bakre, Ravji Mhaiskar, Zunzharrao Pawar

Guniyal Gulab
aka **Patighatini Sati, For Country's Sake**
7632 ft.; **genre:** Social
pc: Sharda Film Co. **d/st/sc:** Harihar Diwana
c: Naval Bhat
lp: Master Vithal, Mary, Tara, Asha

Indrajal
aka **Swarga Kankan, Missing Bracelet**
8473 ft.; **genre:** Costume
pc: Royal Art Studio **d/st/sc:** B.P. Mishra
c: Ardeshir Irani
lp: Zubeida, Fatma Begum, Elizer, Jilloo, S.E. Joshi

▲ Advertisement for variety programme during intermissions

Jangal Ni Jadibutti
aka **Gauhr-e Jungle, Love Rewarded**
9426 ft.; **genre:** Social
pc: Sharda Film Co. **d:** Manilal Joshi **c:** Naval Bhat **st:** Ramashankar Dave
lp: Tara, Balabhai, Bachu

Janki Swayamwar
aka **Dhanurbhang**
7150 ft.; **genre:** Mythological
pc: Hindustan Cinema Film Co., Nasik **d/st/sc:** D.G. Phalke

Joydev
aka **Jaydev**
12000 ft.; **genre:** Devotional
pc: Madan Theatres Ltd. **d:** Jyotish Banerjee **c:** Charles Creed **st:** Haripada Chatterjee
lp: Patience Cooper, Indiradevi, Binapani, Renubala, Manorama, Kalidasi, Kananbala, Satyen Dey, Kartik Dey, Tulsi Banerjee (?)

Kacha Devyani
aka **Vidhyaharan**
7077 ft.; **genre:** Mythological
pc: Pioneer Film Co. **d/c:** S.N. Patankar
lp: Thatte, K.B. Athavale, Bhosle

Kalabaj Ashak
aka **Wooing Tactics**
7126 ft.; **genre:** Comedy
pc: Saurashtra Film Co. Ltd, Rajkot **d:** Vajeshankar Pattani **c:** Champaklal Pattani
st: Manilal M. Vaidya
lp: Dorothy, Manilal M. Vaidya, Nathalal Soni, Monghibai, Gatubhai Vaidya, Shanta, Allarakha Mir, Maganlal Dave, Master Hemant Vaidya

Kashmeera
aka **Dushman Ni Dikri**
7661 ft.; **genre:** Costume
pc: Excelsior Film Co. **d/sc:** Manilal Joshi **c:** D.D. Dabke
st: Gopalji Delwadakar
lp: Zubeida, Madanrai Vakil, W.M. Khan

Kataryu Gap
7807 ft.; **genre:** Comedy
pc: Royal Art Studio **d:** Dinshah J. Jhaveri **c:** A.P. Karandikar **st:** Irfani
lp: Madanrai Vakil, Sakhu

Keechak Vadh
6475 ft.; **genre:** Mythological
pc: Hindustan Cinema Film Co., Nasik **d/st/sc:** D.G. Phalke **c:** Anna Salunke
lp: Bhaurao Datar, Bachu Pawar, Yamuna Gole

Khudoorat Bala
aka **Society Butterfly**
16820 ft.; **genre:** Social serial in 2 parts
pc: Krishna Film Co. **d:** Kanjibhai Rathod **c:** Chaturbhai Patel **st:** Natwar Shyam (C. N. Maniar) **sc:** Krishnakumar
lp: Gulab, Ermeline, Nandram, Vishnu, Hyder Shah, P.R. Joshi, Fayma

Krishna Sakha
6018 ft.; **genre:** Mythological
pc: Aurora Cinema Co., Calcutta **d/sc:** Ahindra Chaudhury **c:** Debi Ghosh
lp: Firoz Bala, Saraswati, Santosh Sinha, Brojendra Sarkar
Remarks: Calcutta CC. No. 8358, dt. 30/12/26 states 7000ft. Bombay release through the Exhibitors Film Service has Bombay CC. No. 6792, dt. 31/7/1928.

Krishnakant's Will
15137 ft.; **genre:** Social
pc: Madan Theatres Ltd. **d:** Amritlal Bose/Priyanath Ganguly **c:** Charles Creed/Jatin Das **st:** Bankimchandra Chatterjee
lp: Durgadas Banerjee, Amritlal Bose, Seeta Devi (of Bengal), Patience Cooper, Prabodh Ch Bose, Chani Dutt, Kartik Dey, Indu Mukherjee, Prafulla, Shanti Gupta

Lagn Ke Lilam
aka **Marriage Market**
6985 ft.; **genre:** Social
pc: Kohinoor Film Co. **d/st/sc:** Bachubabu **c:** K.G. Gokhale
lp: Moti, Siddimiya, Usharani

Lakho Vanjaro
7608 ft.; **genre:** Costume
pc: Kohinoor Film Co. **d:** Homi Master **c:** K.G. Gokhale **st/sc:** Mohanlal G. Dave
lp: Gohar, Jamuna, Khalil

Madan Kala
10619 ft.; **genre:** Costume
pc: Sharda Film Co. **d:** Harihar Diwana **c:** Naval Bhat **st:** Ramashankar Dave **sc:** Nanubhai Desai
lp: Master Vithal, Janibabu, Tara, Mary, Asha

Madhav Kamakundala

8435 feet; **genre:** Legend
pc: Laxmi Pictures **d:** Chandulal Shah **c:** D.D. Dabke **st/sc:** Mohanlal G. Dave
lp: Putli, Raja Sandow, Miss Fiske (Blanche Verne)

Madhu Bansri

aka **Divine Flute**
1105 ft.; **genre:** Mythological
pc: Krishna Film Co.

Mano Vijaya

7048 ft.; **genre:** Mythological
pc: Pioneer Film Co. **d/c:** S.N. Patankar
lp: Nargis, K.B. Athavale, Takle

Mena Kumari

8211 ft.; **genre:** Costume
pc: Kohinoor Film Co. **d:** Mohan Bhavnani **c:** Vishnu B. Joshi **st/sc:** Mohanlal G. Dave
lp: Gohar, Raja Sandow, R.N. Vaidya, Ghanshyam, Sidimiyan

Mohini Avatar

6000 ft.; **genre:** Mythological
pc: Indian Film Co., Madras **d/sc:** R.S. Prakash

Mumtaz Mahal

9101 ft.; **genre:** Historical
pc: Kohinoor Film Co. **d:** Homi Master **c:** Narayan Devare **st/sc:** Mohanlal G. Dave
lp: Gohar, Sulochana, Raja Sandow, Sidimiyan

Neera

aka **Beautiful Snake of Arawalli**
9817 ft.; **genre:** Costume
pc: Laxmi Pictures **co-d/st/sc:** R.S.D. Chaudhary **co-d:** R.G. Torney
c: Pandurang S. Naik
lp: Raja Sandow, Putli, Dabir, K.B. Athavale, Takle, Ghory, Baba Vyas, Chandrarao, Dewanchand, Miss Janubai

Pagal Premi

aka **Girl Mad**
9244 ft.; **genre:** Costume
pc: Imperial Film Co. **d/sc:** Mohan Bhavnani **c:** Adi Irani **st:** A.S. Desai
lp: Sulochana, Madanrai Vakil, B.P. Mishra, Jilloo, Elizer, Jamshetji

Pahadi Pindharo
aka **Midnight Rider**
9422 ft.; **genre:** Costume/Stunt
pc: Imperial Film Co. **d/st/sc:** B.P. Mishra **c:** A.P. Karandikar
lp: Putli, Jilloo, Madanrai Vakil, Miss Jean

Panch Kalyan
aka **Parijatak**
7909 ft.; **genre:** Costume
pc: Krishna Film Co. **d:** Harshadrai Mehta **c:** Chaturbhai Patel **st/sc:** Krishnakumar
lp: Gulab, Ermeline, Nandram

Panch Mahabhut
6362 ft.; **genre:** Social
pc: Pioneer Film Co. **d/st/lp:** Alvaro

Paniman Aag
aka **Niti Vijaya, Sweet Adversity**
8811 ft.; **genre:** Costume
pc: Royal Art Studio **d:** Nagendra Mazumdar **c:** Rustom Irani **st/sc:** Vijay Shankar Bhat
lp: Madanrai Vakil, Putli, Jilloo, Miss Jainu

Panna Ratna
aka **Jewel of Mewad**
8575 ft.; **genre:** Historical
pc: Krishna Film Co. **d:** Harshadrai Mehta **c:** Chaturbhai Patel **sc:** Krishna Kumar
lp: Nandram, Gangaram, Miss Fayma, Master Kamlakar

Prem Sanyas
aka **The Light of Asia**
9437 ft.; **genre:** Biographical
pc: Great Eastern Film Corporation, Delhi/Emelka Film Co., Munich **d:** Franz Osten
c: Joseph Wirsching/Willi Kiermeier **st:** based on Edwin Arnold's *The Light of Asia*
sc: Niranjan Pal
lp: Seeta Devi (Renee Smith), Himansu Rai, Sarada Ukil, Ranibala, Prafulla Roy, Sunit Mitter, Jagit Mathur, Sundar Rajan, Nalini Kumari, Sunil Blemi, Charu Pillai, Ashok Bose, Haren Sen
Remarks: Released in Europe in 1925 with a running length of 7382 ft.

Prithvi Putra
8236 ft.; **genre:** Mythological
pc: Kohinoor Film Co. **d/c:** Gajanan S. Devare **st/sc:** Mohanlal G. Dave
lp: Gohar, Sulochana, Khalil, Jamuna, Siddimiyan

Profulla
aka **Prafulla**
14000 ft.; **genre:** Social
pc: Madan Theatres Ltd. **d:** Jyotish Banerjee **st:** Girish Chandra Ghosh
lp: Patience Cooper, Satyen Dey, Dadibhai Sarkari

Pyari Mamta
aka **Bird of Prey**
8695 ft.; **genre:** Social
pc: Imperial Film Co. **d:** B.P. Mishra **st:** Prof. Sathe
lp: Jilloo, Madanrai Vakil, Putli, Yusuf

Ra Kawat
aka **Pranay Milan**
7952 ft.; **genre:** Historical
pc: Kohinoor Film Co./Saraswati Film Co. **d:** Mohan Bhavnani **c:** Vishnu B. Joshi
st: Dayaram Shah
lp: Sulochana, Gohar, Raja Sandow, Nur Mohamed

Race ki Thes
7728 ft.; **genre:** Comedy
pc: Madan Theatres Ltd.
lp: Master Mohan, Surajram
Remarks: Banned on the grounds that it `transfers to an Indian setting all the worst features of the lowest type of American vulgarity'.

Radha Madhav
7987 ft.; **genre:** Mythological
pc: Royal Art Studio **d/sc:** K.P. Bhave **c:** Rustom Irani **st:** Yeshwant N. Tipnis
lp: Madanrai Vakil, Dwarki, Jilloo, Elizer, Baburao Sansare, Asooji

Raja Bhoj
aka **Kismet Ka Khel, Trial of Destiny**
7995 ft.; **genre:** Legend
pc: Royal Art Studio **d/st/sc:** Dinshah J. Jhaveri **c:** Rustom Irani
lp: Zubeida, Madanrai Vakil, Jilloo, Sakhu

Rajane Gami Te Rani
aka **Love is Blind**
7172 ft.; **genre:** Costume
pc: Krishna Film Co. **d/st/sc:** Kanjibhai Rathod **c:** Chimanlal Luhar
lp: Gulab, Ermeline

Ram Bharose
aka **Per Chance**
8384 ft.; **genre:** Social
pc: Krishna Film Co. **d:** Harshadrai Mehta **c:** Chimanlal Luhar **st:** Shivlal Nayak **sc:** Krishnakumar
lp: Ermeline, Gulab, Nandram, Durga, Kusum, Prabhudas

Rama Rajya Viyog
8071 ft.; **genre:** Mythological
pc: Hindustan Cinema Film Co., Nasik **d:** Gajanan V. Sane

Rang Rakhyo Chhe
aka **Mertle Preserved**
1775 ft.; **genre:** Comedy
pc: Gujarat Studio **d/st/sc:** Vithaldas Panchotia **c:** Narsi Mistry
lp: Vithaldas Panchotia, Ratilal

Ratna Manjri
10023 ft.; **genre:** Costume/Fantasy
pc: Sharda Film Co. **d:** Manilal Joshi **c:** Naval Bhat **st:** Justice Kincaid **sc:** Nanubhai Desai
lp: Master Vithal (first lead role), Kumudini, Janibabu, Balabhai, Bachu

Samrat Shiladitya
9413 ft.; **genre:** Historical
pc: Kohinoor Film Co. **d:** Mohan Bhavnani **c:** D.D. Dabke
lp: Sulochana, Gohar, Raja Sandow, Moti, R.N. Vaidya, Nur Mohamed

Sant Eknath
aka **Saint of Paithan**
6233 ft.; **genre:** Devotional
pc: Hindustan Cinema Film Co., Nasik **d/st/sc:** D.G. Phalke **c:** Anna Salunke
lp: Bhaurao Datar, Gotiram

Sati Jasma
aka **Jasma Odan**
8540 ft.; **genre:** Legend
pc: Kohinoor Film Co. **d:** Homi Master **c:** Gajanan S. Devare **st/sc:** Mohanlal G. Dave
lp: Gohar, Khalil, Jamuna, R.N. Vaidya, Nur Mohamed, Ghanshyam

Sati Menadevi
aka **Bolto Lekh**
8347 ft.; **genre:** Costume
pc: Royal Art Studio **d/st/sc:** P.J. Jhaveri
lp: Zubeida, Jilloo, Madanrai Vakil, M. Udwadia

Sati Saroj
aka **Shiyalni Kasoti**
10022 ft.; **genre:** Devotional
pc: Saraswati Film Co.
lp: Jilloo, Madanrai Vakil, Elizer

Satyavijaya
8534 ft.; **genre:** Social
pc: Pioneer Film Co. **d/c/st/sc:** S.N. Patankar
lp: K.B. Athavale, Thatte, K. Narayan Kale

Shahe Jungle
aka **King of Forest**
7555 ft.; **genre:** Costume
pc: Royal Art Studio **d/st/sc:** K.P. Bhave **c:** Rustom Irani
lp: Jilloo, Madanrai Vakil, B.P. Mishra, M. Udwadia

Shirin Farhad
aka **At the Altar of Love**
10252 ft.; **genre:** Legend
pc: Kohinoor Film Co. **d:** Homi Master **c:** N.G. Devare/ Pandurang Naik
st/sc: Mohanlal G. Dave
lp: Gohar, Khalil, Daji, Jamuna, Heera, Nur Mohamed

Shish Mahal
8756 ft.; **genre:** Costume
pc: Royal Art Studio **d/st/sc:** B.P. Mishra **c:** Rustom Irani
lp: Jilloo, Madanrai Vakil, Elizer,

Slaves of Custom
5000 ft.; **genre:** Social
pc: Royal Art Studio/Bombay Baby Week Committee **d:** B.P. Mishra **st/sc:** Pijam

Suvarna Kamal
aka **Kalika Murti, Golden Lotus**
10176 ft.; **genre:** Mythological/Costume
pc: Sharda Film Co. **d/st/sc:** K.P. Bhave **c:** Naval Bhat
lp: Master Vithal, Mary, Shiraz Ali, Janibabu, Hira, Miss Rosy

Tai Teleen
7632 ft.; **genre:** Historical
pc: United Pictures Syndicate, Poona **d/st/sc:** N.D. Sarpotdar **c:** Pandurang Talegiri/ V. V. Date

lp: Gangubai, Durga Koregaonkar, D. Bilimoria, Dwarkanath Potdar, P .N. Varne, Dattoba Rajwade

Telephone Ni Taruni

aka **Telephone Girl**

8427 ft.; **genre:** Social
pc: Kohinoor Film Co. **d:** Homi Master **c:** Narayan Devare **st/sc:** Mohanlal G. Dave
lp: Sulochana, Khalil, Raja Sandow, Jamuna

Totayache Bund

aka **Dano Diwan, Pretender**

6982 ft.; **genre:** Historical
pc: United Pictures Syndicate, Poona **d/sc:** N.D. Sarpotdar **c:** Pandurang Talegiri **st:** N. C. Kelkar
lp: Bandopant Sohoni, Durga Koregaonkar, P. N. Varne, Wamanrao Kulkarni, Dattoba Rajwade

Typist Girl

aka **Why I Became a Christian**

9518 ft.; **genre:** Social
pc: Kohinoor Film Co. **d:** Chandulal Shah/Gajanan S. Devare **c:** Narayan Devare
st/sc: Mohanlal G. Dave
lp: Sulochana, Gohar, Raja Sandow

Umaji Naik

6366 ft.; **genre:** Historical
pc: United Pictures Syndicate, Poona **d:** N.D. Sarpotdar **c:** Pandurang Talegiri
lp: Baburao Pawar, Dattoba Rajwade, Durga Koregaonkar, Dwarkanath Potdar, P. N. Varne, Dattu Kamble, D. Bilimoria

Vandemataram Ashram

6590 ft.; **genre:** Social
pc: Vande Mataram Film Co. **d/st/sc:** Bhalji Pendharkar **c:** D.D. Dabke
lp: P.Y. Altekar, Yamunadevi, Baburao Pendharkar, Master Vithal
Remarks: Prohibited on 15/9/26 for implied attack on the prestige of University education. Certified on 7th Dec. 1926.

Vasantbala

7894 ft.; **genre:** Costume
pc: Sharda Film Co. **d:** Nanubhai Desai **c:** Naval Bhat
lp: Miss Jones

Veer Kesari

9724 ft.; **genre:** Costume

pc: Krishna Film Co. **d:** Kanjibhai Rathod **c:** Chaturbhai Patel **st:** B.K. Pachbhaya
lp: Ermeline, Gulab, Nandram, Vishnu, Gangaram

Vidhinu Vidhan
aka **Vanthel Vishaya, Flirting Widow**
8345 ft.; **genre:** Social
pc: Royal Art Studio **d:** K.P. Bhave **c:** Rustom Irani **st/sc:** Vijay Shankar Bhat
lp: Jilloo, Madanrai Vakil
Remarks: Censors objected to the original title *Vanthel Vidhva* aka *Flirting Widow*.

Youvan Chakra
aka **Vamp**
9387 ft.; **genre:** Social
pc: Sharda Film Co. **d/st/sc:** Naval Gandhi **c:** Naval Bhat
lp: Yakbal

1927
Adbhut Khoon
aka **Horrible Murder**
1938 ft.; **genre:** Comedy
pc: United Pictures Syndicate, Poona

Alibaba Chalis Chor
aka **Alibaba and Forty Thieves**
10102 ft.; **genre:** Costume
pc: Imperial Film Co. **d:** B.P. Mishra **c:** Rustom Irani **st/sc:** Pessi Karani
lp: Sulochana, Jamshetji, Elizer, Jilloo, Madanrai Vakil, Baburao Sansare, Ghori, Prabhakar Joshi, Mehboob

Allaudin ane Jadui Fanas
aka **Alladin & the Wonderful Lamp**
10643 ft.; **genre:** Costume
pc: Imperial Film Co. **d/sc:** B.P. Mishra
lp: Zebu, Elizer, Yusuf, Sayed Hussein, Baburao Sansare, Ghory, Miss Stewart, Victoria, Leila, Zenu, Miss Thompson, Miss Gordon

Allah ka Pyara
aka **The Guarding Angel**
8465 ft.; **genre:** Costume
pc: Imperial Film Co. **d/st/sc:** K.P. Bhave **c:** Adi Irani
lp: Indira, Elizer, Zebu, Jamshetji, Madanrai Vakil, Yusuf

Anun naam te Bairi
aka **Trust Your Wife**

8756 ft.; **genre:** Social
pc: Imperial Film Co. **d:** Mohan Bhavnani **c:** Rustom Irani
lp: Jilloo, Jamshetji, Miss Mohini (Miss Wood)

Asuri Lalsa
aka **Passion**
10751 ft.; **genre:** Social
pc: Sharda Film Co. **d/sc:** Nanubhai Desai **c:** Naval Bhat **st:** Narayan Visanji Thakur
lp: Master Vithal, Kumudini, Malka, Janibabu

Balidan
aka **Sacrifice**
8282 ft.; **genre:** Adaptation
pc: Orient Pictures Corpn. **d:** Naval Gandhi **c:** Naval Bhat **st:** Rabindranath Tagore
sc: Jamshed Ratnagar
lp: Sulochana, Zubeida, Master Vithal, Janibabu, J. Makhijani, Jal Khambata
Remarks: English titled version for the European release is 5500 ft.

Bansari Bala
aka **Fairy of the Flute**
10442 ft.; **genre:** Costume
pc: Sharda Film Co. **d/st/sc:** A.P. Kapur **c:** Naval Bhat
lp: Master Vithal, Janibabu, Lobo, Asha, Meherbanu

Beghadi Mauj
aka **Pleasure Mad**
9815 ft.; **genre:** Social
pc: Kohinoor Film Co. **d/c:** Narayan Devare **st/sc:** Mohanlal G. Dave
lp: Heera, Jamuna, Thomas, R.N. Vaidya, Rajababu, Rustomji Patel, Usharani

Bhakta Sudama
aka **Sudamache Pohe**
6159 ft.; **genre:** Mythological
pc: Hindustan Cinema Film Co., Nasik **d/st/sc:** D.G. Phalke **c:** Anna Salunke
lp: Bhaurao Datar, Dattatray Kshirsagar

Bhaneli Bhamini
aka **Educated Wife**
9882 ft.; **genre:** Social
pc: Kohinoor Film Co. **d:** Homi Master **c:** Narayan Devare **st/sc:** Mohanlal G. Dave
lp: Gohar, Raja Sandow, R.N. Vaidya, Master Kishore

Bhedi Trishul
aka **Hidden Treasure**

9348 ft.; **genre:** Stunt
pc: Sharda Film Co. **d/st/sc:** Nanubhai Desai **c:** Naval Bhat
lp: Master Vithal, Lobo, Prabhashankar, Miss Mani, Malka, Janibabu, A.P. Kapoor

Bole Te Be Khaay
1115 ft.; **genre:** Comedy
pc: Krishna Film Co. **st:** based on a medieval tale

Chandidas
9315 ft.; **genre:** Devotional
pc: Madan Theatres Ltd. **d:** Jyotish Banerjee
lp: Tulsi Banerjee, Patience Cooper, Manorama, Nilima Devi, Jyotsna, Satyen Dey, Phulanalini, Purnima Devi

Chhel Batao ane Rani Mohana
7762 ft.; **genre:** Costume
pc: Royal Art Studio **d:** Dinshah J. Jhaveri **st:** Pandit Parimal
lp: Jilloo, Putli, Madanrai Vakil

Chitrakar Premi
aka **Artist Lover**
7025 ft.; **genre:** Comedy
pc: Saurashtra Film Co Ltd., Rajkot **d:** Vajeshankar Pattani **c:** Champakbhai Pattani
st: Manilal M. Vaidya
lp: Manilal M. Vaidya, Shanta, Nathabhai Soni, Master Hemant Vaidya

Curse of Ignorance
5845 ft.; **genre:** Educational
pc: Bombay Baby Week Committee **st/sc:** Pijam

Daksha Yagna
5904 ft.; **genre:** Mythological
pc: Hindustan Cinema Film Co., Nasik **d:** Gajanan V. Sane
lp: Bhaurao Datar, Bachu Pawar, Gangubai Mohite

Daya ni Devi
aka **Nurse**
9426 ft.; **genre:** Social
pc: Imperial Film Co. **d:** Mohan Bhavnani **st:** Indulal Yagnik
lp: Sulochana, Jamshetji, D. Bilimoria

Detective Kumar
8150 ft.; **genre:** Social
pc: Excelsior Film Co. **d/st/sc:** K.B. Athavale **c:** D.D. Dabke

lp: K.B. Athavale, Malini, Rampiary, Salvi

Dil Farosh

8062 ft.; **genre:** Costume
pc: Excelsior Film Co. **d:** M. Udwadia **c:** D.D. Dabke **st:** Gopalji Delwadakar, based on Shakespeare's *The Merchant of Venice*
lp: M. Udwadia, K.B. Athavale, Nargis, Saiyed Umer

Draupadi Vastra Haran

6759 ft.; **genre:** Mythological
pc: Hindustan Cinema Film Co., Nasik **d/st/sc:** D.G. Phalke **c:** Anna Salunke
lp: Bhaurao Datar, Gangubai Mohite, Bachu Pawar

Durgesh Nandini

12400 ft.
pc: Madan Theatres Ltd. **d:** Priyanath Ganguli **c:** Manglu **st:** Bankimchandra Chatterjee
lp: Durgadas Banerjee, Naresh Mitra, Seeta Devi, Patience Cooper, Ahindra Chaudhary, Indira Devi, Kanak Narayan Bhup, Geeta, Prabodh Ch Bose, Jainarayan Mukherjee, Ashu Bose, Kanu Banerjee

E Kon

aka **Who**
6343 ft.; **genre:** Historical
pc: Sri Ram Film Co. **d:** Jhaveri **st:** Nathmadhav **sc:** Dayaram Shah
lp: Blanche Verne

Gamdani Gori

aka **Village Girl**
10128 ft.; **genre:** Social
pc: Imperial Film Co. **d:** Mohan Bhavnani **c:** Rustom Irani **st:** Nanubhai Vakil
lp: Sulochana, Jamshetji, Bhatia Sandow, Madanrai Vakil

Gandharva Kanya

aka **The Reunion**
8347 ft.; **genre:** Costume
pc: Krishna Film Co. **st:** Shamal Bhat
lp: Nandram, Lila, Gangaram, Nizam, Chandra, Durga

Gatarnun Gulab

aka **Dancing Girl**
9435 ft.; **genre:** Social
pc: Imperial Film Co. **d/st/sc:** B.P .Mishra **c:** Rustom Irani
lp: Sulochana, Putli, Madanrai Vakil, K.P. Bhave, Sakhu, Jamshetji, Elizer

Gulzar

9291 ft.; **genre:** Costume
pc: Sharda Film Co. **d:** Nanubhai Desai **c:** Naval Bhat
lp: Janibabu, Miss Mani, Malka, Yakub, Atta Mohamed

Gunasundari

aka **Why Husbands Go Astray**
9452 ft.; **genre:** Social
pc: Kohinoor Film Co. **d:** Chandulal Shah **c:** Narayan Devare **st:** Dayaram Shah
lp: Gohar, Raja Sandow, Rampiary, Jamuna, R.N. Vaidya

Hanuman Janma

aka **Birth of Maruti**
5650 ft.; **genre:** Mythological
pc: Hindustan Cinema Film Co., Nasik **d/st/sc:** D.G. Phalke **c:** Anna Salunke
lp: Bhaurao Datar, Laxman Malusare, Yamuna Gole

Jana

9000 ft.; **genre:** Mythological
pc: Madan Theatres Ltd. **d:** Priyanath Ganguli **st:** Girish Chandra Ghosh
lp: Patience Cooper, Tulsi Banerjee, Indira Devi, Dinesh Das

Jane Alam Anjuman Ara

15574 ft.; **genre:** Costume serial in 2 parts
pc: Sharda Film Co. **d/st/sc:** Nanubhai Desai **c:** Naval Bhat
lp: Janibabu, Kumudini, Miss Mani, Malka, A.P. Kapoor

Janjirne Jankare

aka **At the Clang of Fetters**
13496 ft.; **genre:** Costume
pc: Krishna Film Co. **d:** Harshadrai Mehta **c/sc:** Chimanlal Luhar **st:** Champsi Udeshi
lp: Gulab, Nandram, Durga, Gangaram, Hyder Shah, P.R. Joshi, Babi, Sultan Alam

Jugari Dharma

aka **Draupadi Vastraharan , Royal Gambler**
6912 ft.; **genre:** Mythological
pc: United Pictures Syndicate, Poona **d:** P.Y. Altekar **c:** Pandurang Talegiri **sc:** Mama Varerkar
lp: P.Y. Altekar, Baburao Gade, Dattu Kamble, Nanasaheb Phatak

Kailas Kumari

aka **Sansar Shatranj**
8765 ft.
pc: Sharda Film Co. **st/sc/d:** Nanubhai Desai **c:** Naval Bhat
lp: Janibabu, Miss Mani, Malka

KALA PAHAD
aka **Masked Terror**
9567 ft.; **genre:** Stunt
pc: Sharda Film Co. **d:** Nanubhai Desai **c:** Naval Bhat
lp: Master Vithal, Kumudini, Prabhashankar, Budhkar

KALA PANI NO QAIDI
aka **Return of Kala Naag**
9082 ft.; **genre:** Social
pc: Kohinoor Film Co. **d:** Homi Master **c:** Pandurang S. Naik **st/sc:** Mohanlal G. Dave
lp: Homi Master, Khalil, Shakuntala, Janaki

KARMAYELI KALI
aka **Tainted Virtue**
10751 ft.; **genre:** Social
pc: Imperial Film Co. **d/st/sc:** R.S.D. Chaudhary **c:** Rustom Irani
lp: Ermeline, Madanrai Vakil, Yusuf

KESHAVKANT B.A.
10397 ft.; **genre:** Social
pc: Krishna Film Co. **d:** Harshadrai Mehta **c:** Chimanlal Luhar
lp: Keshavlal, Yekbal , Nandram, Rampiary, Nizam,

KIMTI ANSU
aka **Precious Tears**
10610 ft.; **genre:** Social
pc: Krishna Film Co. **d:** Harshadrai Mehta **c/st/sc:** Chimanlal Luhar
lp: Nandram, Yekbal, Nizam, Vishnu, P.R. Joshi

KRISHNA SAMBHAV
aka **8th Incarnation**
6121 ft.; **genre:** Mythological
pc: United Pictures Syndicate, Poona **d:** N.D. Sarpotdar **c:** V.V. Date **st:** K.P. Bhave
lp: Gangubai, Wamanrao Kulkarni

KULDIPAK
aka **Born Hero**
7932 ft.; **genre:** Costume
pc: Krishna Film Co. **d:** Kanjibhai Rathod **c:** Chimanlal Luhar **st:** Natwar Shyam **sc:** Krishnakumar
lp: Gulab, Nandram, Nizam, Hyder Shah, Durga, Fayma

LAILA MAJNU
9541 ft.; **genre:** Legend
pc: Excelsior Film Co. **d/sc:** Manilal Joshi **c:** D.D. Dabke
lp: Zubeida, Madanrai Vakil, Shahzadi

Lohika Lilam
aka **Gulami Jiwan, Soul of Slave**
7346 ft.; **genre:** Social
pc: Excelsior Film Co. **d/st/sc:** Manilal Joshi **c:** D.D. Dabke
lp: Nargis, Heera

Machhavatar
6000 ft.; **genre:** Mythological
pc: Peninsular Film Services, Madras **d:** Thomas E. Huffton

Madalasa
6313 ft.; **genre:** Mythological
pc: Hindustan Cinema Film Co., Nasik **d:** Gajanan V. Sane **c:** Anna Salunke
lp: Bhaurao Datar, Anasuya

Mahasati Anasuya
8250 ft.; **genre:** Mythological
pc: Krishna Film Co. **d:** Kanjibhai Rathod **c:** Chaturbhai Patel
lp: Sakina

Mardna Gha
aka **Master Stroke**
8170 ft.; **genre:** Costume
pc: Krishna Film Co. **d:** Kanjibhai Rathod **c:** Chaturbhai Patel **st:** Natwar Shyam **sc:** Krishnakumar
lp: Nandram, Gulab, Gangaram, Sakina, Chandra, Hyder Shah, Durga

Mission Girl
9200 ft.; **genre:** Social
pc: Kohinoor Film Co. **d:** Homi Master **c:** Pandurang S. Naik **st/sc:** Mohanlal G. Dave
lp: Ruby Fillish, Heera, Khalil, Raja Sandow, Mani

Mohabat Ke Musibat
aka **Love & Romance**
7642 ft.; **genre:** Social
pc: Saurashtra Film Co Ltd., Rajkot **d/st:** Manilal M. Vaidya
lp: Bhimbhai (?), Shiraz Ali Hakim (?)

Mumbai Ni Biladi
aka **Uthavgir Abala, Wild Cat of Bombay**
9724 ft.; **genre:** Social
pc: Imperial Film Co. **d:** Mohan Bhavnani **st:** Desai
lp: Sulochana, D. Bilimoria, Jamshetji

Muralivala
8907 ft.; **genre:** Mythological
pc: Maharashtra Film Co., Kolhapur **d:** Baburao Painter **c:** S. Fattelal
lp: Madhsudan (Lalji Gokhale), Sushila Devi, Bal Gaibar, V. Shantaram, Ravji Mhaiskar, Padmabai, Tulsabai

Nakli Rani
aka **Sham Queen**
8819 ft.; **genre:** Comedy
pc: Sharda Film Co. **c:** Naval Bhat
lp: Harihar Diwana, Mary (Kumudini), Janibabu, Prabhashankar, Gangaram

Nala Damayanti
8123 ft.; **genre:** Mythological
pc: Hindustan Cinema Film Co., Nasik **d:** D.G. Phalke **c:** Trymbak B. Telang
lp: Anna Salunke, Gotiram, Bachu Pawar, Joshi, (Dattatray?) Kshirsagar, Bhaurao Datar, Gangubai Mohite

Nanand Bhojai
aka **The Victim of Society**
9370 ft.; **genre:** Social
pc: Excelsior Film Co. **d/st/sc:** Manilal Joshi **c:** D.D. Dabke
lp: Zubeida, M. Udawadia, Takle, Mani, Nargis, Gangaram, Thatte

Nari ke Nagan
aka **Soul of a Snake**
7412 ft.; **genre:** Social
pc: Imperial Film Co. **d:** K.P. Bhave **c:** Rustom Irani **st:** Shaikh
lp: Jilloo, Baburao Sansare, Dinkar Bidkar, Dhanji, Tara, Madanrai Vakil, Putli (?), Zebu (?)

Nasib ni Leeli
aka **Kicks of Kismet**
10887 ft.; **genre:** Social
pc: Imperial Film Co. **d:** Mohan Bhavnani **st:** Soona Irani **sc:** Hayrat Kapadia
lp: Sulochana, Ermeline, Jilloo, Madanrai Vakil

Netaji Palkar
9815 ft.; **genre:** Historical
pc: Maharashtra Film Co., Kolhapur **d:** V. Shantaram/Keshavrao Dhaiber **c:** S. Fattelal
lp: Balasaheb Yadav, Sushila Devi, Zunzharrao Pawar, Ganpat Bakre, G.R. Mane, Vasantrao Deshpande

Pandav Rajasooya Yagnam

5300 ft.; **genre:** Mythological

Remarks: This film was produced for Exhibitor Film Service, Madras and was probably directed by R.S. Prakash.

Pavitra Saitan

aka **Parse Eblis**

7016 ft.; **genre:** Social

pc: Excelsior Film Co. **d/st/sc:** Manilal Joshi **c:** D.D. Dabke

lp: Nargis, K.B. Athavale

Remarks: Director Manilal Joshi died before this film was completed.

Pita Puja

6000 ft.; **genre:** Social

pc: Madan Theatres Ltd. **st:** Pandit Tulsidutt Shaida

Poonam no Chand

aka **Ratna Baan, Jewelled Arrow**

9465 ft.; **genre:** Mythological

pc: Imperial Film Co./British India Film Co. **d/st/sc:** B.P. Mishra

lp: Zebu, Indira, Jamshetji, Elizer

Prem ni Pratima

aka **Lovers**

5965 ft.; **genre:** Costume

pc: Excelsior Film Co. **d/st/sc:** Manilal Joshi **c:** D.D. Dabke

lp: Blanche Verne

Princess Laila

10804 ft.; **genre:** Costume

pc: La Tosca Production **d:** R.S.D. Chaudhary

lp: Jilloo, Zebu, Blanche Verne, Madam Tosca, Elizer, Madanrai Vakil, Miss Helen

Punar Janma

aka **Incarnation**

9500 ft.; **genre:** Social

pc: Indian Kinema Arts, Calcutta **d:** Jaigopal Pillai **c:** Nitin Bose **st/sc:** Premankur Atorthy

lp: Kedar Chatterji, Miss Hayde (Susheela), Atul Sen, Krishna Haldar (Premankur Atorthy), Indira, Funniman, Aratidevi

Raghunathrao And Saryubala

8025 ft.; **genre:** Historical

pc: Royal Art Studio **d:** Madanrai Vakil **c:** Rustom Irani **st/sc:** Vijay Shankar Bhat
lp: Jilloo, S.E. Joshi

Rangmahel Ni Ramani
aka **Fairy of Delhi**
10709 ft.; **genre:** Historical
pc: Kohinoor Film Co. **d:** Homi Master **c:** Pandurang S. Naik **st/sc:** Mohanlal G. Dave
lp: Shahzadi, Khalil

Reshmi Sari
aka **Follies of the Rich**
10489 ft.; **genre:** Social
pc: Sharda Film Co. **d:** Nanubhai Desai **c:** Bhogilal Dave
lp: Miss Mani, Mary, Janibabu, A.P. Kapur

Roopsundari
aka **Adarsh Virangana**
7663 ft.; **genre:** Costume
pc: Krishna Film Co. **d:** Harshadrai Mehta **c:** Chimanlal Luhar **st:** Natwar Shyam
sc: Krishnakumar
lp: Gulab, Nandram, Durga, Chandra

Rukmangad Mohini
aka **Ekadashi Mahatmya**
8291 ft.; **genre:** Mythological
pc: Hindustan Cinema Film Co., Nasik **d/st/sc:** D.G. Phalke
lp: Ganpat Shinde, Gangubai Mohite

Rukmini Haran
7265 ft.; **genre:** Mythological
pc: Hindustan Cinema Film Co., Nasik **d/st/sc:** D.G. Phalke
lp: Bhaurao Datar, Anasuya

Sansar
aka **Phase of Life**
8462 ft.; **genre:** Social
pc: Saurashtra Film Co Ltd., Rajkot **d/st:** Vajeshankar Pattani **c:** Champaklal Pattani
lp: Harilal M Bhatt (?), Miss Mani (?)

Sati Madri
8470 ft.; **genre:** Mythological
pc: Kohinoor Film Co. **d:** Chandulal Shah/Narayan Devare **c:** Pandurang S. Naik
st/sc: Mohanlal G. Dave
lp: Gohar, Raja Sandow

Sati Savitri

5168 ft.; **genre:** Mythological
pc: Maharashtra Film Co., Kolhapur
d: Baburao Painter **c:** S. Fattelal
lp: Sushila Devi, Balasaheb Yadav, Gulabbai, V. Shantaram, Zunzharrao Pawar, Nimbalkar

▲ Sabita Devi

Satsang

6000 ft.; **genre:** Social
pc: Aurora Cinema Co., Calcutta
st: Bhupendranath Banerjee

Savitri

aka **Ideal Wife**
6750 ft.; **genre:** Mythological
pc: United Pictures Syndicate, Poona **d:** Pandurang Talegiri **st/sc:** Mama Varerkar
lp: Datto Pant Waishampayan, Gangubai, Wamanrao Kulkarni, Baburao Gade, P.N. Varne

Sawalya Tandel

7494 ft.; **genre:** Historical
pc: South Indian Film Co., Sholapur

Shankaracharya

aka **Renaissance of Hinduism**
11500 ft.; **genre:** Biographical
pc: Indian Kinema Arts, Calcutta **d:** Kaliprasad Ghosh **c:** Noni Gopal Sanyal/P. Sanyal
st: Girish Chandra Ghosh
lp: Nirmalendu Lahiri, Jiban Ganguli, Manmath Pal, Ahi Sanyal, Renubala, Prafulla, Kaliprasad Ghosh

Sharad Purnima

9377 ft.; **genre:** Social
pc: Krishna Film Co. **d:** Harshadrai Mehta **c:** Chimanlal Luhar **st:** Natwar Shyam **sc:** Krishnakumar
lp: Gulab, Nandram, Gangaram, Keshavlal

Sheel Prabhav

aka **Glory of Virtue**
7103 ft.; **genre:** Devotional
pc: United Pictures Syndicate, Poona **st:** Vishnupant Aundhkar

Shiraj-Ud-Daula

aka **By Sheer Valour**
8423 ft.; **genre:** Historical

pc: Sharda Film Co./Ideal Pictures Corporation **d:** Dhanji K. Desai **c:** Bhogilal Dave
st: Ramnik Mehta
lp: Master Vithal, Janibabu, Tara, Dwarki, Asha, Kumudini, Gangaram, Zebu (?)

Shoor Killedarini
aka **Fair Warrior**
4988 ft.; **genre:** Historical
pc: United Pictures Syndicate, Poona **d/st/sc:** Vishnupant Aundhkar **c:** Pandurang Talegiri
lp: Gangubai, Wamanrao Kulkarni, Gondhalekar

Shree Krishna Naradi
6541 ft.; **genre:** Mythological
pc: Imperial Film Co./British India Film Co. **d:** K.P. Bhave **c:** Rustom Irani
lp: Madanrai Vakil, Jilloo, Yusuf, Putli, Sakhu

Shrimati Nalini
9377 ft.; **genre:** Social
pc: Excelsior Film Co. **d/sc:** Manilal Joshi **c:** D.D. Dabke **st:** adapted from Ellen Wood's *East Lynne*
lp: Yakbal, Nargis, Takle

Sindh ni Sumri
aka **Sumri of Sindh**
10065 ft.; **genre:** Costume
pc: Kohinoor Film Co. **d:** Chandulal Shah **c:** Pandurang S. Naik/Narayan Devare
st/sc: Mohanlal G. Dave
lp: Gohar, Raja Sandow, Yakbal, Leena, Nur Mohamed

Soneri Jaal
aka **Ex-husband**
7543 ft.; **genre:** Social
pc: Gujarat Studio **d:** Gordhanbhai Patel
c: Chaturbhai Patel **sc:** Krishnakumar
lp: Gulab, Nandram, Durga, Vishnu, Jehangir, Lila, Ramdevi

Sudhrel Shaitan
aka **Cultured Criminal**
6972 ft.; **genre:** Social
pc: Saurashtra Film Co. Ltd., Rajkot **d:** Vajeshankar Pattani **st:** Manilal M. Vaidya (?)
lp: Miss Mani (?), Bhimbhai (?), Shiraz Ali Hakim (?)

▲ Madhuri and E. Bilimoria in an unidentified film

Surat no Sahukar
aka **Why Sons Go Astray**
11578 ft.; **genre:** Social
pc: Kohinoor Film Co. **d:** Homi Master **c:** Narayan Devare **st/sc:** Mohanlal G. Dave
lp: Khalil, Susheela (Miss Hayde), R.N. Vaidya, Nur Mohamed, Behram Vasania, Master Ganapatrao Brahmbhat

Swadesh Seva
aka **My Country**
11863 ft.; **genre:** Costume
pc: Sharda Film Co.
lp: Master Vithal, Lobo

Thoratanchi Kamala
7561 ft.; **genre:** Historical
pc: United Pictures Syndicate, Poona **d:** N.D. Sarpotdar **c:** Pandurang Talegiri
lp: Gangubai, Wamanrao Kulkarni, Baburao Shinde, Bandopant Sohoni, P.N. Varne, Dattoba Rajwade

Vediya Dhor
aka **Unpractical**
7372 ft.; **genre:** Comedy
pc: Krishna Film Co. **d:** Harshadrai Mehta **c:** Chimanlal Luhar **st:** Mast Fakir

Veer Garjana
aka **Rakshasi Mahatvakanksha, Rewards of Blind Passion**
11781 ft.; **genre:** Costume
pc: Sharda Film Co. **d:** A.P. Kapur **c:** Naval Bhat **st/sc:** Nanubhai Desai
lp: Master Vithal, Prabhashankar, Kumudini

Vilasi Kanta
aka **Flirting Wife**
7380 ft.; **genre:** Social
pc: Social Pictures Corporation **d/st/sc:** Vishnupant Aundhkar
c: Vishnu B. Joshi
lp: Nanasaheb Phatak, Vishnupant Aundhkar, Wamanrao Kulkarni, Miss Gulab, Hansa Sohoni, Yamuna Gole, D. Billimoria

1928

Aankh ka Nasha
11202 ft.; **genre:** Social
pc: Madan Theatres Ltd. **st:** Aga Hashr Kashmiri
lp: Patience Cooper, Sarifa, Master Mohan, Soorajram, Manilal, Mohammed Ishaq
Remarks: Calcutta CC. No. 9296; 12000 ft.

Akkalna Bardan
aka **Upto Date**
7835 ft.; **genre:** Comedy
pc: Krishna Film Co. **d:** Prafulla Ghosh **c:** Chaturbhai Patel/Gordhanbhai Patel
st/sc: Maneklal Patel
lp: Gulab, Jehangir, Jamu Patel, Noor Mohammed (Charlie)

Amrit ke Zer
aka **Madira Mohini, Wine and Woman**
9963 ft.; **genre:** Social
pc: Sharda Film Co. **d:** A.P. Kapur **c:** Naval Bhat **st:** S.K. Padwal **sc:** Nanubhai Desai
lp: Zebu, Miss Mani, Balabhai, S.K. Padwal, Barsade

Anarkali
aka **Monument of Tears**
12276 ft.; **genre:** Costume
pc: Imperial Film Co. **d:** R.S.D. Chaudhary **c:** Adi Irani **st:** Narayan Visanji Thakur
lp: Sulochana, D. Bilimoria, Jilloo, Putli, Madanrai Vakil, Sakhu, Mehboob
Remarks: The film was re-censored on June 10, 1931 (CC. No. 10367).

Anarkali
aka **Rajmahal ni Ramani, Loves of a Moghul Prince**
9525 ft.; **genre:** Costume
pc: Great Eastern Film Corporation, Delhi **d:** Charu Roy/Prafulla Roy **c:** Vishnu B. Joshi
st: from Imtiaz Ali Taj's play *Anarkali* **sc:** Hakim Ahmed Shuja
lp: Seeta Devi, Sawan Singh, Charu Roy, Maya Devi, Shakuntala, Dewan Sharar, Rajkumari, Imtiaz Ali Taj

Arya Mahila
aka **Ideal Wife**
8956 ft.; **genre:** Social
pc: Aryan Film Co., Poona **d/st/sc:** N.D. Sarpotdar **c:** Y.D. Sarpotdar
lp: Sada Bhau Bhopatkar, Durga Koregaonkar, Sushila, P.N. Varne, Baburao Athavale

Bhai ke Kasai
aka **His Father's Honour**
10568 ft.; **genre:** Social
pc: Shree Jagdish Film Co. **d/st/sc:** Ramakant Gharekhan **c:** G.G. Gogate
lp: Shantakumari, Khalil, R.N. Vaidya, Janibabu

Bhakta Damaji
7281 ft.; **genre:** Devotional
pc: Hindustan Cinema Film Co., Nasik **d/st/sc:** D.G. Phalke **c:** Ganpat Shinde
lp: Gotiram, Bhaurao Datar

Bhakta Kabirdas
genre: Devotional
pc: Peninsular Film Services, Madras **d:** Thomas E. Huffton

Bharmaylo Bharthar
aka **Foolish Husband**
9433 ft.; **genre:** Social
pc: Kohinoor Film Co. **d:** Narayan Devare **st/sc:** Mohanlal G. Dave
lp: Jamuna, Fatma Jr. Behram Vasania, Faram Sethna

Bhasmasur
1672 ft.; **genre:** Mythological
pc: Prativa Cinema Co., Calcutta **d/c/st/sc:** Tarapada Saha
lp: Deben Mullick

Bhranti
aka **Vranti**
13000 ft.; **genre:** Historical
pc: Madan Theatres Ltd. **d:** Jyotish Banerjee **st:** Girish Chandra Ghosh
lp: Danibabu (Surendra Nath Ghosh), Patience Cooper, Satyen Dey

Bisha Briksha
aka **Poison Tree**
11000 ft.; **genre:** Social
pc: Madan Theatres Ltd. **d:** Jyotish Banerjee **c:** Jatin Das **st:** Bankimchandra Chatterjee
lp: Durgadas Banerjee, Miss Light (Tarakbala), Manoranjan Bhattacharya, Jainarayan Mukherjee, Kartik Dey, Leelavati

Bodku Mathu
aka **Indulal Advocate**
7473 ft.; **genre:** Comedy
pc: Gujarat Studio **d:** Kanjibhai Rathod **c:** Chaturbhai Patel **st:** Mast Fakir **sc:** Krishnakumar
lp: Jehangir, Jamu Patel

Chamakti Chanda
8223 ft.; **genre:** Costume
pc: Jagtap Pictures **d:** M. Udwadia **c:** V.B. Jagtap **st/sc:** Manilal Joshi
lp: Zubeida, R.B. Jagtap, Yvonne Wallace, Mohanlal

Chandrahas
8034 ft.; **genre:** Costume
pc: Krishna Film Co. **d:** Kanjibhai Rathod **c:** Chaturbhai Patel **st:** Narayan Visanji Thakur
lp: Gangaram, Lila, Wamanrao Abhyankar, Nizam, Kusum, Sakina

Chandravali
aka **Taje Neki, Crown of Virtue**
11985 ft.; **genre:** Costume
pc: Victoria Fatma Film Co. **d.** Fatma Begum **c:** V.V. Date
lp: Sultana, Shahzadi, Janibabu, Yakub

Chaturkanta
8167 ft.; **genre:** Social
pc: Excelsior Film Co. **d/sc:** Ramakant Gharekhan **c:** Ambadas Pawar **st:** Gokuldas Raichura
lp: Kumudini, K.B. Athavle, K.C. Roy

Dev Kanya
aka **Daughter of God / Nymph of God**
10525 ft.; **genre:** Costume
pc: Krishna Film Co. **d:** Kanjibhai Rathod **c:** Chaturbhai Patel **st:** Giraja Shankar Joshi
sc: Natwar Shyam
lp: Gulab, Nandram, Lila, Vishnu, P.R. Joshi, Babi

Devdas
8000 ft.; **genre:** Social
pc: Eastern Films Syndicate, Calcutta **d:** Naresh Mitra **c:** Nitin Bose **st:** Saratchandra Chatterjee
lp: Phani Burma, Naresh Mitra, Tincowri Chakraborty, Tarakbala, Nihar Bala, Ramadevi, Parul, Mani Ghosh, Kanak Narayan Bhup

Ek Abala
aka **Sainted Devil**
10181 ft.; **genre:** Social
pc: Imperial Film Co. **d/st/sc:** B.P. Mishra
lp: Ermeline, Putli, Jilloo, B.P. Mishra, Yusuf, Ghory, Lakhibai, Asooji, Rustom Irani
Remarks: The original version was prohibited on the grounds that its morals are very low. Revised version passed on 28/8/1928.

Ekaj Chumban
aka **Fatal Kiss**
6119 ft.; **genre:** Social
pc: Excelsior Film Co. **d:** K.B. Athavale **c:** D.D. Dabke **st/sc:** Manilal Joshi
lp: Yakbal, K.B. Athavale

For Money
1200 ft.; **genre:** Social
pc: Little Film Co. **d:** Saki

Ganimi Kawa
aka **Dav Pech, Guerilla Tactics**
7225 ft.; **genre:** Historical
pc: Aryan Film Co., Poona **d/st/sc:** N.D. Sarpotdar **c:** Y.D. Sarpotdar
lp: Durga Koregaonkar, Amboo (Lalita Pawar), K. Budhkar, P.N. Varne, Jadavrao, Dattoba Rajwade

Ghosh Yatra
5969 ft.; **genre:** Mythological
pc: Hindustan Cinema Film Co., Nasik **d:** Gajanan V. Sane **c:** Ganpat Shinde
lp: Bhaurao Datar

Gita Rahasya
aka **Friend in Need**
9790 ft.; **genre:** Social
pc: Imperial Film Co. **d/st/sc:** K.P. Bhave **c:** A.P. Karandikar
lp: Ermeline, E. Bilimoria, J.P. Gidwani

Grihalakshmi
aka **Sansar Leela**
9170 ft.; **genre:** Social
pc: Shree Jagdish Film Co. **d/st/sc:** Chandulal Shah **c:** Pandurang S. Naik/G.G. Gogate
lp: Gohar, Raja Sandow, R.N. Vaidya, Baba Vyas

Gul Badan
10650 ft.; **genre:** Costume
pc: Sharda Film Co. **d:** Harshadrai Mehta **c:** Naval Bhat **st/sc:** Nanubhai Desai
lp: Master Vithal, Zebu

Gul Sanobar
12099 ft.; **genre:** Legend
pc: Kohinoor Film Co. **d:** Homi Master **c:** K.G. Gokhale **st/sc:** Mohanlal G. Dave
lp: Heera, Yakbal, Khalil, Thomas, Ganibabu

Gulru Zarina
11752 ft.; **genre:** Costume
pc: Sharda Film Co. **d:** A.P. Kapur **c:** Naval Bhat
lp: Janibabu, Lobo

Haiyano Haar
aka **Fatal Garland**
9870 ft.; **genre:** Costume
pc: Imperial Film Co. **d:** B.P. Mishra **st:** Suvarna Kumari **sc:** Soona Irani/Hayrat Kapadia
lp: Ermeline, Putli, Madanrai Vakil, Jamshetji, Mazhar Khan

Heer Ranjah
8570 ft.; **genre:** Legend
pc: Victoria Fatma Film Co. **d/st:** Fatma Begum
lp: Zubeida, Janibabu, Shahzadi

Hira Sundari
8545 ft.; **genre:** Costume
pc: Sharda Film Co. **d:** A.P. Kapur **c:** Naval Bhat **st:** Narayan Visanji Thakur
lp: Master Vithal, Janibabu, Nirasha

Hoor-E-Arab
10147 ft.; **genre:** Costume
pc: Madan Theatres Ltd. **d:** Ratansha Sinor **c:** Jal Ariya
lp: Patience Cooper, Bapuji Punegar, Ratansha Sinor, Miss Belle and members of Parsi Imperial Theatrical Co.

Hoor-E-Bagdad
aka **Forbidden Love**
11165 ft.; **genre:** Costume
pc: Saraswati Film Co. **d:** B.P. Mishra **c:** Rustom Irani **st:** A.S. Desai
lp: Ermeline, Mazhar Khan, W.M. Khan, Khatoon

Jai Bhavani
7891 ft.; **genre:** Historical
pc: Jagtap Pictures **d/st/sc:** K.P. Bhave **c:** M.R .Jagtap
lp: R.B. Jagtap, Dwarki

Kaal Ratrinun Khuni Khanjar
aka **Vile Woman**
8925 ft.; **genre:** Social
pc: Krishna Film Co. **d:** Kanjibhai Rathod **c:** Chaturbhai Patel **st:** Satyendra Prasad Mehta
sc: Krishnakumar
lp: Rampiary, Gulab, Nandram, Vishnu, Hyder Shah

Kamala Kumari
aka **Sabur Shah**
9876 ft.; **genre:** Costume
pc: Imperial Film Co. **d/st/sc:** B.P. Mishra **c:** Rustom Irani
lp: Ermeline, Madanrai Vakil, Gohar Jr., Yakub

Kamsena Lilavati
5943 ft.; **genre:** Legend
pc: Excelsior Film Co.
lp: Yakbal, Mary, K.B. Athavale, Vithaldas Panchotia

Kanak Kanta
aka **Navlakha Haar**
9524 ft.; **genre:** Costume
pc: Sharda Film Co. **d:** A.P. Kapur **c:** Chimanlal Luhar **st:** Ata Mohamed **sc:** Nanubhai Desai
lp: Master Vithal, Nirasha, Lobo, Prabhashankar, Ata Mohamed, Meherbanu

Karuna Kumari
8501 ft.; **genre:** Costume
pc: Sharda Film Co. **d:** Harshadrai Mehta **c:** Naval Bhat **sc:** Nanubhai Desai
lp: Master Vithal, Zebu, Lobo, Prabhashankar, Balabhai

Katil Kathiyani
aka **La Belle**
10482 ft.; **genre:** Social
pc: Imperial Film Co. **d/st/sc:** Nagendra Mazumdar **c:** Adi Irani
lp: Jilloo, Putli, D. Bilimoria, Jal Merchant, Jamshetji

Kelor Kirti
10665 ft.; **genre:** Social
pc: Aurora Film Co., Calcutta **d:** Sudhangsu Mustafi **c:** Debi Ghosh **st:** Bhupendranath Banerjee
lp: Nihar Bala, Lalu Bose, Belarani

Khoon-E-Nahak
aka **Hamlet**
7353 ft.
pc: Excelsior Film Co. **d:** K.B. Athavale **c:** Ambadas Pawar
lp: Yakbal, Rampiary, K.C. Roy, Salvi

Kichak Vadha
aka **Sairandhri**
5860 ft.; **genre:** Mythological
pc: United Pictures Syndicate, Poona

Kunj Kishori
9945 ft.; **genre:** Social
pc: Gujarat Studio **d:** Kanjibhai Rathod **c:** Chaturbhai Patel **st:** Satyendra Prasad Mehta
sc: C.N. Maniar
lp: Gulab, Rampiary, Nandram, Durga, Nizam, Hyder Shah, Haridas

Kusum Kumari
6451 ft.; **genre:** Costume
pc: Little Film Co. **d:** Saki
lp: Elizer, Saki

Lakho Phulani

9334 ft.; **genre:** Historical
pc: Royal Art Studio/Lokmanya Film Co. **d:** Dinshah J. Jhaveri **st/sc:** Vijay Shankar Bhat
lp: Zebu, Yusuf
Remarks: The film was ready for release in 1926.

Lekh Par Mekh

aka **Destiny Defied**
10243 ft.; **genre:** Costume
pc: Kohinoor Film Co. **d:** Homi Master **c:** K.G. Gokhale **st/sc:** Mohanlal G. Dave
lp: Panna, Heera, Thomas, Ganibabu, Nur Mohamed

Mad

1200 ft.: **genre:** Comedy
pc: Little Film Co.

Madan Manjari

aka **Wise Fool**
10174 ft.; **genre:** Costume
pc: Imperial Film Co. **d/sc:** Pessi Karani **st:** Harihar Diwana
lp: Ermeline, Jamshetji, Dinkar Bidkar, Tara

Madhuri

10875 ft.; **genre:** Costume
pc: Imperial Film Co. **d:** R.S.D. Chaudhary **c:** Adi Irani/Ardeshir Irani **st:** Vasantrai Desai
lp: Sulochana, D. Bilimoria, Jilloo, Madanrai Vakil

Maharathi Karna

aka **Karna, The True Battler**
9793 ft.; **genre:** Mythological
pc: Maharashtra Film Co., Kolhapur **co-d/c:** S. Fattelal **co-d:** V. Damle
lp: Balasaheb Yadav, Kamladevi, B. Nandrekar, Zunzharrao Pawar, V. Shantaram, Vasantrao Deshpande, Tukaram Mandhre, Ravji Mhaiskar, Chimasaheb Bhosle, Kishabapu Bakre, G.R. Mane, I.T. Nimbalkar, Sushila Devi

Malhari Martand

6654 ft.; **genre:** Mythological
pc: Hindustan Cinema Film Co., Nasik **d:** Ganpat Shinde **c:** Trymbak B. Telang
lp: Bhaurao Datar, Kashibai Phatak, Shelar, Joshi

Marathyachi Mulgi

aka **Daughter Of The Marathas**

9908 ft.; **genre:** Historical
pc: United Pictures Syndicate, Poona **d:** N.G. Kamatnurkar **c:** Pandurang Talegiri
st: Saraswati Kumar
lp: Gangubai

Maya Mahal
aka **Magic Valley**
9118 ft.; **genre:** Costume
pc: Sharda Film Co. **d/sc:** Nanubhai Desai **c:** Naval Bhat **st:** Sukumar Chatterjee
lp: Zebu, Janibabu, Lobo, Meherbanu, Abdul Hamid Kasam

Maya Mohini
7787 ft.
pc: Gujarat Studio **d:** Keshavlal Joshi **c:** Gordhanbhai Patel **st:** Harilal M. Bhatt **sc:** Keshavlal Joshi
lp: Gulab, Gangaram, Nizam, Durga, Harilal

Mayana Rang
aka **Enticement**
10525 ft.; **genre:** Costume
pc: Suvarna Pictures **d:** P.V. Chauhan/Dhirubhai Desai/Sundarrao Nadkarni **c:** Ambadas Pawar **st:** Narayan Visanji Thakur
lp: Zebu, Bachu, Gangubai, Baburao Gade

Moh Jal
aka **Lure of Lust**
6992 ft.; **genre:** Social
pc: Saurashtra Film Co. Ltd., Rajkot **d:** M. Udwadia **st:** Thakkar Nirbhay
lp: Nanbai

Nag Padmini
aka **Shepherd King**
9482 ft.; **genre:** Costume
pc: Kohinoor Film Co. **d/c:** Narayan Devare **st/sc:** Mohanlal G. Dave
lp: Raja Sandow, Yakbal, Jamuna, Fatma Jr., Thomas, Nargis

Nara Kesari
aka **Lion of Maharashtra**
8236 ft.; **genre:** Historical
pc: Jagtap Pictures **d/st/sc:** K.P. Bhave **c:** V.B. Jagtap
lp: Dwarki, R.B. Jagtap, M. Udwadia, Hirani

Narad Sansar
aka **Narada's Worldly Life**

5122 ft.; **genre:** Mythological
pc: Hindustan Cinema Film Co., Nasik **d/c:** Ganpat Shinde
lp: Bhaurao Datar, Sakharam Jadhav, Jadhavrao

Neelam Manek
11525 ft.; **genre:** Social
pc: Krishna Film Co. **d:** Kanjibhai Rathod **c:** Gordhanbhai Patel **st:** Gopalji Delwadakar
sc: Kanjibhai Rathod/C.N. Maniar
lp: Gulab, Rampiary, Keshavlal, Gangaram, Durga, Chandra, Haridas, Baby Asha

Nimak Haram
aka **Traitor**
5956 ft.; **genre:** Historical
pc: Aryan Film Co., Poona **d/st/sc:** N.D. Sarpotdar **c:** V.V. Date/Y.D. Sarpotdar
lp: P.N. Varne, Jadhavrao, Meera, Dattoba Rajwade, Govindrao Shinde
Remarks: The original title was *Har Har Mahadeo.*

Nisiddha Phal
aka **Forbidden Fruit**
6500 ft.; **genre:** Social
pc: Indian Kinema Arts, Calcutta **d:** Kaliprasad Ghosh **c:** Noni Gopal Sanyal **st:** Prabhat Mukherjee
lp: Renubala, Bhanu Banerjee, Prafulla, Nimai Saha, Nivanani Devi, Kaliprasad Ghosh

Padmalata
aka **Kantakman Gulab, Lily in the Mud**
8327 ft.; **genre:** Costume
pc: Gujarat Studio **d/sc:** D.A. Dandekar **c:** Gordhanbhai Patel **st:** Satyendra Prasad Mehta
lp: Nandram, Lila, Nizam, Gangaram, P.R. Joshi, Salma, Rambha

Pandav Patrani
aka **Celestial Lotus**
8659 ft.; **genre:** Mythological
pc: Imperial Film Co./British India Film Co. **d:** Nagendra Mazumdar **c:** Adi Irani
lp: Jilloo, P.S. Wagle

Panhalgad
5972 ft.; **genre:** Historical
pc: South Indian Films, Sholapur

Parashuram
6730 ft.; **genre:** Mythological
pc: Hindustan Cinema Film Co., Nasik **d/st/sc:** D.G. Phalke **c:** Ganpat Shinde
lp: Bhaurao Datar, Gotiram, Asarabai

Patalketu
6356 ft.; **genre:** Adaptation
pc: Imperial Film Co. **d/sc:** K.P. Bhave **c:** Adi Irani
lp: K. Narayan Kale, Tara, Sakhu, Rustom Irani, Dinkar Bidkar, Jamshetji

Patitodhar
aka **Reclamation**
7147 ft.; **genre:** Social
pc: Aryan Film Co., Poona **d:** N.D. Sarpotdar **c:** Y.D. Sarpotdar
lp: Amboo, Durga Koregaonkar, Jadhavrao, Master Shantaram, P.N. Varne

Pavagadh nu Patan
aka **Fall of Pavagadh**
11082 ft.; **genre:** Historical
producer/st/sc: Indulal Yagnik **d:** Nagendra Mazumdar **c:** Ambadas Pawar
lp: Navinchandra, Iris Crawford (Mohini), Zaverbhai Kaiser, K.B. Athavle, Vasanti

Pita ke Parmeshwar
aka **Father O' Mine**
9580 ft.; **genre:** Social
pc: Imperial Film Co. **d/st/sc:** R.S.D.Chaudhary **c:** Rustom Irani
lp: Jilloo, Putli, Jamshetji, Elizer, Yusuf

Prem ane Vasana
aka **Sansar Nauka, Wife and Vampire**
9065 ft.; **genre:** Social
pc: Saurashtra Film Co. Ltd., Rajkot/British India Film Co. **d:** Lalitarai Vyas **st:** Prataprai Mehta

Prem Pariksha
aka **Daughter of Today**
7448 ft.; **genre:** Social
pc: Premier Film Co., Lahore **d/c:** G.K. Mehta
lp: Miss Billie Love, Vijay Kumar, Miss Maya, Hiralal, M. Ismail

Punarlagna ni Patni
aka **Second Wife**
7976 ft.; **genre:** Social
pc: Kaiser-E-Hind Film Co. **d:** Nagendra Mazumdar **c:** Rustom Irani
lp: Mehtab, Yusuf, Gangu, Salvi, Miss Anasuya

Puran Bhagat
10925 ft.; **genre:** Devotional
pc: Imperial Film Co. **d/sc:** Pessi Karani **c:** Rustom Irani
lp: Ermeline, Jilloo, Jamshetji, Gohar Jr., Sakhu, Rustom Irani

Raj Kumar
8170 ft.; **genre:** Costume
pc: New India Film Co., Nasik
lp: Krishna Bai

Raj Tarang
aka **Prisoners of Love**
10896 ft.; **genre:** Costume
pc: Sharda Film Co. **d:** Harshadrai Mehta **c/sc:** Chimanlal Luhar **st:** Arvind
lp: Master Vithal (double role), Zebu, Prabhashankar, Alibux, Lobo

Rajani Bala
10737 ft.; **genre:** Social
pc: Kohinoor Film Co. **d:** Homi Master **c:** K.G. Gokhale **st/sc:** Mohanlal G. Dave
lp: Yakbal, Heera, Khalil, Thomas

Rajba
aka **Hans Nauka, Daughter of India**
9739 ft.; **genre:** Costume
pc: Kohinoor Film Co./ Saraswati Film Co. **d/c:** Narayan Devare **st:** Shaida **sc:** Mohanlal G. Dave
lp: Khalil, Jamuna, Heera, Thomas

Rajrang
aka **Vengeance**
10147 ft.; **genre:** Costume
pc: Imperial Film Co. **d/st/sc:** B.P. Mishra **c:** Rustom Irani
lp: Sulochana, Jilloo, Elizer, Jamshetji, D. Billimoria
Remarks: Narendra Film Co. re-released this film as *Sood* aka *Vengeance*.

Rajwadana Rang
aka **Female Feat**
9930 ft.; **genre:** Costume
pc: Krishna Film Co. **co-**d/**sc:** Maneklal Patel **co-d:** Kanjibhai Rathod **c:** Chaturbhai Patel
st: Chunilal Hirji
lp: Gulab, Abdul Pahelwan, Rampiary, Hyder Shah, Gangaram, Vishnu, Keshavlal

Ramdas
12000 ft.; **genre:** Devotional
pc: Peninsular Film Services, Madras **d:** Thomas E. Huffton

Razalati Rajkumari
aka **Pauper Princess**
9390 ft.; **genre:** Costume

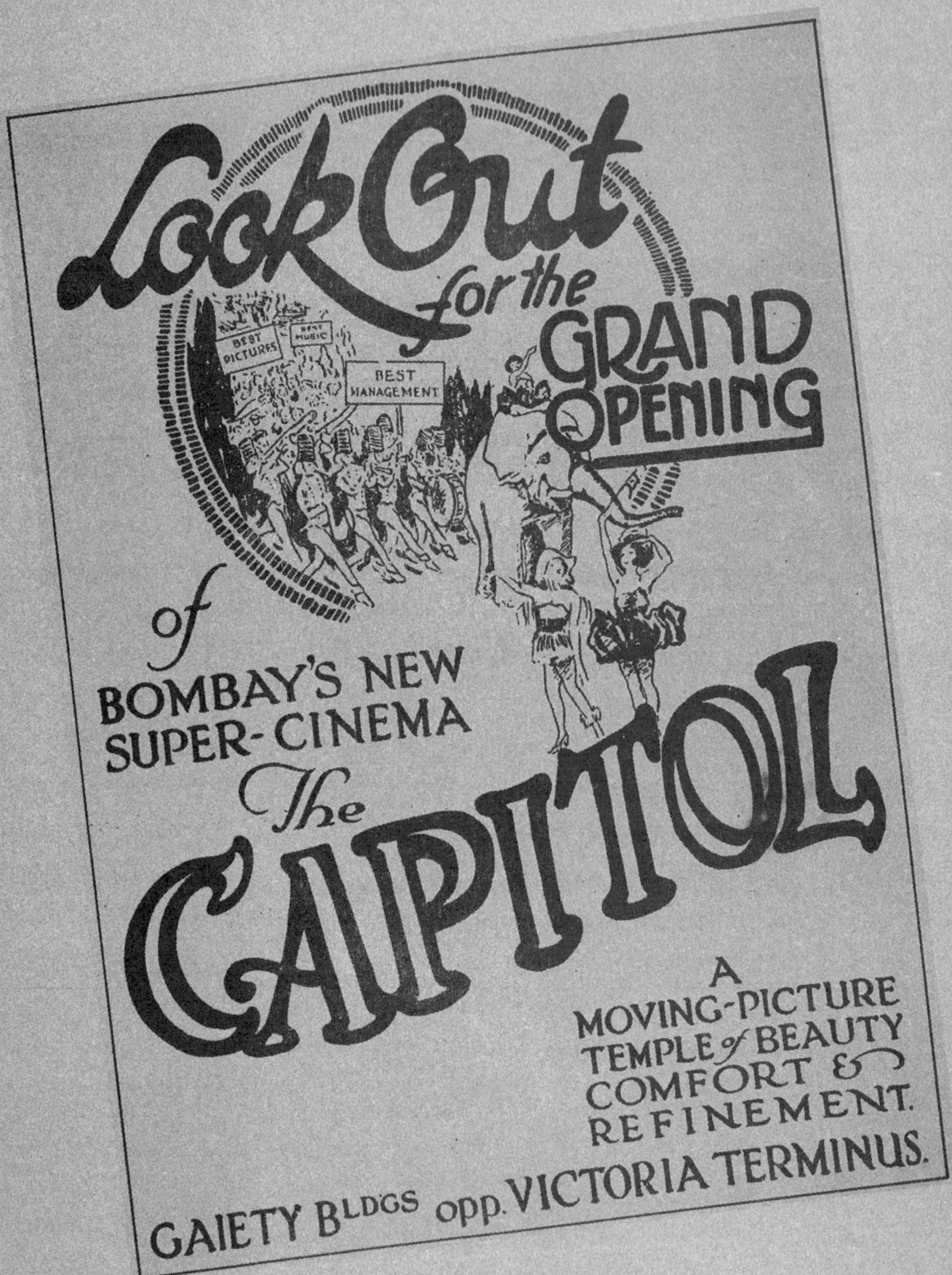

▲ Advertisement for Capitol Cinema

pc: Shree Jagdish Film Co. **d:** Ramakant Gharekhan **c:** G.G. Gogate
lp: Mohini (Iris Crawford), Mary (Kumudini), J.K. Nanda, Drupad Roy, Baba Vyas

Rup Basant
aka **Madan Mohana**
10591 ft.
pc: Suvarna Pictures, Poona **d:** P.V. Chavan **c:** D.B. Chavan **st:** Nanubhai Desai
lp: Bachu, Baburao Gade, Miss Mohna, Wamanrao Kulkarni, Hansa, Fayma

Samrat Ashok
aka **Emperor Ashok**
6769 ft.; **genre:** Biographical
pc: Royal Art Studio/Lokmanya Film Co. **d:** B.P. Mishra
lp: Zubeida, Jilloo, Putli, M. Udwadia, Madanrai Vakil, Asooji, Dwarki
Remarks: The film was ready for release in 1926.

Samsher Pratigna
8334 ft.; **genre:** Costume
pc: Shree Jagdish Film Co. **d:** R.N. Vaidya/Jamnadas Subedar **st:** Ramchandra Davec/D.D. Dabke
lp: Kumudini, R.N. Vaidya, Ghanshyam, Baba Vyas

Sarla
9726 ft.; **genre:** Social
pc: Madan Theatres Ltd. **d/sc:** Amritlal Bose **c:** Jatin Das **st:** Taraknath Ganguly
lp: Tarasundari, Seeta Devi, Durgadas Banerjee, Naresh Mitra, Chittaranjan (Goswamy?), Sailen Choudhary, Rani Sundari, Manorama

Sarojini
aka **Ghor Pratigna**
7989 ft.; **genre:** Social
pc: Kohinoor Film Co. **d:** Homi Master **c:** K.G. Gokhale **st:** Bachu Babu
lp: Panna, Heera, Thomas, Usharani, Ganibabu, Fatma Jr.

Sarovarani Sundari
aka **Lady of the Lake**
10380 ft.; **genre:** Costume
pc: Imperial Film Co. **d:** R.S.D. Chaudhary **c:** Boman Irani **st/sc:** J.B.H. Wadia
lp: Ermeline, Jilloo, Zebu, Madanrai Vakil, Yusuf, Yakub, Elizer, Baburao Sansare, R.S.D. Chaudhary, Mazhar Khan

Sati Pingala
6848 ft.; **genre:** Mythological
pc: Hindustan Cinema Film Co., Nasik **d:** Gajanan V. Sane
lp: Gangubai Mohite, Bhaurao Datar

Saundarya Sura
aka **Wine of Youth**

9858 ft.; **genre:** Social

pc: Sharda Film Co. **d:** Harshadrai Mehta **c/sc:** Chimanlal Luhar **st:** Narayan Visanji Thakur

lp: Master Vithal, Zebu, Lobo, Miss Mani, A.P. Kapur

Shashi Punhu

10866 ft.; **genre:** Costume

pc: Sharda Film Co. **d:** Harshadrai Mehta

st: Nanubhai Desai **c:** Chimanlal Luhar

lp: Master Vithal, Zebu, Balabhai

Shashikala
aka **Machchhavedh, Tit for Tat**

7434 ft.; **genre:** Costume

pc: Royal Art Studio/Lokmanya Film Co. **d:** B.P. Mishra

lp: Jilloo, Putli, M. Udwadia

Shasti ki Shanti

12000 ft.; **genre:** Social

pc: Madan Theatres Ltd. **d:** Jyotish Banerjee **st:** Girish Chandra Ghosh

lp: Tara Sundari, Durgadas Banerjee, Ahindra Choudhary, Tulsi Banerjee, Dani Babu, Jainarayan Mukherjee, Kartik Dey, Satyen Dey, Prabhavati, Tarakbala

Shekhchally

2472 ft.; **genre:** Comedy (2 Parts)

pc: Excelsior Film Co.

lp: Vithaldas Panchotia

Shiraz

9308 ft.; **genre:** Costume

pc: British Instructional Film Co, London/UFA, Germany/ Himansu Rai Film **d:** Franz Osten **c:** Emil Schünemann/H. Harris **st:** Niranjan Pal **sc:** W. Burton

lp: Himansu Rai, Seeta Devi Jr. (Percy Smith), Charu Roy, Enakshi Rama Rao, Maya Devi, Profulla Roy, Esther Ricks

Remarks: This film was prohibited in August 1928. Revised version released in Bombay on 16/3/1929.

◄ Jairaj and Zebu

Shree Jagat Guru
aka **World Teacher**
8862 ft.; **genre:** Biographical
pc: Imperial Film Co. **d:** P.Y. Altekar **c:** A.P. Karandikar
lp: P.Y. Altekar, K. Narayan Kale, Ermeline, Jilloo, Putli, Gohar Jr., Sakhu, Rustom Irani, Nazir, Baburao Sansare

Shri Dwarkadhish
8160 ft.; **genre:** Mythological
pc: Shree Jagdish Film Co. **d/st/sc:** Ramakant Gharekhan
lp: Kadambari, Promoth Bose, Baba Vyas, Ghanshyam

Shri Krishna Shishtai
6097 ft.; **genre:** Mythological
pc: Hindustan Cinema Film Co., Nasik **d:** D.G. Phalke

Sneh Jyoti
aka **Love Flame**
9619 ft.; **genre:** Social
pc: Shree Jagdish Film Co. **d:** Raja Sandow/R.N. Vaidya **c:** Pandurang S. Naik
st: Nanubhai Vakil
lp: Raja Sandow, Shantakumari, Putli, R.N. Vaidya, Dabir, Baba Vyas, Ghanshyam

Soneri Toli
aka **Golden Gang**
8891 ft.; **genre:** Social
pc: Jagtap Pictures **d/st/sc:** K.P. Bhave
lp: Zubeida, R.B. Jagtap, M. Udwadia

Soni Mahiwal
aka **Suni Meyar**
10890 ft.; **genre:** Legend
pc: Sharda Film Co. **d:** A.P. Kapur **c/st/sc:** Chimanlal Luhar
lp: Master Vithal, Zebu, Miss Mani, Himatlal

Soni Mahiwal
aka **Suni Meyar**
9958 ft.; **genre:** Legend
pc: Imperial Film Co. **d:** K.P. Bhave **c:** Adi Irani
lp: Gohar Jr., Jamshetji, Neelam

Sudarshan
8870 ft.; **genre:** Mythological
pc: Hindustan Cinema Film Co., Nasik **d:** Gajanan V. Sane

Swarga Vihar
aka **Dreamland**
7855 ft.; **genre:** Costume
pc: Krishna Film Co. **d:** Maneklal Patel **c:** Chaturbhai Patel **st/sc:** Raja Sandow
lp: Gulab, Rampiary, Gangaram, Vishnu

Tajayali Taruni
aka **Forsaken Wife**
10955 ft.; **genre:** Social
pc: Kohinoor Film Co. **d:** Narayan Devare **st/sc:** Mohanlal G. Dave
lp: Jamuna, Heera, Baheram Vasania

Tarunina Tarang
aka **Brother to Brother**
7886 ft.; **genre:** Costume
pc: Krishna Film Co. **d/sc:** Prafulla Ghosh **c:** Gordhanbhai Patel
lp: Gulab, Durga, Haridas, Keshavlal, Takle

Udantappu
aka **Vagabond**
7734 ft.; **genre:** Social
pc: Aryan Film Co, Poona **d/st/sc:** N.D. Sarpotdar **c:** Y.D. Sarpotdar
lp: Dattoba Rajwade, Krishnaji Ghanekar, Durga Koregaonkar, Hansa, P.N. Varne, Jadhavrao, C.R. Das

Vara Chatan Vidhawa
aka **Silver Cloud**
7353 ft.; **genre:** Social
pc: Excelsior Film Co. **d/sc:** Maneklal Joshi **c:** Ambadas Pawar **st:** S.K. Padwal
lp: Rampiary, Kumudini, Salvi

Vasant Leela
aka **Sons of the Rich**
10937 ft.; **genre:** Social
pc: Artistic Pictures **d:** D.A. Dandekar **c:** Gajanan S. Devare **st/sc:** J.B.H. Wadia
lp: Shakuntala, Panna, Faram Sethna, Faram Balsara, Rajababu, Charubala, Fatma Jr., Siraj, Nur Mohamed

Vasavadatta
aka **Sonano Suraj**
9351 ft.; **genre:** Adaptation
pc: Kaiser-E-Hind Film Co. **d/sc:** Nagendra Mazumdar **c:** Ambadas Pawar **st:** based on Bhasa's play
lp: Putli, Janibabu, K.B. Athavale, Salvi

Veerangana
10531 ft.; **genre:** Costume
pc: Kohinoor Film Co. **d:** Homi Master **c:** K.G. Gokhale **st/sc:** Mohanlal G. Dave
lp: Khalil, Yakbal, Heera, Ganibabu, Shivlal

Vigathakumaran
d/st/sc: J.C. Daniel
lp: J.C. Daniel

Vilasi Vandho
aka **Tarrangi Vandho, Mad Bachelor**
993 ft.; **genre:** Comedy
pc: Excelsior Film Co. **st/sc:** Manhar Vartejwalla
lp: Vithaldas Panchotia

Vishva Mohini
9791 ft.; **genre:** Social
pc: Shree Jagdish Film Co. **d/st/sc:** Chandulal Shah **c:** Pandurang S. Naik
lp: Gohar, Raja Sandow, Menadevi, R.N. Vaidya, Baba Vyas, Promoth Bose (?)

1929

Akkalmand Bewakoof
aka **Foolish Wisdom**
11765 ft.; **genre:** Parsi Comedy
pc: Madan Theatres Ltd. **d/lp:** Dadi Sarkari

Amarun Hindustan
aka **Our India**
7113 ft.; **genre:** Social
pc: Elphin Cinema Co. **d/c/st/sc:** C.H. Shah
lp: Shahzadi, Dinsha, Tayeb, Anasuya

Anarbala
aka **Fairy of Anar**
8556 ft.; **genre:** Costume
pc: Sharda Film Co. **d:** B.P. Mishra **c:** K.V. Machhwe
lp: Navinchandra, Zebu, Nirasha, Ata Mohamed

Apahrita
aka **The Kidnapped Girl**
8000 ft.; **genre:** Social
pc: Indian Kinema Arts, Calcutta **d:** Kaliprasad Ghosh **c:** Jatin Das **st:** S.K. Banerjee
lp: Renubala, B.S. Rajhans, Bhumen Roy, Prafulla, Nimai Saha, Amitav Bose, Sukriti Devi

Arab ki Ladki
aka **Gulshan-e-Arab**

11904 ft.; **genre:** Costume

pc: Imperial Film Co. **d/sc:** K.P. Bhave **c:** Rustom Irani **st:** Faizal Mohammed

lp: Ermeline, Gohar Jr., Jamshetji, Jilloo, Sakhu, Rustom Irani

Baghdad no Baharvatio
aka **Bandit of Bagdad**

11464 ft.; **genre:** Costume

pc: Kohinoor United Artists **d:** Narayan Devare **st/sc:** Mohanlal G. Dave

lp: Jamuna, J.K. Nanda, Elizer, Rajababu, Ganibabu, Usharani

Bahadur Baharvatio
aka **Terror of the Hill**

9265 ft.; **genre:** Costume

pc: Sharda Film Co. **d:** Dhirubhai Desai **c:** G.K. Mehta **st:** M.R. Kapoor

lp: Navinchandra, Rajkumari, Kukreja

Baji Deshpande
aka **Valley of Immortals**

10481 ft.; **genre:** Historical

pc: Maharashtra Film Co., Kolhapur **d:** Baburao Painter **c:** Yashvant Gune (?)

st: Shivram Washikar

lp: Balasaheb Yadav, Ganpat Bakre, Baburao Painter, Tulsabai, Babasaheb Nandrekar, I.T. Nimbalkar, V. Shantaram, Kamladevi, K. Dhaiber

Bangabala
11000 ft.; **genre:** Social

pc: Graphics Arts, Calcutta **d/c:** Dwarka Khosla

st: Bijay Ratna Mazumdar

lp: Umashashi, Phani Burma, Moni Burma, Bankim Dutta

Be Dhari Talwar
aka **Challenge**

9244 ft.; **genre:** Costume

pc: Imperial Film Co. **d/st/sc:** B.P. Mishra

lp: Ermeline, E. Bilimoria, Mazhar Khan, Asooji, W.M. Khan

Bhedi Swar
aka **Masked Cavalier**

10188 ft.; **genre:** Stunt

▲ Ganpat Bakre in **Baji Deshpande**

pc: Sharda Film Co. **d:** A.P. Kapur **st:** Arvinda **c:** Naval Bhat
lp: Master Vithal, Lobo, Prabhashankar, Ata Mohammed

Bhikharn
aka **Beggar Girl**
9974 ft.; **genre:** Social
pc: Ranjit Film Co. **d/st/sc:** Chandulal Shah **c:** Pandurang S. Naik
lp: Gohar, K. Narayan Kale, Baba Vyas, Baburao Sansare, Thatte

Bhul Bhulaiya
aka **Comedy of Errors**
2933 ft.; **genre:** Comedy
pc: Sharda Film Co. **d/lp:** Vithaldas Panchotia

Bicharak
aka **Judge**
genre: Social
pc: Eastern Films Syndicate, Calcutta **d:** Sisir Bhaduri **c:** Nitin Bose **st:** Rabindranath Tagore
lp: Sisir Bhaduri, Tara Kumar Bhaduri, Miss Kanakvati, Shefalika
Remarks: The film was banned, but re-censored and released in 1932.

Bilwamangal
aka **Bhakta Surdas, Surdas**
11562 ft.; **genre:** Devotional
pc: Kohinoor Film Co. **d:** Homi Master **st/sc:** Mohanlal G. Dave
lp: Neelam, Bhopatkar, Elizer, Jamuna

Bolki Tapeli
aka **Bolti Tapeli, Talking Pot**
10708 ft.; **genre:** Social
pc: Hindustan Cinema Film Co., Nasik **d/st/sc:** D.G. Phalke

Chalta Purja
aka **Terror**
pc: Sharda Film Co.
Remarks: The film was banned on the grounds that it brought disrepute to the rulers of the Indian princely states.

Chandrahas
6631 ft.; **genre:** Mythological
pc: Hindustan Cinema Film Co., Nasik **d:** D.G. Phalke

Chandramukhi
11151 ft.; **genre:** Social

pc: Shree Jagdish Film Co. **d/st/sc:** Chandulal Shah **c:** Pandurang S. Naik
lp: Gohar, Raja Sandow, R.N. Vaidya, Ghanshyam, Baba Vyas

Chirage Kohistan
aka **Lamp of the Hut**
7925 ft.; **genre:** Costume
pc: Sharda Film Co. **d/st/sc:** A.P. Kapur **c:** Naval Bhat
lp: Master Vithal, Zebu, Lobo, Rajkumari, Prabhasankar, Promoth Bose

Collegian
6209 ft.; **genre:** Social
pc: Saee Films/Gunjal Production **d:** Dada Gunjal
lp: Miss Bunda, Hasam

Dagakhor Dilbar
aka **King's Paramour**
6510 ft.; **genre:** Costume
pc: British India Film Co.
lp: Jilloo, Elizer

Dasa Avathar
9000 ft.; **genre:** Mythological
pc: Guarantee Film Co., Madras **d:** R.S. Prakash

Dashrathi Ram
6589 ft.; **genre:** Mythological
pc: Aryan Film Co., Poona **d:** Sane Mama **c:** Y.D. Sarpotdar **st/sc:** N.D. Sarpotdar
lp: Bhaurao Datar, Durga Koregaonkar, Meera (Chandrika), P.N. Varne, Patankar, Anant Khule, Amboo

Dehna Dan
aka **Mrignayani, Divine Dowry**
9439 ft.; **genre:** Social
pc: Ranjit Film Co. **d:** Nanubhai Vakil **c:** Jamnadas Subedar **st:** Kavi Vairati
lp: Putli, Inamdar, Manilal, Baba Vyas,Thatte

Dharmapathini
aka **The Virtuous Wife**, **The Ideal Hindu Wife**
8000 ft.; **genre:** Social
pc: General Pictures Corporation, Madras **d:** A. Narayan
lp: Devaki, T.P. Kailasam

Dilruba
aka **Belle of Bombay**

10427 ft.; **genre:** Social
pc: Sharda Film Co. **d:** Harshadrai Mehta **c/st/sc:** Chimanlal Luhar
lp: Zohu, Nirasha, Nandram, Janibabu, P.R. Joshi, Meharbanu, P.N. Varne

Domingo
genre: Social
pc: Usha Pictures, Mangalore **d/c/st/sc:** K. Shivrama Karanth
Remarks: Short film on the theme of untouchability.

Falak Numa
aka **Soundarya Jwala**
8890 ft.; **genre:** Costume
pc: Indira Film Co. **d/sc:** Madhusudan Smart **st:** F. Rustomji
lp: Faredoon, Miss Esther Ricks, Abdul Razak, Kisan Lal

Garud Garva Bhangam
aka **Pride of Satyabhama**
6451 ft.; **genre:** Mythological
pc: General Pictures Corporation, Madras **d:** A. Narayan
lp: Devaki, Y.V. Rao

Gnana Sundari
9000 ft.
pc: General Pictures Corporation, Madras **d:** A. Narayan
lp: Devaki

Gopal Krishna
9557 ft.; **genre:** Mythological
pc: Prabhat Film Co., Kolhapur **d:** V. Shantaram **co-d:** K. Dhaiber (?)
c: S. Fattelal **st/sc:** Shivram Washikar
lp: Suresh, Kamladevi, Anant Apte, Sakribai, G.R. Mane

Hatimtai
35891 ft.; **genre:** Legend-serial in 4 parts
pc: Krishna Film Co. **d:** Prafulla Ghosh **c:** Chaturbhai Patel
lp: Rampiary, Abdul Pehelwan, Gulab, Gangaram, Bapurao Apte, Hyder Shah, Durga, Rosy, Leslie, Miss Hormez, Haridas, Nizam

Hawai Sawar
aka **Flying Prince**
11812 ft.; **genre:** Social
pc: Imperial Film Co. **d:** Mohan Bhavnani **c:** Rustom Irani **st:** A.S. Desai
lp: D. Bilimoria, Maya (Diana), Jilloo, Mazhar Khan, Baburao Chinchgar

Heer Ranjah
aka **Hoor-e-Punjab**
11289 ft.; **genre:** Legend
pc: Imperial Film Co. **d/sc:** Pessi Karani **co-d:** R.S.D. Chaudhary **c:** Adi Irani **st:** Vijay Shankar Bhat
lp: Sulochana, D. Bilimoria, Neelam, Jamshetji, Ismail, Faruki, A.R. Kardar

Hungry
1695 ft.; **genre:** Comedy
pc: Saee Films/Gunjal Production **d:** Dada Gunjal
lp: Miss Bunda, Hasam

Husna ka Daku
aka **Mysterious Eagle**
12332 ft.; **genre:** Costume
pc: United Players Corporation, Lahore **d:** A.R. Kardar **c:** D.D. Dabke
lp: M. Esmail, Iris Crawford, A.R. Kardar, G.R. John, S.F. Shaw, Gulam Quadir

Indira
8000 ft.; **genre:** Social
pc: Madan Theatres Ltd. **d:** Jyotish Banerjee **c:** Manglu
st: Bankimchandra Chatterjee
lp: Durgadas Banerjee, Tulsi Banerjee, Tarakbala, Leelavati, Jainarayan Mukherjee, Satyen Dey, B.S. Rajhans

Indira
aka **Cinema ni Sundari**
10737 ft.; **genre:** Social
pc: Imperial Film Co. **d:** R.S.D. Chaudhary **c:** Adi Irani **st:** Vasantrai H. Desai
lp: Sulochana, Jilloo, Mehtab, Sakhu, Jamshetji, Dinkar Bidkar, Salvi, Asooji

◄ Prabhat logo

Jaheri Saap
aka **Bholi Kulsum**
9915 ft.; **genre:** Costume
pc: New Excelsior Film Co. **d/st/sc:** K.B. Athavale
lp: Gangubai, Wamanrao Kulkarni
Remarks: Released in 1931 under K.B. Athavale Productions.

Jakhmi Jigar
aka **Broken Hearts**
11125 ft.; **genre:** Costume
pc: Kohinoor United Artists/N.G. Devare Production Co. **d:** Narayan Devare **c:** V.M. Vyas
st: A.S. Desai
lp: Jamuna, Mary, Thomas, Miss Jones, Elizer

Jawani Diwani
aka **Flaming Youth**
12232 ft.; **genre:** Social
pc: Kohinoor United Artists **d:** Nandlal Jaswantlal **c:** K.G. Gokhale **st/sc:** Mohanlal G. Dave
lp: Thomas, Kumudini, Heera, Panna

Jay Bharati
aka **Young India**
10951 ft.; **genre:** Social
producer/st/sc: Indulal Yagnik **d:** B.P. Mishra **c:** Naval Bhat
lp: Sultana, Zubeida, Navinchandra, Promoth Bose, C.C. Shah

Jay Somnath
11902 ft.; **genre:** Costume
pc: Krishna Film Co. **d:** Harshadrai Mehta c/**st/sc:** Chimanlal Luhar
lp: Rampiary, Gulab, Bapurao Apte, K. Narayan Kale, Hyder Shah, Ibrahim

Jayant
11125 ft.; **genre:** Social
pc: Kaiser-e-Hind Film Co. **d:** Nagendra Mazumdar **c:** Ambadas Pawar
st: Ramanlal V. Desai
lp: Madanrai Vakil, Mehtab, Salvi, Blanche Verne

Jugal Anguriya
aka **Two Rings**
9000 ft.
pc: Madan Theatres Ltd. **d:** Jyotish Banerjee **st:** Bankimchandra Chatterjee
lp: Tarakbala, Tulsi Banerjee

Julia Dalia
8925 ft.; **genre:** Costume
pc: United Pictures Syndicate, Poona **d:** N.G. Kamatnurkar **c:** Pandurang Talegiri
st: V.S. Gurjar
lp: Gangubai, Sunderrao Nandkarni, Wamanrao Kulkarni, Jairampant Desai (?)

Kacha Devayani
8444 ft.; **genre:** Mythological
pc: Hindustan Cinema Film Co., Nasik **d/st/sc:** D.G. Phalke

Kanak Tara
7985 ft.; **genre:** Costume
pc: Victoria Fatma Film Co. **d:** Fatma Begum
lp: Zubeida, Sultana, Shahzadi

Kapal Kundala
12985 ft.
pc: Madan Theatres Ltd. **d:** Priyanath Ganguli **c:** Marconi **st:** Bankimchandra Chatterjee
lp: Seeta Devi, Patience Cooper, Durgadas Banerjee, Naresh Mitra, Danibabu, Tulsi Banerjee, Indira Devi, Lalita Devi

Kaya Palat
992 ft.; **genre:** Comedy
pc: Shree Vithal Films **d/st/sc/lp:** Vithaldas Panchotia

Khuni Kon
aka **Not Guilty**
6855 ft.; **genre:** Social
pc: Little Film Co. **d/st/sc:** Saki
lp: Saki, Umar, Sayani

Khwabe Hasti
aka **Magic Flute**
10525 ft.; **genre:** Costume
pc: Imperial Film Co. **d:** Mohan Bhavnani **c:** Adi Irani **st:** A.S. Desai
lp: Sulochana, D. Bilimoria, Gohar Jr., Mazhar Khan, Baburao Sansare, Rustom Irani, Ghory, Diana

Kishori
aka **Choice of a Bride**
10930 ft.; **genre:** Costume
pc: Surya Film Co., Bangalore **d/st/sc:** Haribhai Desai **c:** D.B. Chavan
lp: Laxmi, Bachu, Ganpat Bakre, Baburao Gade, Zunzharrao Pawar

Kodanddhari Ram
aka **Seeta Swayamvar**
6502 ft.; **genre:** Mythological
pc: United Pictures Syndicate, Poona
lp: Gangubai, Sunderrao Nadkarni, Hansa, Wamanrao Kulkarni

Kono Wank
aka **Whose Fault**
12861 ft.; **genre:** Social
pc: Krishna Film Co. **d:** Kanjibhai Rathod **c:** Gordhanbhai Patel **st:** K.M. Munshi
lp: Gulab, Bapurao Apte

Kovalan
11000 ft.; **genre:** Adaptation
pc: Guarantee Film Co., Madras **d:** R.S. Prakash **st:** based on Ilango Adigal's Tamil classic *Silappadikaram*

Kovalan
aka **Fatal Anklet**
8547 ft.; **genre:** Adaptation
pc: General Pictures Corporation, Madras **d:** A. Narayan **st:** based on *Silappadikaram*
lp: T.P. Rajalakshmi, Devaki

Krishna Kaushalya
aka **Imitator**
7380 ft.; **genre:** Mythological
pc: Mahavir Photoplays, Hyderabad DN

Kumud Kumari
8042 ft.
pc: Shree Jagdish Film Co. **d/st/sc:** Nanubhai Vakil/R.N. Vaidya **c:** Bimal C. Mitra/Jamnadas Subedar
lp: Shantakumari (triple role), Putli, R.N. Vaidya, Dabir, Baba Vyas, Manilal, Inamdar

Kusum Kumari
3710 ft.; **genre:** Costume
pc: Madan Theatres Ltd.

Kusum Lata
aka **Lily of the Valley**
9525 ft.; **genre:** Costume
pc: Suvarna Pictures **d:** Dhirubhai Desai **c:** K.V. Machwe **st:** Giraja Shankar Joshi
lp: Gangubai, Bachu, Wamanrao Kulkarni, K. Budhkar

Lal Vavto
aka **Red Signal**
10610 ft.; **genre:** Social
pc: Imperial Film Co. **d/st/sc:** K.P. Bhave
lp: Ermeline, E. Bilimoria, Mazhar Khan, Baburao Sansare, Dongre

Lanka ni Laxmi
12905 ft.; **genre:** Costume
pc: Kohinoor United Artists **d:** Homi Master **c:** K.G. Gokhale **st/sc:** Mohanlal G. Dave
lp: Panna, Khalil, Jamuna, Nur Mohamed, Neelam, Fatma Jr.

Lutaru Lalna
aka **Dacoit's Damsel**
13940 ft.; **genre:** Costume
pc: Kohinoor United Artists **d:** Homi Master **c:** V.M. Vyas **st/sc:** Mohanlal G. Dave
lp: Heera, Jamuna, Ebrahim, Nur Mohamed, Fatma Jr.

Madhu Bansari
10525 ft.; **genre:** Costume
pc: Sharda Film Co. **d/sc:** A.P. Kapur **c:** Naval Bhat **st:** Giraja Shankar Joshi
lp: Zebu, Nandram, Lobo, P.R. Joshi

Maha Sunder
8962 ft.; **genre:** Costume
pc: Precious Pictures Corporation **c:** Ambadas Pawar
lp: Zubeida, Sultana, Janibabu, Yakub, Shahzadi, Fatma Begum, Ata Mohamed

Malti Madhav
8123 ft.; **genre:** Adaptation
pc: Hindustan Cinema Film Co., Nasik **d:** D.G. Phalke **c:** Anna Salunke **st:** based on Bhavbhuti's play
lp: Anasuya, Krishna Kumbhar

Malvikagnimitra
9717 ft.; **genre:** Adaptation
pc: Hindustan Cinema Film Co., Nasik **d:** D.G. Phalke **c:** Anna Salunke **st:** based on Kalidasa's play
lp: Shakuntala, Kishori Pathak, Krishna Kumbhar

Mard ki Jaban
aka **His Old Debt**
9304 ft.; **genre:** Costume
pc: United Pictures Syndicate, Poona **d:** N.G. Kamatnurkar **c/st:** Pandurang Talegiri
lp: Sundarrao Nadkarni, Gangubai, Wamanrao Kulkarni

Maurya Patan
aka **Chanchal Nari, Fall of the Mauryas**
8725 ft.; **genre:** Historical
pc: Royal Art Studio **d:** R.S.D. Chaudhary
lp: Zebu, Jilloo, Putli, Madanrai Vakil, Elizer, Mehboob

Mayavi Nagri
aka **Magic City**
8019 ft.; **genre:** Costume
pc: Young India Pictures **d/st/sc:** Dhirubhai Desai **c:** G.K. Mehta
lp: Mumtaz, Promoth Bose

Mewadnun Moti
aka **Jewel of Rajputana**
10686 ft.; **genre:** Costume
pc: Imperial Film Co. **d:** B.P. Mishra **c:** Rustom Irani **st:** A.S. Desai
lp: Sulochana, D. Bilimoria, Jilloo, Mazhar Khan, Madanrai Vakil

Milan Dinar
aka **Prem Ni Kasoti**
6125 ft.; **genre:** Costume
pc: Victoria Fatma Film Co. **d:** Fatma Begum
lp: Zubeida, Shahzadi, Yakub, Janibabu, Aziz, Mia Khan

Mirza Sahiba
8290 ft.; **genre:** Legend
pc: Sharda Film Co. **d:** B.P. Mishra **c:** K.V. Machhwe
lp: Zebu, Nandram, Ata Mohamed, P.R. Joshi, Meherbanu

Miss Dolly
9859 ft.; **genre:** Comedy
pc: Krishna Film Co. **d:** Harshadrai Mehta **c/st/sc:** Chimanlal Luhar
lp: Rampiary, Bapurao Apte, Gangaram, Durga, Haridas, Wamanrao Abhyankar

Mumbai No Mawali
aka **The Blackguard**
7664 ft.; **genre:** Social
pc: Little Film Co. **d/c/st/sc:** Saki
lp: Saki, Umar, Sayani, Master Rehman, Gulzar, Mohanlal

Mumbai no Satodio
aka **Speculator**
12291 ft.; **genre:** Social

pc: Kohinoor United Artists **d:** Narayan Devare/R.N. Vaidya **c:** Bimal C. Mitra
st/sc: Mohanlal G. Dave
lp: Jamuna, Mary, Thomas, R.N. Vaidya, Jijibhai, Allavali, Pawar, Malvankar, Ganibabu, Manjula, Charubala, Baby Shirin

Nasib na Nakhara
aka **Shattered Hopes**
7848 ft.; **genre:** Comedy
pc: Sharda Film Co. **d/st/sc:** Vithaldas Panchotia **c:** Naval Bhat
lp: Zebu, Lobo, Nirasha, Vithaldas Panchotia, Meharbanu, Kusum, Ata Mohamed

Nasib ni Devi
aka **Goddess of Luck**
7097 ft.; **genre:** Social
pc: Victoria Fatma Film Co. **d:** Fatma Begum
lp: Sultana, Fatma Begum

Natun Janma
genre: Social
d: Dwarka Khosla

Nisha Sundari
aka **Midnight Girl**
8034 ft.; **genre:** Social
pc: Maharashtra Film Co., Kolhapur **d:** Moti B. Gidwani **c:** D.G. Gune **st:** based on *Cinderella*
lp: Kamaladevi, I.T. Nimbalkar, Bhagwat, Shinde, Sarojini

Nishan Danka
aka **Flag of Honour**
11494 ft.; **genre:** Costume
pc: Sharda Film Co. **d/sc:** Dhirubhai Desai **c:** K.V. Machhwe/Ambadas Pawar **st:** Nanubhai Desai
lp: Master Vithal, Zebu, Lobo, Prabhashankar, P.R. Joshi, Ata Mohamed, P.N.Varne

Paisa na Gulam
aka **All for Money**
8937 ft.; **genre:** Social
pc: Krishna Film Co. **d:** Prafulla Ghosh **c:** Gordhanbhai Patel
lp: Gulab, Rampiary, Vishnu, Hyder Shah, Takle

Pardeshi Saiyan
aka **Lovers**
11985 ft.; **genre:** Costume
pc: Kohinoor United Artists **d:** Nandlal Jaswantlal **c:** K.G. Gokhale **st/sc:** Mohanlal G. Dave
lp: Shantakumari, Khalil, Aziz, Fatma Jr., Kumudini

▲ I.T. Nimbalkar and Gulabbai in
Nisha Sundari

Parijatak
aka **The Flowers of Heaven**
4876 ft.; **genre:** Mythological
pc: Aryan Film Co., Poona **d/st/sc:** N.D. Sarpotdar
lp: Amboo (Lalita Pawar), Bhaurao Datar, Durga Koregaonkar, Meera (Chandrika), Jadhavrao

Parivartan
aka **Revolution in Life**
8975 ft.; **genre:** Social
pc: Krishna Film Co. **d:** Prafulla Ghosh **c:** Gordhanbhai Patel **st:** Shaida
lp: Rampiary, Durga, Bapurao Apte, Hyder Shah

Patal Padamini
11321 ft.; **genre:** Costume
pc: Sharda Film Co. **d:** Harshadrai Mehta **c:** Chimanlal Luhar **st/sc:** Giraja Shankar Joshi
lp: Zebu, Nirasha, Nandram, Janibabu, P.R. Joshi

Pati Patni
aka **Husband and Wife**
8855 ft.; **genre:** Social

pc: Ranjit Film Co. **d/st/sc:** Chandulal Shah **c:** Pandurang S. Naik
lp: Gohar, Raja Sandow, Mubarak, Baba Vyas

Pitru Prem
aka **A Father's Love**
9868 ft.; **genre:** Social
pc: Mahavir Photoplays, Hyderabad DN **d/sc:** Harilal M. Bhatt
lp: Miss Mani, Gaby Hill, Yusuf, Y.L. Chinchunkar, S.P. Niphadkar, Maganlal Dave, Master Madanlal

Prabhavati
7609 ft.; **genre:** Costume
pc: Hindustan Cinema Film Co., Nasik **d:** Gajanan V. Sane

Prem Pash
aka **Law of Love**
6717 ft.; **genre:** Social
pc: Aryan Film Co., Poona **d:** Dinkar Bidkar
lp: Bhaurao Datar, Jadhavrao, Rajkumari, Himmat, Madhav Kale, Amboo

Prem Yatra
aka **Pilgrims of Love**
9931 ft.; **genre:** Social
pc: Shree Jagdish Film Co. **d:** Ramakant Gharekhan/R.N. Vaidya **c:** G.G. Gogate
lp: Shantakumari, R.N. Vaidya, Baba Vyas

Prithviraj Sanyogita
9055 ft.; **genre:** Historical
pc: Aryan Film Co., Poona **d/st/sc:** N.D. Sarpotdar **c:** Y.D. Sarpotdar
lp: Amboo, Bhaurao Datar, Meera (Chandrika), Ghodke, Jadhavrao, C.R. Das

Punjab Kesari
11985 ft.; **genre:** Costume
pc: Kohinoor United Artists **d:** Homi Master **c:** V.M. Vyas **st/sc:** Mohanlal G. Dave
lp: Panna, Bulbule, Bhopatkar, Fatma Jr.

Punjab Mail
11767 ft.; **genre:** Stunt
pc: Imperial Film Co. **d/st/sc:** R.S.D. Chaudhary **c:** Adi Irani
lp: Sulochana, Jal Merchant, Jilloo, D. Bilimoria, J.P. Gidwani, Tara, Gohar Jr., Zaverbhai Kaiser, Mazhar Khan

Punya Prabhav
12440 ft.; **genre:** Social

▲ A title card from **Pitru Prem**

pc: Kohinoor United Artists **d:** Homi Master **c:** V.M. Vyas **st/sc:** Mohanlal G. Dave
lp: Tara, Khalil, R.N. Vaidya, Jamuna, Fatma Jr.

Radio Girl
10383 ft.; **genre:** Social
pc: Indira Film Co. **d/sc:** Baren Roy **st:** R.J. Ruparel
lp: Pratibha, Baren Roy, Miss Vedi

Raj Dharma
aka **Prince of the People**
10994 ft.; **genre:** Costume
pc: Mahavir Photoplays, Hyderabad DN **d/st/sc:** Harilal M. Bhatt **c:** Gatubhai Vaidya
lp: Miss Mani, Shankar

Raj Hansa
8902 ft.; **genre:** Costume
pc: Krishna Film Co. **d:** Kanjibhai Rathod **c:** Gordhanbhai Patel **st:** Narayan Visanji Thakur
sc: Natwar Shyam
lp: Gulab, Rampiary, Vishnu, Hyder Shah

Raj Hriday
aka **Heart of a King**
8773 ft.; **genre:** Costume

pc: Surya Film Co., Bangalore **st/sc:** Bhalji Pendharkar
lp: Ganpat Bakre, Laxmi, Baburao Gade, Zunzharrao Pawar, K. Rangarao

Raj Ramni
aka **Vanishing Hopes**
11943 ft.; **genre:** Costume
pc: Imperial Film Co. **d/st/sc:** B.P. Mishra **c:** Adi Irani
lp: E. Bilimoria, Ermeline, Mazhar Khan

Raj Sanyas
9049 ft.; **genre:** Historical
pc: United Pictures Syndicate, Poona
lp: Gangubai, Saku, Wamanrao Kulkarni

Raja Harishchandra
6566 ft.; **genre:** Mythological
pc: Aryan Film Co., Poona **d/c:** Y.D. Sarpotdar **st/sc:** N.D. Sarpotdar
lp: Amboo, Bhaurao Datar, Jadhavrao, Ghodke, P.N. Varne, Durga Koregaonkar, Master Shantaram, Dattoba Rajwade

Rajani
10000 ft.; **genre:** Social
pc: Madan Theatres Ltd. **d:** Jyotish Banerjee **c:** Manglu **st:** Bankimchandra Chatterjee
lp: Durgadas Banerjee, Tarakbala, Lalita Devi, Leelavati, Manoranjan Bhattacharya, Satyen Dey, Sashimukhi

Raja Shriyal
aka **Great Devotee**
8675 ft.; **genre:** Devotional
pc: Asian Film Co., Indore **d/c/st/sc:** V.H. Palnitkar

Rajput Swar
aka **Rajput Cavalier**
8409 ft.; **genre:** Costume
pc: Young India Pictures **d:** Ramakant Gharekhan/ Indulal Yagnik **c:** D.R. Barodekar
lp: Madhuri, Mohan, Manorama, Mumtaz, Ramesh Niranjan, Kapoor

Rajputani
10905 ft.; **genre:** Costume
pc: Ranjit Film Co. **d/st/sc:** Chandulal Shah
c: Pandurang S. Naik
lp: Gohar, D. Bilimoria, Baburao Sansare, Baba Vyas, Thatte

▲ Ranjit logo

Raktacha Sood
aka **Lohini Vasulat, Blood for Blood**

9810 ft.; **genre:** Adaptation

pc: United Pictures Syndicate, Poona **d:** Pandurang Talegiri **st:** based on Sheridan's *Pizarro*

lp: Gangubai, Sunderrao Nadkarni, Wamanrao Kulkarni, Baburao Gade, Jairampant Desai

Ran Garjana
aka **What Price Loyalty?**

10925 ft.

pc: Sharda Film Co. **d:** Harshadrai Mehta **c:** Chimanlal Luhar

lp: Zebu, Nandram, Ata Mohamed, Vithaldas Panchotia, P.R. Joshi

Ranaghelo Rajput
aka **Warrior**

10915 ft.; **genre:** Costume

pc: Sharda Film Co. **d:** A.P. Kapur **c:** Naval Bhat **st:** Arvind **sc:** Nanubhai Desai

lp: Master Vithal, Zebu, Lobo, Prabhashankar, Ata Mohamed

Rank Ramani
aka **Sitamgar Samaj**

7925 ft.; **genre:** Social

pc: Union Stars Film Co.

lp: Mani, Dumasia

Rank Nu Ratan
aka **Anathno Nath, Mill Mazdoor, Saviour**

10090 ft.; **genre:** Social

pc: Sharda Film Co. **d:** A.P. Kapur **c:** Naval Bhat **st:** A.S. Desai **sc:** Arvinda Supervision: Nanubhai Desai

lp: Master Vithal, Lobo, Miss Mani, Prabhashankar, Promoth Bose, Harischandra Nayak, Miss Rani

Rukmini Haran

8921 ft.; **genre:** Mythological

pc: Krishna Film Co. **d:** Kanjibhai Rathod **c:** Maneklal Patel

lp: Gulab, Vishnu

Sanmitra ke Saitan
aka **Friend or Fiend**

9825 ft.; **genre:** Social

pc: Krishna Film Co. **d/st/sc:** Bhaidas Kewalram **c:** Chaturbhai Patel

lp: Rampiary, Miss Sardar, Abdul Pahelwan, Hyder Shah

Sant Meerabai

8810 ft.; **genre:** Devotional
pc: Hindustan Cinema Film Co., Nasik **d/st/sc:** D.G.Phalke
lp: Shakuntala Tembe

Sattano Mad

aka **Wages of Virtue**
10099 ft.; **genre:** Social
pc: Suresh Film Co. Ltd. **d:** Harshadrai Mehta **c/st/sc:** Chimanlal Luhar
lp: Lobo, Navinchandra, Prabhashankar, Ata Mohamed, Janibabu

Shahi Chor

aka **Wonderful Prince**
7635 ft.; **genre:** Costume
pc: Victoria Fatma Film Co. **d:** Janibabu **c:** Pranjiwan Shukla **st/sc:** Fatma Begum
lp: Zubeida, Shahzadi, Janibabu, Yaqub, Sherwani, Hamid

Shakuntala

9709 ft.; **genre:** Adaptation
pc: Victoria Fatma Film Co. **d:** Fatma Begum: **st:** based on Kalidasa's *Shakuntala*
lp: Sultana, Yakub
Remarks: The film was re-certified in 1933.

Shirin Khusharu

9331 ft.; **genre:** Costume
pc: Imperial Film Co./New Excelsior Film Co. **d:** R.S.D. Chaudhary
lp: Madanrai Vakil, Gohar Jr., Jamshetji, Mehboob

Shri Balaji

8560 ft.; **genre:** Mythological
pc: Aryan Film Co., Poona **d:** Sane **c:** Y.D. Sarpotdar **st/sc:** N.D. Sarpotdar
lp: Amboo, Bhaurao Datar, Jadhavrao

Sinhaka Bacha Sinha

aka **Roaring Lion**
10165 ft.; **genre:** Costume
pc: Kohinoor United Artists **d:** Homi Master **c:** V.M. Vyas **st:** Pessi Karani
lp: Heera, Jamuna, Bulbule, Elizer, Ghanshyam

Sinhaldwip ni Sundari

aka **Fairy of Sinhaldwip**
9625 ft.; **genre:** Costume
pc: Ranjit Film Co. **d/st/sc:** Nanubhai Vakil **c:** Jamnadas Subedar
lp: Putli, Inamdar, Manilal, Thatte

Sneh Samadhi

aka **Martyrs of Love**

8225 ft.; **genre:** Social

pc: Artists Union **d:** Ramakant Gharekhan **c:** D.R. Barodekar **st:** Surabhi Raiji

lp: Manorama, Dilip Raiji, Dhansukhlal Mehta

Sorathi Samsher

aka **Benamun Balidan, Noblesse Oblige**

11564 ft.; **genre:** Costume

pc: Young India Pictures **d:** Dhirubhai Desai **c:** D.R. Barodekar **st:** Zaverchand Meghani

sc: Indulal Yagnik

lp: Mohini, Ramesh Niranjan, Madhuri, Hilal Bin Gani, R. Dinshaw, Miyankhan, Manorama, Mumtaz

Stage Girl

8000 ft.; **genre:** Social

pc: Guarantee Film Co., Madras **d:** R.S. Prakash

Subhadra Haran

7399 ft.; **genre:** Mythological

pc: Aryan Film Co., Poona **d/st/sc:** N.D. Sarpotdar **c:** Y.D. Sarpotdar

lp: Amboo, Bhaurao Datar, Meera (Chandrika), Durga Koregaonkar

Sundariothi Savchet

aka **Sundariothi Savadhan, Beware of Women**

8951 ft.; **genre:** Social

pc: Saurashtra Film Co Ltd., Rajkot **d/st:** Manilal M. Vaidya (?)

lp: Gatubahi Vaidya, Maganlal Dave, Nathabhai Soni, Miss Leela (?)

Tal Bhairav

4200 ft.; **genre:** Social

pc: Omkar Films, Sholapur

Talwar Ka Dhani

aka **Sword to Sword**

11825 ft.; **genre:** Costume

pc: Imperial Film Co. **d/st/sc:** R.S.D. Chaudhary **c:** Adi Irani

lp: Sulochana, Jal Merchant, Jilloo, Yusuf

Tarun Tapswini

aka **Young Ascetic**

9649 ft.; **genre:** Social

pc: Gujarat Studio **d:** Prafulla Ghosh **c:** Chaturbhai Patel **st:** Satyendra Prasad Mehta

lp: Gulab, Abdul Pahelwan, Vishnu, Durga, Takle, Ibrahim

Tawangar Ni Talwar

8547 ft.

pc: Vivekanand Pictures **d:** M. Udwadia **c:** V.B. Jagtap **st/sc:** Vijay Shankar Bhat

lp: Mumtaz, M. Udwadia, Janaki

Thaksen Rajputra

aka **Sawai Vikram, Mysterious Prince**

9334 ft.; **genre:** Costume

pc: Aryan Film Co., Poona **d:** G.P. Pawar **sc:** N.D. Sarpotdar **c:** Y.D .Sarpotdar

lp: Amboo, Bhaurao Datar, Jadhavrao, Ghodke

Ulphat-E-Mohamad

aka **Loves of Prince Mehmood**

12371 ft.; **genre:** Costume

pc: Kohinoor Film Co/N.G. Devare Production Co. **d/st/sc:** Narayan Devare **co-d:** Nandlal Jaswantlal **c:** V.M. Vyas

lp: Khalil, Jamuna, Nur Mohamed, Panna, Fatma Jr., Ganibabu, Rajababu, Behram Vasania

Vasal Ki Rat

aka **Wedding Night**

9737 ft.; **genre:** Costume

pc: Imperial Film Co. **d:** P.Y. Altekar **c:** A.P. Karandikar **st:** based on Victor Hugo's *Hernani* **sc:** Raymino Asher

lp: Jilloo, Nayampalli, P.Y. Altekar, Mubarak, Mazhar Khan

Vasant Padmini

6512 ft.; **genre:** Costume

pc: South Indian Films, Sholapur

Vasantsena

9111 ft.; **genre:** Adaptation

pc: Hindustan Cinema Film Co., Nasik **d:** D.G. Phalke **c:** Anna Salunke

lp: Shankutala, Gotiram

Veer Baji

6225 ft.; **genre:** Historical

pc: Omkar Films, Sholapur

Veer Hak

aka **The Triumph**

10785 ft.; **genre:** Costume

pc: Vishnu Film Co. **d:** A.P. Kapur **c:** Naval Bhat **st:** Shaida

lp: Bachu, Lobo, Tara, Ata Mohamed, Promoth Bose

Veer Pujan
aka **Hero Worship**
10326 ft.; **genre:** Costume
pc: Kohinoor United Artists/Shree Jagdish Film Co. **d/st/sc:** Nanubhai Vakil **c:** Bimal C. Mitra
lp: Shantakumari, Inamdar, Dabir

Veer Rathod
aka **Daring Rathod**
9954 ft.; **genre:** Costume
pc: Krishna Film Co. **d:** Kanjibhai Rathod **c:** Haribhai Patel **st:** Natwar Shyam
lp: Rampiary, Abdul Pahelwan, Miss Sardar, Durga, Hyder Shah

1930

Abad Veer
aka **Shadow**
9425 ft.; **genre:** Costume
pc: Saroj Film Co. **d/st/sc:** Dhirubhai Desai **c:** Ambalal Patel
lp: Janibabu, Iqbal, Lobo, Prabhashankar, Kamla

Adal-E-Jahangir
aka **Justice of Jahangir**
10925 ft.; **genre:** Historical
pc: Sharda Film Co. **d:** A.P. Kapur **c:** Naval Bhat
lp: Zebu, Nandram, Promoth Bose, Sankatha, Miss Rukma, Balabhai, Wilson, B. Khan

Adarsh Abala
aka **Ideal Woman**
7863 ft.; **genre:** Social
pc: Mahavir Photoplays, Hyderabad DN **d:** Vajeshankar Pattani
lp: Miss Mani, Shankar

Aghor Lalsa
aka **Avarice**
8537 ft.; **genre:** Social
pc: Mahavir Photoplays, Hyderabad DN **d:** Harilal M. Bhatt **c:** Gatubhai Vaidya
lp: Miss Mani, Shankar, Maganlal Dave

Albelo Sawar
aka **Beloved Rogue**
10980 ft.; **genre:** Costume
pc: Ranjit Film Co. **d/st/sc:** Nagendra Mazumdar
lp: Putli, E. Bilimoria

ALIK BABU
aka **Master Liar**
7000 ft.; **genre:** Comedy
pc: British Dominion Films Ltd., Calcutta **d:** Dhiren Ganguly **c:** Krishna Gopal/P. Sanyal
st: Jyotindranath Tagore
lp: Dhiren Ganguly, Radharani, Dinesh Das, Kalidas

AMAR KIRTI
aka **Immortal Glory**
9807 ft.; **genre:** Costume
pc: Krishna Film Co. **d:** Prafulla Ghosh **c:** Gordhanbhai Patel **st:** Jayant Desai **sc:** Natwar Shyam
lp: Abdul Pahelwan, Rampiary, Hyder Shah, Vishnu, Wamanrao Abhyankar, Haridas

AMARUN HINDUSTAN
aka **Father India**
11621 ft.; **genre:** Social
pc: Imperial Film Co./Patel Bros. **d:** R.S.D. Chaudhary **c:** Adi Irani
lp: Sulochana, Jal Merchant, Jilloo, Madanrai Vakil, Jamshetji, Mazahar Khan, Mehtab, Yusuf

ANADHAI PENN
aka **Orphan's Daughter**
8525 ft.; **genre:** Social
pc: Associated Films Ltd., Madras **d/st/sc:** Raja Sandow **c:** G.G. Gogate
lp: Raja Sandow, Leela, Hiroji, Dr Ernest Wood

ARUNODAYA
aka **Rising Sun**
9555 ft.; **genre:** Costume
pc: Sagar Film Co. **d/st/sc:** B.P. Mishra **c:** Boman Irani
lp: Master Vithal, Manorama, Nirasha, Yakub, Boman Irani, Vamanrao, Syed Hoosen, Manekbai, W.M. Khan

ARYA KANYA
10725 ft.; **genre:** Social
pc: Kohinoor United Artists **d/c:** K.G. Gokhale **st/sc:** Narayan Devare
lp: Shantakumari, Bapurao Apte

BAHARVATIA NI BETI
aka **Daughter of an Outlaw**
11725 ft.; **genre:** Costume
pc: Kohinoor United Artists **d:** Narayan Devare **c:** K.G. Gokhale **st/sc:** Mohanlal G. Dave
lp: Jamuna, Ebrahim, Fatma Jr., Ganibabu, Malwankar, Pawar

Baharvatio Behram
aka **Behram the Bandit**
7200 ft.; **genre:** Stunt
pc: Asiatic Film Co. **d/st/sc:** Saki
lp: Shahazadi, Saki

Bakawali
aka **Tajj-Ul-Mulk**
12525 ft.; **genre:** Legend
pc: Krishna Film Co. **d:** Mohanlal Shah **c:** Chaturbhai Patel **st/sc:** Natwar Shyam
lp: Gulab, Rampiary, Vishnu, Miss Sardar, Durga, Nanasaheb Chapekar

Bal Gopal
aka **Keshi Vadh**
8425 ft.; **genre:** Mythological
pc: British India Film Co.

Beguman Ashak
aka **The Gallant**
5925 ft.; **genre:** Costume
pc: Chandrakala Film Co., Berar

Bhagyawan Bharwad
aka **Son of a Shepherd**
9525 ft.; **genre:** Costume
pc: Kohinoor United Artists **d:** Hiralal Doctor **c:** Chaturbhai Patel **st:** H.E. Khatib
lp: Shakuntala, Chudekar, Jal Sardar, Surangi

Bhagyodaya
aka **Destiny at Play**
7725 ft.; **genre:** Social
pc: Sharda Film Co. **d:** R.N. Vaidya **c:** R.G. Kukde **st:** M.R. Kapoor
lp: Thomas, Mary, R.N. Vaidya

Bhanto Bhot
959 ft.; **genre:** Comedy
pc: Chandrakala Film Co., Berar

Bharat Ramni
12250 ft.; **genre:** Costume
pc: Madan Theatres Ltd. **d:** Jyotish Banerjee **st:** Aga Hashr Kashmiri
lp: Seeta Devi, Patience Cooper, Leelavati

Bharter Fer
aka **Wheel of Fortune**
6000 ft.; **genre:** Social
pc: Star Of India Film Co., Calcutta (?)

Bhavani no Bhog
aka **Temple of Tortures**
10525 ft.; **genre:** Costume
pc: Young India Pictures **d/st/sc:** Dhirubhai Desai **c:** Ambalal Patel
lp: Iqbal, Madhav Kale, Jairaj, Nazir, Jahanara, Chandrika, Malti, Indira

Bhimsen the Mighty
7781 ft.; **genre:** Mythological
pc: Aryan Film Co., Poona **d/st/sc:** N.D. Sarpotdar **c:** Y.D. Sarpotdar
lp: Joraswamy Sandow, Jadhavrao, Bhaurao Datar, Amboo, P.N. Varne, Miss Umrao, Durga Koregaonkar

Bhola Shikar
aka **Brand of Fate**
11834 ft.; **genre:** Social
pc: Imperial Film Co. **d:** Ramakant Gharekhan **c:** Rustom Irani **st:** Soona Irani
lp: Sultana, Madanrai Vakil, Salvi, Gohar Jr.

Bigraha
aka **The God and the Image**
12000 ft.; **genre:** Social
pc: Graphics Arts, Calcutta **d:** Charu Roy **c:** Debi Ghosh **st:** Jyoti Bachaspati
lp: Jiban Ganguly, Umashashi, Renuka Ghosh, Phani Burma, Renubala

Birth of Shivaji
7825 ft.; **genre:** Historical
pc: Gajanan Film Co.

Bishyut Barer Barbela
aka **On the Afternoon of Thursday, Unlucky Hour of Thursday**
genre: Social (short)
pc: Provincial Film Co., Calcutta **d/c:** Debi Ghosh **st:** Kanai Banerjee
lp: A. Husaini, Bina

Buker Bojha
aka **The Burden**
6500 ft.; **genre:** Social
pc: Arya Films, Calcutta **d/c:** Nitin Bose **st:** Harendra Ghosh
lp: Durgadas Banerjee, Bina Dutt, Renuka Ghosh

Chabuk Swar

aka **Whipman**

9625 ft.; **genre:** Stunt

pc: Sun Art Film Studio **d/st/sc:** Chunilal H. Parekh

lp: Gulab, Mohini, Kusum, Chandulal

Chabukne Chamkare

aka **Flogged into Love**

10175 ft.; **genre:** Stunt

pc: Surya Film Co., Bangalore **d:** Baburao **c:** Mohamed **st:** Nanubhai R. Desai

lp: Zebu, Bachu, Baburao Gade, Zunzharrao Pawar

Chatur Sundari

aka **Wily Heroine**

8938 ft.; **genre:** Costume

pc: Aryan Film Co., Poona **d/st/sc:** N.D. Sarpotdar **c:** Y.D. Sarpotdar/Baburao Shirswade

lp: Amboo, Joraswamy Sandow, Jadhavrao, Bhaurao Datar

Chauhani Talwar

aka **Fighting Cavalier**

10525 ft.; **genre:** Stunt

pc: Surya Film Co., Bangalore **d:** Baburao **c:** D.B. Chavan **st:** Chimanlal Luhar **sc:** Haribhai Desai

lp: Ganpat Bakre, Jena, Baburao Gade, K. Rangrao, Jamu Patel

Chitachor

aka **Cavalier of Love**

9625 ft.; **genre:** Costume

pc: Sharda Film Co. **d:** Faram Shethna **c:** R.G. Kukde

lp: Khalil, Heera, Thomas, Kumudini, R.N. Vaidya

Chitod ni Virangana

aka **Valiant Angel**

9525 ft.; **genre:** Costume

pc: Saraswati Film Co. **d:** Dhirubhai Desai **st:** Giraja Shankar Joshi

lp: Madhuri, Iqbal, Ramesh Niranjan, Fali Cooper

Cinema Girl

10925 ft.; **genre:** Social

pc: Imperial Film Co. **d/st/sc:** B.P. Mishra **c:** Rustom Irani

lp: Ermeline, Prithviraj, Mazhar Khan, Baburao Sansare, Baby Devi

Daily Mail

11925 ft.; **genre:** Social

pc: Kohinoor United Artists **d:** Narayan Devare **st:** A.S. Desai
lp: Khalil, Kumudini, Jamuna, Thomas, Allawali, Bhopatkar

Daivi Khadga
aka **Divine Sabre**

11525 ft.; **genre:** Costume
pc: Surya Film Co., Bangalore **d:** G.P. Pawar **c:** D.B. Chauhan **st:** Nanubhai R. Desai
lp: Ganpat Bakre, Laxmi, Zunhzarao Pawar, Tara, Roshanali, K. Rangrao, Hakimjee, Miss Jaya, Miss Prabha

Daku ke Dilbar
aka **Laughing Cavalier**

10825 ft.; **genre:** Costume
pc: Suresh Film Co. Ltd. **d:** Harshadrai Mehta c/**st/sc:** Chimanlal Luhar
lp: Navinchandra, Prabhashankar, Mumtaz (Queenie), Manjula

Dalia
6000 ft.; **genre:** Social
pc: Madan Theatres Ltd. **d:** Madhu Bose **c:** Jatin Das **st:** Rabindranath Tagore
lp: B.S. Rajhans, Kartik Roy, Ramoladebi, Miss Ruby

Dash Lakh no Dallo
aka **Dashing Youth**

9070 ft.; **genre:** Social
pc: Krishna Film Co. **d:** Prafulla Ghosh **c:** Gordhanbhai Patel **st/sc:** Natwar Shyam
lp: Rampiary, Hyder Shah, Madhukar Gupte, Abdul Pahelwan, Durga, Prafulla Ghosh, Noor Mohamed

Dav Pech
aka **The Web**

9569 ft.; **genre:** Social
pc: Sagar Film Co. **d:** Moti B. Gidwani **c:** Boman Irani **st:** M.M. Wadia
lp: Master Vithal, Gohar Jr., Yakub, Godrej

Desh Dipak
aka **Patriot**

10819 ft.; **genre:** Costume
pc: Ranjit Film Co. **d/st/sc:** Nanubhai Vakil **c:** Jamnadas Subedar
lp: Putli, Inamdar, Manilal, Damayanti, Thatte
Remarks: The film was refused a certificate on 6/10/1930 on the grounds that it was objectionable in the existing political situation. Reissued as *Chalak Chor* aka *Mysterious Man* on January 21, 1931 (CC. No. 9852).

DEVDASI
aka **Bride of Gods, Temple Maid**
6625 ft.; **genre:** Costume
pc: Orient Pictures Corpn. Ltd. **d:** Naval Gandhi
lp: Zubeida, Jal Khambata, Lavji Lavangia, Rupmavati, J. Makhijani

DHRUV NARAYAN
8525 ft.; **genre:** Mythological
pc: British India Film Co.

DHUMKETU
aka **The Comet**
10525 ft.; **genre:** Stunt
pc: Surya Film Co., Bangalore **d:** Sundarrao Nadkarni **c:** D.B. Chauhan **st/sc:** Haribhai Desai
lp: Bachu, Laxmi, Baburao Gade, Miss Sultana (of Bangalore)

DILDARIA
12000 ft.; **genre:** Costume
pc: Prativa Cinema Co., Calcutta **d/st/sc:** Tarapada Saha **c:** Jiten Banerjee
lp: Tarapada Saha, Deben Mullick, Miss Zoe Michael, Gaby Hill, A. Husaini, Kamla, Uma

DIVANI DILBAR
aka **My Darling**
9503 ft.; **genre:** Social
pc: Ranjit Film Co. **d/st/sc:** Chandulal Shah **c:** Pandurang S. Naik
lp: Gohar, D. Bilimoria, Thatte, Baba Vyas, Baburao Sansare

DUKHIARI
aka **Street Girl**
9725 ft.; **genre:** Social
pc: Kohinoor United Artists **d/c:** V.M. Vyas **st/sc:** H.E. Khatib
lp: Panna, Bulbule, Bhopatkar, Ushadevi, Mijjan (Kumar)

FAREBI SHAHZADA
aka **Junglenun Jawahir, Shepherds**
11000 ft.; **genre:** Costume
pc: United Players Corporation, Lahore **d:** A.R. Kardar
lp: Hiralal, Gulzar, M. Esmail

GAIBI SWAR
aka **Masked Rider**
8616 ft.; **genre:** Stunt

pc: Vivekanand Pictures **d/st/sc:** Vithaldas Panchotia **c:** V.B. Jagtap
lp: Gangu, Waman Talpade, M. Udwadia, Vithaldas Panchotia, Mary

Gajendra Moksham
7854 ft.; **genre:** Mythological
pc: General Pictures Corporation, Madras **d:** R.S. Prakash
lp: Rajanamma, Y.V. Rao, K.R. Sarma, R.S. Prakash

Gandhariyin Pulambal
aka **Lament of Gandhari**
10935 ft.; **genre:** Mythological
pc: General Pictures Corporation, Madras **d:** R.S. Prakash
lp: Vilochana, T.S. Mani, Tara

Ganesh Janma
10000 ft.; **genre:** Mythological
pc: Madan Theatres Ltd. **d:** Jal Ariya
lp: Indira Devi, Patience Cooper

Garib ni Hai
aka **Curse**
9725 ft.; **genre:** Costume
pc: Sharda Film Co. **d/sc:** Asooji **c:** D.K. Patel
lp: Gulab, Asooji, Sarla, P.R. Joshi, Salu, Miss Nagamma, Miss Sardar, Balabhai

Garva Khandan
aka **Fall of Pride**
9657 ft.; **genre:** Costume
pc: Jagtap Pictures **d:** M. Udwadia **c:** V.B. Jagtap **st/sc:** Jayant Desai
lp: Zubeida, Waman Talpade, M. Udwadia

Giribala
8000 ft.; **genre:** Social
pc: Madan Theatres Ltd. **d:** Madhu Bose **c:** Jatin Das **st:** Rabindranath Tagore
lp: Dhiraj Bhattacharya, Naresh Mitra, Tincowri Chakraborty, Shanti Gupta, Lalita Devi, Leelavati
Remarks: Screenplay was revised by Rabindranath Tagore who also wrote additional dialogues.

Golden Pathway
6925 ft.; **genre:** Costume
pc: Royal Art Studio/Patel Bros.
Remarks: Royal Art Studio had closed down by 1927 and the film was censored and released in 1930 by Patel Bros.

Gori Bala
aka **Hell's Paradise**
10195 ft.; **genre:** Social
pc: Imperial Film Co. **d:** P.Y. Altekar **c:** A.P. Karandikar **st/sc:** Mama Varerkar
lp: Jilloo, Nayampalli, Manorama, P.S. Wagle, Mubarak, Sakhu

Gulanar
11717 ft.; **genre:** Costume
pc: Kohinoor United Artists **d:** D.A. Dandekar **c:** Bimal C. Mitra **st/sc:** Mohanlal G. Dave
lp: Nurjehan, Khalil, Bapurao Apte

Gul-e-Arab
aka **Arabian Girl**
8921 ft.; **genre:** Costume
pc: Venus Film Co.

Hanuman Vijay
7414 ft.; **genre:** Mythological
pc: British India Film Co.

Himmate Marda
aka **Dare Devil**
9525 ft.; **genre:** Crime
pc: Krishna Film Co. **d:** Prafulla Ghosh **c:** Gordhanbhai Patel **st:** Dhanshankar Tripathi
lp: Abdul Pahelwan, Rampiary, Hyder Shah, Arab Sandow

Hridaya Jwala
aka **Women's Vengeance**
10877 ft.; **genre:** Costume
pc: Sharda Film Co. **d:** R.N. Vaidya **c:** D.R. Barodekar **st:** Krishnaswamy
lp: Khalil, Heera, R.N. Vaidya, Sankatha

Husnara
9336 ft.; **genre:** Costume
pc: Krishna Film Co. **d:** Mohanlal Shah **c:** Thakorbhai Patel **st:** B.J. Upadyay **sc:** Amrutlal R. Trivedi
lp: Vishnu, Jessi, Durga, Wamanrao Abhyankar, Arab Sandow

Inteqam
aka **Revenge**
8320 ft.; **genre:** Social
pc: Imperial Film Co. **d/st/sc:** K.P. Bhave **c:** Rustom Irani
lp: Sultana, E. Bilimoria, Madanrai Vakil, Baburao Sansare, W.M. Khan, Mazhar Khan

Jai Shree Shankar
aka **Bhasmasur Vadh**
8525 ft.; **genre:** Mythological
pc: British India Film Co.

Jai Vijay
9525 ft.; **genre:** Stunt
pc: Aryan Film Co., Poona **d/st/sc:** N.D. Sarpotdar **c:** Y.D. Sarpotdar
lp: Durga Koregaonkar, Meera (Chandrika), C.R. Das, P.N. Varne

Jalim Jadugarin
aka **Enchantress**
8720 ft.; **genre:** Costume
pc: Sharda Film Co. **d:** A.P. Kapur **c:** Naval Bhat
lp: Nandram, Zebu, P.R. Joshi, Asooji, Rajkumari, Promoth Bose

Jawanmarda
aka **Dashing Hero**
9323 ft.; **genre:** Stunt
pc: Ranjit Film Co. **d:** Jayant Desai **c:** Jamnadas Subedar **st/sc:** Jayant Desai
lp: Putli, Baburao Sansare, Manilal

Jigarna Gha
aka **Rajput Ramani, Wronged Wife**
10451 ft.; **genre:** Costume
pc: Sharda Film Co. **d/st/sc:** Pessi Karani **c:** Naval Bhat
lp: Nandram, Zebu, Asooji, P.R. Joshi, Rajkumari, Kashar Butt

Jobanna Jadu
aka **Love Angle**
9425 ft.; **genre:** Social
pc: Ranjit Film Co. **d:** Jayant Desai **c:** Jamnadas Subedar **st:** Chaturbhuj Doshi
lp: Zubeida, Inamdar, Ishwarlal

Josh-e-Jawani
aka **Romance of a Youth**
10751 ft.; **genre:** Historical (based on a true story)
pc: Sagar Film Co. **d:** Moti B. Gidwani **c:** Rustom Irani
lp: Master Vithal, Mazhar Khan, Gohar Jr., Chandrarao Kadam
Remarks: Original title was objected to by the censors viz., *Bhistino Bhagyoday* aka *Romance of Bhisti, Bacha-i-Sakka.*

Jugal Jugari
aka **Gambler**

11765 ft.; **genre:** Social
pc: Kohinoor United Artists **d:** Farum Shethna **c:** Bimal C. Mitra, K.G. Gokhale **st:** A.S. Desai
sc: Mohanlal G. Dave
lp: Heera, Jamuna, Bapurao Apte, Miss Jones, Rajababu

Kabir Kamal
7589 ft.; **genre:** Devotional
pc: Hindustan Cinema Film Co., Nasik **d:** Gajanan V. Sane

Kal Parinaya
aka **Fatal Marriage**
10000 ft.; **genre:** Social
pc: Madan Theatres Ltd. **d:** Priyanath Ganguly **c:** Jatin Das **st:** based on a Ramlal Banerjee play
lp: Dhiraj Bhattacharya, Naresh Mitra, Seeta Devi, Prakash Moni, Patience Cooper, Dipti Sanyal, B.S. Rajhans, Kartick Dey, Sudhir Sanyal, Bhanu Banerjee, Shanti Gupta

Kalikano Kop
aka **Royal Savage**
9625 ft.; **genre:** Costume
pc: Surya Film Co., Bangalore **d:** Sundarrao Nadkarni **c:** Vishnu Sawant
st: Nanubhai R. Desai
lp: Laxmi, Ganpat Bakre, Zunzharrao Pawar, Baburao Gade, Jena

Kalino Ekko
aka **Ace of Spades**
11332 ft.; **genre:** Social
pc: Young India Pictures **d/st/sc:** Nagendra Mazumdar
lp: Madhuri, Madhav Kale, Dikshit

Kamale Samsher
9235 ft.; **genre:** Costume
pc: New Excelsior Film Co. **d:** Ramakant Gharekhan **c:** Boman Irani **st/sc:** H.E. Khatib
lp: Mehtab, W.M. Khan

Kamaner Aagun
aka **Padmini Of Chittor, Flames of Flesh**
12000 ft.; **genre:** Historical
pc: British Dominion Films Ltd., Calcutta **d:** Dinesh Ranjan Das **c:** Krishna Gopal
st/sc: Debaki Kumar Bose
lp: Dhiren Ganguly, Ramola Devi, Sabita Devi, Debaki Bose, Radharani, K.N. Tagore, Hem Gupta, Dinesh Das, Harold Lewis (Majnu)

Kanthahar
aka **Diamond Necklace**

12000 ft.; **genre:** Crime

pc: Indian Kinema Arts, Calcutta **d:** Kaliprasad Ghosh **c:** Noni Gopal Sanyal/Bibhuti Das

st: Dasarathi Mukherjee

lp: Durgadas Banerjee, Sabita Devi, Renubala, Tincowry Chakraborty, Sarat Chatterjee, Prakash Ghosh, Samar Ghosh, Prabhat Sinha, B.S. Rajhans, Prafulla, Nimai Saha, Boken Chatterjee

Khandana Khel
aka **Fight Unto Death**

9315 ft.; **genre:** Costume

pc: Young India Pictures **d/st/sc:** Maneklal Joshi **co-d:** Nagendra Mazumdar **c:** Dwarka Khosla

lp: Madhuri, Madhav Kale, Jairaj, Radhakumar Bhaduri, Fali Cooper

Khooni Khanjar
aka **Fighting Blade**

8353 ft.; **genre:** Costume

pc: Prabhat Film Co., Kolhapur **d:** V. Shantaram/Keshavrao Dhaiber **c:** S. Fattelal/V. Damle

st/sc: Shivram Washikar

lp: Miss Vijya, Jai, G.R. Mane, Sakribai, Ganpat Shinde

Khuda Parashta
9000 ft.; **genre:** Costume

pc: Hindustan Cinema Film Co., Nasik **d:** Ganpat Shinde **c:** Anna Salunke

lp: Anasuya, Gotiram, Kishori Pathak, Shelar

Khuni Taj
aka **Raktacha Rajmukut, All for the Crown**

12542 ft.; **genre:** Costume

pc: United Pictures Syndicate, Poona

d/c/sc: Pandurang Talegiri **st:** based on Shakespeare's *Macbeth*

lp: Wamanrao Kulkarni, Gangubai, Jairampant Desai

Khuni Teer
aka **Fatal Arrow**

10925 ft.; **genre:** Costume

pc: Sharda Film Co. **d:** A.P. Kapur **c:** Naval Bhat

st: M.R. Kapoor

lp: Nandram, Zebu, Sankatha, Promoth Bose, P.R. Joshi

▲ Madhav Kale and Jairaj in **Khandana Khel**

King Bhoj
8000 ft.; **genre:** Legend
pc: General Pictures Corporation, Madras **d:** A. Narayan
lp: Y.V. Rao, Vilochana, Tara, Devaki

Komalner Ni Kusum
aka **Rose of Komalner**
10625 ft.; **genre:** Costume
pc: Suresh Film Co. Ltd. **d/st/sc:** Dhirubhai Desai **c:** G.K. Mehta
lp: Janibabu, Lobo, Prabhashankar, Datar

Krishna Kumari
aka **Flower of Rajasthan**
10530 ft.; **genre:** Costume
pc: Young India Pictures **d:** Maneklal Joshi astt: P. Jairaj **c:** Dwarka Khosala, Ambalal Patel
lp: Madhuri, Jairaj, Madhav Kale, Yekbal, Dikshit, Master Bachu

Krishnabarna Tirandaj
aka **Black Archer**
7000 ft.: **genre:** Costume
pc: Madan Theatres Ltd. **d:** B.S. Rajhans **c:** S. Marconi
lp: Lalita Devi, B.S. Rajhans, Kartik Roy, Samar Ghosh

Krur Sinha
aka **The Terror**
8430 ft.; **genre:** Costume
pc: Kamar Film Co.

Lanka
aka **Land of Lust**
7241 ft.; **genre:** Mythological
pc: Maharashtra Film Co., Kolhapur **d:** Baburao Painter **c:** D.G. Gune
lp: Balasaheb Yadav, B. Nandrekar, I.T. Nimbalkar, Krishnakumari, Shankarrao Gurav, Padmavati

Madabhar Mohini
aka **Magic Flame**
11277 ft.; **genre:** Costume
pc: Ranjit Film Co. **d:** Nanubhai Vakil **c:** Pandurang S. Naik
lp: Putli, Baburao Sansare

Madan Kokila
aka **Devi Kalika's Vengeance**

8525 ft.; **genre:** Costume
pc: Asian Film Co., Indore **d:** V.H. Palnitkar
lp: Shakuntala

MADHABI KANKAN
aka **Slave Girl of Agra**
10000 ft., **genre:** Historical
c: Madan Theatres Ltd. **d:** Jyotish Banerjee **c:** Charles Creed/ Marconi **st:** R.C. Dutt
lp: Mumtaz Begum, Lalita Devi, Bhanu Banerjee, Leelavati, Jainarayan Mukherjee, Farida Begum, Nawab
Remarks: The film was initially banned. Re-censored and released in 1932.

MANIK JORE
aka **Fortune Hunters**
8000 ft.
pc: Madan Theatres Ltd. **d:** Jyotish Banerjee **c:** Charles Creed
lp: Meherji Surveyor, Bapuji Punegar, Rahim Bux, Savitridevi

MARD KA BACHCHA
aka **The Valiant**
8800 ft.; **genre:** Social
pc: Krishna Film Co. **d:** Prafulla Ghosh **c:** Gordhanbhai Patel **sc:** Natwar Shyam
lp: Abdul Pahelwan, Rampiary, Hyder Shah

▼ **Lanka**

Masta Fakir
aka **Fall of Vijaynagar**

11525 ft.; **genre:** Costume

pc: Kohinoor United Artists **d:** Homi Master **c:** V.M. Vyas **st/sc:** Mohanlal G. Dave

lp: Bulbule, Nurjehan, Ghanshyam, Rajababu

Mathano Sadhu
aka **Devil of the Cave**

11981 ft.; **genre:** Social

pc: Kohinoor United Artists **d:** Kanjibhai Rathod **c:** Chaturbhai Patel **st:** Shaida

lp: Tara, Ghanshyam, Ramesh Niranjan, Jeejibhai, Leena

Mayabee
aka **Mystery Man**

9875 ft.; **genre:** Mystery Thriller

pc: Indian Film Producing Co., Calcutta **d:** Becharam Ghosh **c:** D.D. Dabke **st:** Panchkari Dey

lp: Becharam Ghosh, Renubala, Bachu, Bhola

Mewad no Mawali
aka **Rogue of Rajasthan**

11425 ft.; **genre:** Costume

pc: Sagar Film Co. **d:** Madanrai Vakil **c:** Adi Irani **st/sc:** H.E. Khatib

lp: E. Bilimoria, Nirasha, Elizer, Mehboob

Mitha Jahar
aka **She Wolf**

10525 ft.; **genre:** Adaptation

pc: Sharda Film Co. **d:** A.P. Kapur **c:** A.D. Pawar **st:** M.R. Kapoor, based on Shakespeare's *Cymbeline*

lp: Nandram, Heera, Promoth Bose, Salu

Mohabatnun Phool
aka **Love Triumphant**

6925 ft.; **genre:** Costume

pc: Royal Art Studio/Patel Bros.

Remarks: Royal Art Studio had closed down by 1927. The film was censored and released in 1930 by Patel Bros.

Moroo
7525 ft.

pc: Indian Pictures **d:** Aseer

Mrinalini
14000 ft.; **genre:** Social

pc: Madan Theatres Ltd. **d:** Jyotish Banerjee **c:** Manglu **st:** Bankimchandra Chatterjee
lp: Dhiraj Bhattacharya, Renubala, Kartik Dey, Kalipada, Phani Burma, Krishnadas Banerjee, Jainarayan Mukerjee

Nai Roshni
aka **Royal Rivals**
11490 ft.; **genre:** Costume
pc: Sagar Film Co. **d/st/sc:** B.P. Mishra **c:** Boman Irani
lp: Jal Merchant, Ermeline, Yakub, Rajkumari

Nand Kumar
8353 ft.; **genre:** Mythological
pc: Asian Film Co., Indore **d:** V.H. Palnitkar **c:** M.P. Joshi
lp: Indumati , Zohra, Raja Vaidya, H. Benjamin

Nandnar
aka **Nand the Naynar, Elevation of the Downtrodden**
7600 ft.; **genre:** Adaptation
pc: Associated Films Ltd., Madras **d/sc:** Raja Sandow **c:** G.G. Gogate
lp: Raja Sandow, Leela, Mangudi Durairaju Aiyer

Nasib ni Nauka
aka **Winds of Fate**
10925 ft.; **genre:** Costume
pc: New Kohinoor Film Co. **d:** Ratansha Sinor **st/sc:** Mohanlal G. Dave
lp: Panna, Aziz

Nirbhagi Nirmala
aka **Woman in Wilderness**
12527 ft.; **genre:** Social
pc: Krishna Film Co. **d:** Kanjibhai Rathod **c:** Chaturbhai Patel
lp: Gulab

Noor-e-Watan
aka **Glory of India**
10925 ft.; **genre:** Costume
pc: Ranjit Film Co. **d:** Jayant Desai **c:** Jamnadas Subedar
lp: Sultana, Inamdar, Thatte, Manilal, Baba Vyas, Shanti

Pahari Kanya
aka **The Wild Flower**
11920 ft.; **genre:** Costume
pc: Ranjit Film Co. **d:** Nandlal Jaswantlal **c:** Pandurang S. Naik **st/sc:** Mohanlal G. Dave
lp: Gohar, D. Bilimoria, Kamla, Baba Vyas, Thatte

Panchasar
aka **The Blind God**
10000 ft.
pc: British Dominion Films Ltd., Calcutta **d/st/sc:** Debaki Kumar Bose **c:** Krishna Gopal/P Sanyal
lp: Dhiren Ganguly, Debaki Bose, Radharani, Dinesh Das, Hem Gupta, Nimai Saha, Mihirlal, Premkumari Nehru

Pandava Nirvahan
7925 ft.; **genre:** Mythological
pc: General Pictures Corporation, Madras **d:** Y.V. Rao **c:** Dhiren Dey
lp: Devaki, T.S. Mani

Patan Ni Panihari
aka **Damsel of Patan**
10925 ft.; **genre:** Costume
pc: Kohinoor United Artists **d:** Homi Master **c:** V.M. Vyas **st/sc:** Mohanlal G. Dave
lp: Yakbal, Panna, Bhopatkar, Ratansha Sinor, Mijjan

Peyum Pennum
aka **Devil and the Damsel**
11525 ft.; **genre:** Social
pc: Associated Films Ltd., Madras **d/st/sc:** Raja Sandow **c:** G.G. Gogate
lp: Raja Sandow, Leela, Dr & Mrs Ernest Wood, Hiroji, K.T. Rukmini

Piari
aka **Pyari**
8000 ft.; **genre:** Costume
pc: Movie Producers Co., Calcutta **d/c:** Bimal Pal **st:** Soumendra Mohan Mukherjee
lp: Ardhendu Banerjee, Nilmani De, Kalipada, Chandravati Devi

Prameela Arjun
7925 ft.; **genre:** Mythological
pc: General Pictures Corporation, Madras **d:** S. Gopalan
lp: Vilochana, T.S. Mani, Tara, M.V. Raju

Prapancha Pasha
aka **Prapanchana Pash, A Throw of Dice**
7630 ft.; **genre:** Costume
pc: British Instructional Films Ltd., London/ U.F.A., Germany/ Himansu Rai Film
d: Franz Osten **c:** Emil Schünemann **st:** Niranjan Pal **sc:** W. Burton/Max Jungk
lp: Seeta Devi, Himansu Rai, Charu Roy, Tincowri Chakraborty, Sarada Gupta, Lala Bijoykishen, Modhu Bose
Remarks: German version: 8277 ft. Released in Europe in 1929.

Prem Diwani
aka **Devotee**

9525 ft.; **genre:** Costume

pc: Suryodaya Film Co. **d:** A.P. Kapur **c:** Naval Bhat **st/sc:** M.R. Kapoor

lp: Sankatha, Salu, Pramoth Bose, Balabhai, B. Khan, Bijlee, Devsingh

Raat ki Baat
aka **Secret of the Night**

10605 ft.; **genre:** Thriller

pc: Imperial Film Co. **d/st/sc:** K.P. Bhave **c:** A.P. Karandikar

lp: Sulochana, Jal Merchant, Elizer, Salvi

Radha Krishna
7925 ft.; **genre:** Mythological

pc: Asian Film Co., Indore **d:** V.H. Palnitkar

lp: Indumati, Zohra

Radharani
8000 ft.; **genre:** Social

pc: Madan Theatres Ltd. **d:** Jyotish Banerjee **c:** Manglu **st:** Bankimchandra Chatterjee

lp: Durgadas Banerjee, Lalita Devi, Jainarayan Mukherjee, Satyen Dey, Kartik Dey, Leelavati

Radhe Shyam
9725 ft.; **genre:** Mythological

pc: Surya Film Co., Bangalore **d:** Madhusudan Smart/P.V. Chavan

c: Telang/D.B. Chavan **st/sc:** Haribhai Desai

lp: Bachu, Kamala, K. Rangarao

Raigad nu Patan
aka **Fall of Raigad**

9732 ft.; **genre:** Historical

pc: United Pictures Syndicate, Poona **d:** Pandurang Talegiri **st:** V.S. Gurjar

lp: Gangubai, Wamanrao Kulkarni, Dattopant Sohoni, Jairampant Desai, V.S. Bapat

Raj Kumari
aka **The Princess**

9532 ft.; **genre:** Costume

pc: Suresh Film Co. Ltd. **d:** Ramakant Gharekhan **c/co-st/sc:** G.K. Mehta **co-st:** Appu Mehta

lp: Navinchandra, Mumtaz, Ata Mohamad, Vasant Mengale

Raj Laxmi
8625 ft.; **genre:** Costume

pc: Shree Jagdish Film Co. **d/st/sc:** Chandulal Shah **c:** Pandurang S. Naik
lp: Gohar, Raja Sandow, Baba Vyas, Putli

Raj Prapanch
aka **State Intrigues**
10925 ft.; **genre:** Costume
pc: Surya Film Co., Bangalore **d:** Keshavlal Joshi **c:** Vishnu Sawant **st:** Nanubhai R. Desai
lp: Laxmi, Drupad Bhatt, Mansur, Manohar Ghatwai, Baburao Gade, Saraswati, Jamu Patel

Raj Sinha
genre: Historical
pc: Madan Theatres Ltd. **d:** Jyotish Banerjee **c:** Mohamed Hanif
st: Bankimchandra Chatterjee
lp: Ahindra Chaudhary, Indira Devi, Patience Cooper, Manorama

Rajdoot
aka **Beggar Meets Beggar**
10525 ft.; **genre:** Costume
pc: Surya Film Co., Bangalore **d/sc:** Haribhai Desai **st:** Nanubhai R. Desai
lp: Zebu, Bachu, Zunzharrao Pawar, Baburao Gade, Abbasi

Rajeswari
10525 ft.; **genre:** Social
pc: Associated Films Ltd., Madras **d/st/sc:** Raja Sandow **c:** V.J. Bhave
lp: Raja Sandow, Leela, T.P. Rajalakshmi

Rajkumari Ni Ranagarjana
aka **Valiant Princess**
11221 ft.; **genre:** Costume
pc: Kohinoor United Artists **d/st/sc:** Kanjibhai Rathod **c:** Chaturbhai Patel
lp: Gulab, Gangram, Bapurao Apte, Nur Mohamed, Ghanshyam, Pawar

Rajmukut
aka **Royal Crown**
11393 ft.; **genre:** Costume
pc: New Kohinoor Film Co. **d:** Behram Vasania **c:** S.N. Patankar **st:** Jaman **sc:** Mohanlal G. Dave
lp: Tara, Nurjehan, Aziz, Ratansha Sinor

Ram Rahim
9599 ft.; **genre:** Social
pc: Imperial Film Co. **d/st/sc:** K.P. Bhave **c:** Sohrab R. Irani
lp: E. Bilimoria, Gohar Jr., W.M. Khan, R.B. Jagtap, Mazhar Khan

RAMA DOOTA
aka **Lanka Dahanam**
7809 ft.; **genre:** Mythological
pc: General Pictures Corporation, Madras **d:** R.S. Prakash
lp: Devaki, M.V. Raju, T.S. Mani

RANAKDEVI
9735 ft.; **genre:** Historical
pc: Ranjit Film Co. **d/st/sc:** Nanubhai Vakil **c:** Jamnadas Subedar
lp: Putli, Baburao Sansare, Thatte, Manilal, Bhagavat, Ishwarlal

RANCHANDI
aka **Goddess of War**
11326 ft.; **genre:** Costume
pc: Kohinoor United Artists **d:** Homi Master **c:** K.G. Gokhale **st/sc:** Mohanlal G. Dave
lp: Khalil, Panna, Jamuna, Thomas, Kumar, Maganlal Dave

RANDHIR
aka **Dauntless**
10525 ft.; **genre:** Stunt
pc: Surya Film Co., Bangalore **d:** Sundarrao Nadkarni **st:** Nanubhai R. Desai
lp: Laxmi, Ganpat Bakre, K. Rangarao

RANI SAHEBA
aka **My Queen**
10351 ft.; **genre:** Comedy
pc: Prabhat Film Co., Kolhapur **d:** V. Shantaram/Keshavrao Dhaiber **c:** S. Fattelal/V. Damle
st/sc: Bhalji Pendharkar
lp: Kamladevi, Baburao Pendharkar, K. Dhaiber, Anant Apte

RASILI RADHA
aka **Romance of Radha**
10925 ft.; **genre:** Costume
pc: Ranjit Film Co. **d/st/sc:** Nanubhai Vakil **c:** G.G. Gogate
lp: Shantakumari, D. Bilimoria, Ishwarlal, Thatte

RASILI RANI
aka **Triumph of Love**
10214 ft.; **genre:** Costume
pc: Young India Pictures **d:** Nagendra Mazumdar **c:** V.V. Date
lp: Madhuri, Jairaj, Mohanlal

SAFADARJUNG
9000 ft.; **genre:** Stunt

pc: United Players Corporation, Lahore **d:** A.R. Kardar **c:** K.V. Machhwe **st:** Akhtyar
lp: Hiralal, Mumtaz, Gulzar

Safed Swar
aka **White Rider**
8895 ft.; **genre:** Costume
pc: Sharda Film Co./Seven Arts Group **d:** Faram Sethna **c:** R.G. Kukde **st:** M.R. Kapoor
lp: Khalil, Mary (Kumudini), Sarala, Usman, Faram Sethna, Jehangir, Moosa, Hanmantrao, Sarifa, Phodke

Samsher Bahadur
aka **Champion of Sword**
6972 ft.; **genre:** Stunt
pc: Aryan Film Co., Poona **d/st/sc:** N.D .Sarpotdar **c:** Baburao Shirswade
lp: Amboo, Bhaurao Datar, Jadhavrao, Ghodke, P.N. Varne, C.R. Das

Samsherbaz
aka **Swordsman**
7925 ft.; **genre:** Stunt
pc: Asiatic Film Co. **d/c/st/sc:** Saki
lp: Saki, Roshanara, Sayani

Sarangthara
8700 ft.; **genre:** Costume
pc: General Pictures Corporation, Madras **d:** Y.V. Rao

Sarfarosh
aka **Brave Heart**
9529 ft.; **genre:** Stunt
pc: United Players Corporation, Lahore **d/st/sc:** A.R. Kardar **c:** K.V. Machhwe
lp: Gulam Quadir, Hiralal, Gulzar, Miss Mumtaz, Gul Hamid, Rafiq Gazanavi

Sati Sarla
10282 ft.; **genre:** Devotional
pc: Hindustan Cinema Film Co., Nasik **d:** Abhaya Charan Lahiri
lp: Anasuya, Kishori Pathak, Krishna Kumbhar

Sati Ushasundari
9800 ft.; **genre:** Mythological
pc: Associated Films Ltd., Madras **d/st/sc:** Raja Sandow **c:** G.G. Gogate/V.J. Bhave
lp: Raja Sandow, Leela, T.P. Rajalakshmi, K.B. Vathsal, P.V. Rao

Sati Vijaya
8725 ft.; **genre:** Mythological

pc: British India Film Co.
lp: Laxmanrao Pahelwan, Roshanara

Savati Matsar
aka **Jealous Co-Wife**
7570 ft.; **genre:** Mythological
pc: Hindustan Cinema Film Co., Nasik **d:** Ganpat Shinde

Seeta Haran
7525 ft.; **genre:** Mythological
pc: Asian Film Co., Indore **d:** C. Vainkunth Rao **c:** M.P. Joshi/M.H. Palnitkar
lp: Shakuntala, Raje, Raja Vaidya

Shahi Ishq
aka **Royal Romance**
7950 ft.; **genre:** Costume
pc: Sun Art Film Studio **d:** Chunilal H. Parekh

Sharif Badmash
9000 ft.; **genre:** Costume
pc: Madan Theatres Ltd.

Sheikh Challi
aka **Castles in the Air**
10626 ft.; **genre:** Comedy
pc: Ranjit Film Co. **d:** Nanubhai Vakil **c:** G.G. Gogate
lp: Shantakumari, Inamdar, Ishwarlal

Sher-e-Arab
aka **Arabian Knight**
10729 ft.; **genre:** Costume
pc: Zarina Pictures **d/st/sc:** B.P. Mishra **c:** G.K. Karkhanis
lp: Indira (Miss Eugene Peterson), Prithviraj, Jagdish Sethi, Dewan Sharar

Shere Jawan
aka **Daring Youth**
9840ft.; **genre:** Costume
pc: Kohinoor United Artists **d:** R. Ghare Khan **st:** Surendra Nath **c:** Naval Bhat
lp: Jaswant Vaidya, Mumtaz, Ata Mohamed, Mengle, Nizam, Fazlu

Sheshpath
aka **Only Way**
7000 ft.; **genre:** Social
pc: Independent Producers **d:** Phani Burma **c:** Dwarka Khosla **st:** Moni Burma
lp: Sushilabala, Phani Burma, Bankim Datta, Moni Burma

Shree Kannika Parmeswari
aka **Shree Kanyaka Parmeswari**
8000 ft.; **genre:** Mythological
pc: Guaranteed Pictures Corpn., Madras

Shree Subrahamaniyam
aka **Vallikumari's Wedding**
5720 ft.; **genre:** Mythological
pc: Hindustan Cinema Film Co., Nasik **d:** Rao (?) **c:** Anna Salunke
lp: Kishori Pathak, Madhav Mistry, Brahmadeo

Shrikanta
12000 ft.; **genre:** Social
pc: Radha Film Co., Calcutta **d:** Tara Kumar Bhaduri **c:** Bimal C. Mitra **st:** Saratchandra Chatterjee
lp: Tara Kumar Bhaduri, Molina, Shanta Kumari, Kanti Banerjee

Shurana Sangram
aka **Benevolent Bravery**
10725 ft.; **genre:** Costume
pc: Krishna Film Co. **d:** Mohanlal Shah **c:** Chaturbhai Patel **st/sc:** Natwar Shyam
lp: Gulab, Gangaram, Miss Sardar, Vishnu, Haridas, Durga

Shurveer Sharada
aka **Gallant Girl**
8525 ft.; **genre:** Costume
pc: Kohinoor United Artists/Shree Jagdish Film Co. **d:** Homi Master
st/sc: Vithaldas Panchotia
lp: Shakuntala, Aziz, Nur Mohamed, Leena

Sindbad Khalasi
aka **Sindbad the Sailor**
10537 ft.; **genre:** Costume
pc: Imperial Film Co. **d/sc:** R.G. Torney **c:** Rustom Irani
lp: Jamshetji, Elizer, P.S. Waghle, Sushila, Mazhar Khan, Sakhu, Trikamlal

Sinhano Punjo
aka **Lion's Claw**
9874 ft.; **genre:** Social
pc: Sharda Film Co. **d/sc:** Pessi Karani **c:** Ambadas Pawar **st:** H.E. Khatib
lp: Zebu, Nandram, Asooji, Promoth Bose, Balabhai

Sitamghar
aka **Tyrant**

10789 ft.; **genre:** Stunt
pc: Surya Film Co., Bangalore **d:** Haribhai Desai
lp: Ganpat Bakre, Laxmi, Dhrupad Bhatt

Soneri Khanjar
aka **Kindred of the Dust**
11596 ft.; **genre:** Stunt
pc: Suresh Film Co. Ltd. **d:** Harshadrai Mehta **c/st/sc:** Chimanlal Luhar
lp: Lobo, Navinchndra, Prabhashankar, Datar, Ata Mohamed, Fazlu, Mengle, Dorothy, Kamla, Ranjit Budhakar

Song of Life
pc: Karnatak Pictures Corpn., Bangalore **d:** G.P. Pawar
lp: Gubbi Veerana, G.P. Pawar, Champadevi (Amboo/Lalita Pawar)

Sorathi Baharvatio
aka **Outlaw of Sorath**
9980 ft.; **genre:** Costume
pc: Ranjit Film Co. **d:** Nanubhai Vakil **c:** Jamnadas Subedar
lp: Putli, Inamdar, Thatte

Subrahmanyam
7825 ft.; **genre:** Mythological
pc: Aryan Film Co., Poona **d/st/sc:** N.D. Sarpotdar **c:** M.D. Wadadekar
lp: Bhaurao Datar, Jadhavrao, Amboo

Surya Prabha
8925 ft.; **genre:** Costume
pc: Surya Film Co., Bangalore **d:** Keshavlal Joshi **st:** Nanubhai R. Desai
lp: Zebu, Dhrupad Bhat, K. Rangarao

Suvarnamala
8525 ft.; **genre:** Costume
pc: Krishna Film Co. **d:** Mohanlal Shah **c:** Haribhai Patel **st:** Giraja Shankar Joshi **sc:** Natwar Shyam
lp: Miss Sirdar, Miss Vasanti, Vishnu

Talwar ka Pani
aka **Ace of Sword**
10525 ft.; **genre:** Costume
pc: Suresh Film Co. Ltd. **d:** Harshadrai Mehta **c/st/sc:** Chimanlal Luhar
lp: Janibabu, Mumtaz, Nizam, Ata Mohamed

Tati Talwar
aka **Glittering Sword**

12525 ft.; **genre:** Costume
pc: Krishna Film Co. **d:** Kanjibhai Rathod **c:** Haribhai Patel **st:** Champsi Udeshi **sc:** Natwar Shyam
lp: Gulab, Durga, Wamanrao Abhyankar, Vishnu, Hyder Shah, Nanasaheb Chapekar

Udaykal
aka **Thunder of the Hills**
10804 ft.; **genre:** Historical
pc: Prabhat Film Co., Kolhapur **d:** V. Shantaram/Keshavrao Dhaiber **c:** V. Damle/S. Fattelal
st/sc: Baburao Pendharkar
lp: V. Shantaram, Baburao Pendharkar, G.R. Mane, Kamladevi, Anant Apte, Ibrahim, Rahim Miyan, K. Dhaibar
Remarks: Original title *Swaraj Toran* was prohibited on 14/10/1930 on the grounds that it was objectionable in the existing political situation. Certified as *Udaykal.*

Valli Kalyanam
aka **Subrahamanyam**
7925 ft.; **genre:** Mythological
pc: United Pictures Syndicate, Poona/Shree Niwas Film Co. **d:** Gajanan V. Sane **c:** R.A. Kamble
lp: Gangubai, Wamanrao Kulkarni, Sundarrao Nadkarni

Vaman Avtaar
9000 ft.; **genre:** Mythological
pc: Madan Theatres Ltd.
lp: Patience Cooper, Indira Devi, Kusum Kumari

Vanaraj
aka **King of Jungles**
9980 ft.; **genre:** Costume
pc: Ranjit Film Co. **d:** Nanubhai Vakil **c:** G.G. Gogate
lp: Putli, Inamdar

Vasant Bengali
aka **Bengali Bomb**
10787 ft.; **genre:** Social
pc: Imperial Film Co. **d/st/sc:** Pessi Karani **c:** Rustom Irani
lp: Jal Merchant, Jilloo, Zaverbhai Kaiser, Ermeline (?)
Remarks: The original title of the film was *Bomb.*

Vasantsena
aka **Toy Cart**
9826 ft.; **genre:** Adaptation
pc: Indian Art Productions **d:** Mohan Bhavnani **c:** K.V. Machhwe **st:** based on Shudraka's *Mrichakatika*

lp: Enakshi Rama Rao, Nalini Tarkhad, Kamladevi Chattopadhyay, J.K. Nanda, Master Bhardwaj, Master Chattopadhyay, T.P. Kailasam, Shakuntala, K. Sitaram, Sriniwas, Namdar

Veer Bhushan
aka **Prince Indeed**
11725 ft.; **genre:** Costume
pc: Surya Film Co., Bangalore **d:** Keshavlal Joshi **c:** Vishnu Sawant
lp: Laxmi, Bachu, Suleman Master, Drupad Bhatt

Veer Rajput
aka **Rajput Chivalry**
6263 ft.; **genre:** Costume
pc: Orient Pictures Corpn. Ltd. **d:** Naval Gandhi **c:** Keki B. Homji **st:** Baldeo Singh
lp: Zubeida, Baldeo Singh, Jal Khambata, Lavji Lavangia, Rupmati

Veer Vairagi
8730 ft.; **genre:** Costume
pc: Venus Film Co.
lp: Jalejar, Homi Nagoria

Veer Vijaysingh
9525 ft.; **genre:** Costume
pc: Kohinoor United Artists **d/c:** V.M. Vyas **st/sc:** Vithaldas Panchotia
lp: Shakuntala, Leela, Nur Mohamed, Aziz

Veer na Ver
aka **Conqueror**
9985 ft.; **genre:** Costume
pc: Sagar Film Co. **d:** Moti B. Gidwani
lp: Master Vithal, Gohar Jr. Elizer, W.M. Khan

Ver Vasul
aka **Avenged**
genre: Stunt
pc: Vivekanand Pictures/Mahesh Film Co. **d:** M. Udwadia **st/sc:** Harihar Diwana
lp: Shahazadi, Malka, M. Udwadia

Vifreli Waghan
aka **Tigress**
10164 ft.; **genre:** Costume
pc: Ranjit Film Co. **d/st/sc:** Nanubhai Vakil **c:** Jamnadas Subedar
lp: Putli, Manilal

Vijay Kumar
8616 ft.; **genre:** Costume
pc: Imperial Film Co. **d:** H.M. Reddy **c:** Rustom Irani
lp: Ermeline, Jilloo, Prithviraj, Jamshetji, Mazhar Khan, Zaverbhai Kaiser

Vijeta
aka **Victor**
7708 ft.; **genre:** Stunt
pc: Satyesh Pictures **d:** Dada Gunjal **c:** Ambadas Kasture **st:** A.K. Pandit
lp: Dwarki, Janki, Jayshree, Boman Shroff

Vipranarayan
13750 ft.; **genre:** Mythological
pc: Peninsular Film Services, Madras **d:** Thomas E. Huffton
lp: K.T. Rukmini, T.S. Bhaskaran

Yasmina
aka **Love's Paradise**
8652 ft.; **genre:** Costume
pc: Krishna Film Co. **d:** Prafulla Ghosh **c:** Gordhanbhai Patel **st:** R.K. Rele
lp: Rampiari, Abdul Pahelwan, Hyder Shah, Arab Sandow

Zagmagti Jawani
aka **Sparkling Youth**
9923 ft.; **genre:** Costume
pc: Chandrika Film Co. **d/st/sc:** Nagendra Mazumdar **c:** V.V. Date
lp: Jairaj, Madhav Kale, Roshanara, Dikshit

Zalim Zulekha
10209 ft.; **genre:** Costume
pc: Surya Prakash Film Co. **d:** C.N. Thakore **st/sc:** Alvaro **c:** G.K. Karkhanis
lp: Fayma, Sunita, Yasmin

1931

Abhishek
11985 ft.; **genre:** Costume
pc: Graphics Arts, Calcutta **d:** Prafulla Roy **c:** Debi Ghosh/Panchanan Chaudhary/Gupi Ghosh **st/sc:** Sukumar Das Gupta
lp: Jiban Ganguly, Umashashi, Purnima Shome, Bhaskar Paul, Chani Dutta, Keshab, Belarani

Abla
aka **The Orphan Girl**
11465 ft.; **genre:** Social

pc: Punjab Film Co. **d:** Jaigopal Pillai **c:** M.K. Sandell
lp: Lalita Devi, Tilakraj Bhasin, Sunita

Afghan Abla
aka **Throne of Delhi**
13926 ft.; **genre:** Historical
pc: Kohinoor United Artists **d:** Narayan Devare **c:** K.G. Gokhale **st/sc:** Mohanlal G. Dave
lp: Jamuna, Fatma Jr., Ebrahim, Rajababu, Ganibabu, Usharani, Mijjan

Aflatoon Abla
aka **Pratigna Bandhan, Bondage**
10226 ft.; **genre:** Costume
pc: Kohinoor United Artists/G.S. Devare Production **d:** Gajanan S. Devare **c:** A.D. Devare
st/sc: J.B.H. Wadia
lp: Panna, Fatma Jr., Shakuntala, Bulbule, Bapurao Apte, Bhopatkar, Matin

Alak Kishori
aka **Sister**
10627 ft.; **genre:** Costume
pc: Saroj Film Co. **d:** Dhirubhai Desai **c:** Dwarka Khosla
lp: Yeqbal, Queenie, Madhav Kale, Janibabu, Prabhashankar, Ghory, Gangaram

Albelu Mumbai
aka **Bombay, the Mysterious**
11526 ft.; **genre:** Social
pc: Ranjit Film Co. **d/st/sc:** Nanubhai Vakil **c:** G.G. Gogate
lp: Shantakumari, E. Bilimoria, Ghory, Kamla

Alladin & the Wonderful Lamp
10000 ft.; **genre:** Costume
pc: Madan Theatres Ltd. **d/c:** Jal Ariya **st:** Aga Hashr Kashmiri
lp: Patience Cooper (Alladin), Ratansha Sinore, Miss Sylvia

Amirkhan
aka **Chivalrous Adventurer**
10325 ft.; **genre:** Costume
pc: Hindustan Cinema Film Co., Nasik **d:** Ganpat Shinde **c:** Anna Salunke
lp: Anasuya, Mathura, Khambete, Sakharam Jadhav

Aparadhi
11500 ft.; **genre:** Social
pc: Barua Film Unit, Calcutta **d/st/sc:** Debaki Kumar Bose **c:** Krishna Gopal
lp: Pramathesh Barua, Sabita Devi, Renubala, Radhikanand Mukherjee, Nirmal Banerjee,

Samar Ghosh, Shanti Gupta, Prabhavati, Arti Devi, Sushil Mazumdar

▲ Sabita Devi and P.C. Barua in **Aparadhi**

Apsara Uravashi
aka **Divine Mare**
8400 ft.; **genre:** Mythological
pc: British India Film Co.
lp: Keki Damania, Sunita

Asire Hirs
aka **Nemesis of Lust**
9756 ft.; **genre:** Costume
pc: Surya Film Co., Bangalore **d:** Sundarrao Nadkarni **st:** Nanubhai R. Desai **sc:** Haribhai Desai
lp: Baby Garbo, Jena, Jamadagni, Manohar Ghatwai, Zunzharrao Pawar, Jamu Patel, Baburao Gade

Atish-e-Ishq
aka **Gypsy Love**
9225 ft.; **genre:** Costume
pc: Saroj Film Co. **d:** Dhirubhai Desai **c:** Dwarka Khosla
lp: Jani Babu, Mumtaz, Prabhashankar, P.R. Joshi, K. Budhakar, Ranjit Budhakar, Chandrarao Kadam, Hamid

Awara Raqasa
aka **Bhataktun Joban, Wandering Dancer**
10756 ft.; **genre:** Stunt
pc: United Players Corporation, Lahore **d:** A.R. Kardar **c:** M.L. Dhody **st:** Akhtar
lp: Hiralal, Rukaiya Khatoun, Gul Hamid, M. Esmail

Azadi na Jung
aka **Bugles of War**
9441 ft.; **genre:** Costume
pc: Ranjit Film Co. **d/st/sc:** Nanubhai Vakil **c:** Pandurang S. Naik
lp: Putli, Baburao Sansare, Thatte, Bhagwat, Kamla

Badmash
aka **Rascal**
9876 ft.; **genre:** Social
pc: Navjawan Film Co. **d:** R.S.D. Chaudhary **c:** V.V. Date
lp: Jal Merchant, Yasmin, Dikshit, Jyotsna

Baghdad nu Bulbul
aka **Siren of Baghdad**

11450 ft.; **genre:** Costume
pc: Ranjit Film Co. **d/st/sc:** Nanubhai Vakil **c:** G.G. Gogate
lp: Madhuri, D. Bilimoria, Thatte, Baba Vyas, Bhagvat, Hiroji

Bahadur Beti
aka **She**
8557 ft.; **genre:** Costume
pc: Sharda Film Co. **d:** A.P. Kapur **c:** Ambalal Patel
lp: Zebu, Jairaj, Salu, Meherbanu

Bahare Jindgi
aka **Jazz of Life**
9626 ft.; **genre:** Social
pc: Rohini Film Co. **d:** Maneklal Joshi
lp: Bulbule, Panna

Baj Bahadur
aka **Hawk**
11456 ft.; **genre:** Stunt
pc: Surya Film Co., Bangalore **d:** Sundarrao Nadkarni **c:** Vishnu Sawant **st:** Nanubhai R. Desai, based on Victor Hugo's *The Hunchback of Notre-Dame*
lp: Laxmi, Bachu, Zunzharrao Pawar, Wamanrao Kulkarni, Jamu Patel, Holms, Ata Mohamed, Baburao Gade

Balika Badhu
aka **Baby Bride**
9000 ft.; **genre:** Social
pc: Asiatic Film Corporation, Calcutta **d/st/sc:** Pandit Tulsidutt Shaida **c:** Vernon Studio
lp: Pandit Tulsidutt Shaida, Miss Alley, Tarak Bagchi

Banke Sanvaria
aka **Prince Charming**
9846 ft.; **genre:** Costume
pc: Ranjit Film Co. **d:** Jayant Desai **c:** Jamnadas Subedar
lp: Shantakumari, E. Bilimoria, Ishwarlal, Ghory, Manilal

Bar Ke Pobar
aka **Bara ke Pobara, A Wager in Love**
11313 ft.; **genre:** Costume
pc: Imperial Film Co. **st/d:** H.M. Reddy **c:** Sorab Irani
lp: Prithviraj, Leelavati, Mubarak, Brown, Godrej, Elizer, Babu H.V.

Bewafa Ashak
aka **Discarded Love**

11236 ft.; **genre:** Costume
pc: Surya Prakash Film Co. **d:** Alvaro **c:** G.N. Thakore **st:** Mrs. Alvaro
lp: Lilavatee, Fayma, Master Bhagwan

Bhaktha Vatsala
aka **Durvasa Garva Bhangam**
10000 ft.; **genre:** Mythological
pc: Associated Films Ltd., Madras/National Theatres Ltd., Madras **d:** P.V. Rao
lp: Raja Sandow, Leela

Bhangela Sikkano Bhed
aka **Broken Coin**
8628 ft.; **genre:** Costume
pc: Asiatic Film Co. **d:** Saki **c:** Badridas
lp: Saki, Roshanara

Bharari the Bandit
8726 ft.; **genre:** Stunt
pc: Vishwesh Film Co. **d/sc:** Dada Gunjal **c:** Ambadas Kasture
lp: Ramkunvar, Muradali, Bachu, Ganpat, Sushila, Dada Bhosle

Bhut Rajya
aka **Devil Land**
7911 ft.; **genre:** Ghost Story
pc: Usha Pictures, Mangalore
d/c/st/sc/lp: K. Shivram Karanth

Bibaha Bibhrat
10000 ft.; **genre:** Social
pc: Madan Theatres Ltd.
d: Jyotish Banerjee **c:** Jatin Das **st/sc:** Amritlal Bose
lp: Patience Cooper, Naresh Mitra, Rani Sundari, Amritlal Bose (?)

Bijli
aka **Miss Lightning**
9425 ft.; **genre:** Costume
pc: Navjawan Film Co. **d:** Ramakant Gharekhan **c:** V.V. Date **st:** Maneklal Thakkar
lp: Indira, Jaswant Vaidya, Dikshit, Bhagwandas

Blood Feud
6935 ft.
pc: University Art Federation, Kolhapur **c:** V.B. Joshi (?)

Bulbul-e-Shiraz

10177 ft.; **genre:** Costume
pc: Bharat Pictures Corporation **d:** Homi Master **st/sc:** Mohanlal G. Dave

Chandbibi
aka **Queen of Ahmednagar**

10545 ft.; **genre:** Historical
pc: Aryan Film Co., Poona **d:** N.D. Sarpotdar **c:** Baburao Shirswade/Y.D. Sarpotdar
st: Munshi Aziz
lp: Heera Dharwadkar, Bhaurao Datar, Kamladevi, Jadhavrao, P.N. Varne

Chandramani
aka **Necklace**

10577 ft.; **genre:** Costume
pc: Sharda Film Co. **d/st/sc:** Mohanlal Shah **c:** Naval Bhat
lp: Madhav Kale, Nurjehan, Promoth Bose, Mona

Chandrasena

9853 ft.; **genre:** Mythological
pc: Prabhat Film Co., Kolhapur **d:** V. Shantaram **co-d/c:** Keshavrao Dhaiber
st/sc: Shivram Washikar
lp: Leela Chandragiri, Kamladevi, Jai, G.R. Mane, Ebrahim

Charitraheen

12000 ft.; **genre:** Social
pc: British Dominion Films Ltd., Calcutta **d:** Dhiren Ganguly **c:** P. Sanyal **st:** Saratchandra Chatterjee
lp: Hem Gupta, Nomita Bose, Kalidas, Sheeladevi, Mayadevi, Sudhir Bose

Chasar Meye
aka **Farmer's Daughter**

11900 ft.; **genre:** Social
pc: International Film Crafts, Calcutta **d:** Prafulla Roy **c:** Nitin Bose **st/sc:** Premankur Atorthy
lp: Jiban Ganguly, Renubala, Amar Mullick, Boken Chatterjee, Bhanu Banerjee, Chani Dutta, Premankur Atorthy, Manorama, Jyotsna Gupta, Premkumari Nehru, Kunjilal Sen

Chorekanta

11000 ft.; **genre:** Social
pc: International Film Crafts, Calcutta **d:** Charu Roy **c:** Nitin Bose **st:** Charu Bannerjee
lp: Shanti Gupta, Amar Mullick, Rajib Roy, Boken Chatterjee, Jyotsna Gupta, Manorama, Dilip Gupta

Chup
aka **Hush**
9999 ft.; **genre:** Comedy
pc: Unique Pictures Corporation, Calcutta **d:** Hiren Bose **c:** Subodh Ganguly **st:** Pramod Das Gupta
lp: Hiren Bose, Renubala, Nivanani Devi, Tarakbala, Satya Datta, Avabati, Nripen Mazumdar

Cinema Shrusti
aka **Filmland**
10667 ft.; **genre:** Social
pc: Kohinoor United Artists **d/st/sc:** Hiralal Doctor
lp: Shakuntala, Surekha, Chudekar, Jal Sardar

Dagabaz Dushman
aka **Betrayer**
9927 ft.
pc: East India Film Co. **d:** Kantilal Patel **c:** Chaturbhai Patel **st:** Amrutlal R. Trivedi
lp: Gulab, Yusuf, Surangi, Aziz

Dano Dushman
aka **Chivalry**
9526 ft.; **genre:** Costume
pc: Navjawan Film Co. **d:** Ramakant Gharekhan **c:** V.V. Date
lp: Mumtaz, Jaswant Vaidya, Bhagwandas, Dikshit

Dard-E-Jigar
aka **Song of Sorrow**
8728 ft.; **genre:** Costume
pc: Sharda Film Co. **d:** R.N.Vaidya **c:** Naval Bhat
lp: Khalil, Nurjehan, Sharifa

Dariai Devangana
aka **Sea Goddess**
9922 ft.; **genre:** Costume
pc: Saroj Film Co. **d:** Dhirubhai Desai **c:** Dwarka Khosla **st:** Giraja Shankar Joshi
lp: Zebu, Chandrarao Kadam, Padma, Prabhashankar, Ata Mohamed, Alexander, Pawar, Budhakar

Darkness To Light
7626 ft.; **genre:** Social
pc: Bapsey Sabavala Production **d:** Bapsey Sabavala
lp: Bapsey Sabavala, Manek Karaka, Roshan Vakil, Dr Jal Patel, Rati Talyarkhan

Debi Choudharani
12000 ft.
pc: Madan Theatres Ltd. **d:** Priyanath Ganguly **c:** Jatin Das **st:** Bankimchandra Chatterjee
lp: Naresh Mitra, Rani Sundari, Kartik Dey, Kartik Roy, Nani, Anupama

Deshbandhu
aka **Mohibe Watan**
10636 ft.
pc: National Pictures Corpn., Lahore **d:** G.R. Shethi
lp: Harold Lewis

Dharmi Daku
aka **Charitable Outlaw**
7981 ft.; **genre:** Stunt
pc: Fire Mount Pictures **d/st/sc:** Jitendra Mehta

Dhartikamp
aka **Thunder**
9726 ft.; **genre:** Stunt
pc: Mehta Luhar Productions **d:** Harshadrai Mehta **c/st/sc:** Chimanlal Luhar
lp: Navinchandra, Lobo, Bapurao Apte, Nizam, Sultan Alam, Bheem, Mohini, Manilal

Digvijay
9926 ft.; **genre:** Historical
pc: Sharda Film Co. **d:** Asooji **c:** Ambadas Pawar
lp: Gulab, Jairaj, Sitara, Rashid, Bijlee

Dilawar
10124 ft.; **genre:** Costume
pc: Sagar Film Co. **d:** R.G. Torney **c:** Adi Irani/Rustom Irani/Boman Irani/A.P. Karandikar
st: H.E. Khatib
lp: Master Vithal, Jilloo, Pramila (Laxmi), Mubarak, Khatoon, R.B. Jagtap, Gulam Kadar, Mehboob

Diler Daku
aka **Thunder Bolt**
8767 ft.; **genre:** Stunt
pc: Young United Players **d:** A.K. Pai **co-d:** B. Rumwalla **c/st/sc:** Homi Wadia
lp: Yashwant Dave, Fatma Jr., N. Jagtap, Laxmikant

Diler Jigar
aka **Gallant Hearts**
9632 ft.; **genre:** Stunt
pc: Agarwal Film Co., Poona **d/st/sc:** G.P. Pawar **c:** Shyam Sundar Agarwal
lp: Amboo, Hamir, Ezak Daniel, Gopinath

Diwani Duniya
aka **Underworld**
10528 ft.; **genre:** Social
pc: Kohinoor United Artists **d/st/sc:** Naval Gandhi **c:** Keki B. Homji
lp: Zubeida, Thomas, Rajababu

Diwano
aka **All for Love**
10671 ft.; **genre:** Costume
pc: Sharda Film Co. **d:** Nagendra Mazumdar **c:** Naval Bhat
lp: Madhav Kale, Nurjehan, Jairaj, Mehtab, Sushila, Mona

Dushmane Iman
genre: Costume
pc: Pratap Pictures **d:** Homi Master **c:** V.M. Vyas **st/sc:** Mohanlal G. Dave
lp: Jamuna, Ebrahim, Rajababu

Dushman ki Raat
aka **Night of Terror**
8576 ft.; **genre:** Social
pc: Maharashtra Film Co., Kolhapur **d:** Balasaheb Yadav **c:** D.G. Gune **st:** S.D. Bhute/D.S. Ambapkar
lp: Sushila Devi, Balasaheb Yadav, B. Nandrekar, Padmabai, Manajirao

Family Feuds
13500 ft.; **genre:** Social
pc: Madan Theatres Ltd.

Farari
aka **Outlaw**
7636 ft.; **genre:** Stunt
pc: University Art Federation, Kolhapur **c:** V.B. Joshi (?)
lp: Madhav Kale

Farebi Daku
aka **Mysterious Bandit**
9000 ft.; **genre:** Costume
pc: United Players Corporation, Lahore **d:** A.R. Kardar
lp: Gulam Quadir

Gayabe Garud
aka **Black Eagle**
9682 ft.; **genre:** Costume

pc: Mahavir Photoplays, Hyderabad DN **d:** Harilal M. Bhatt **c:** Gatubhai Vaidya
st: Munshi Abbas
lp: Miss Mani, Paro Nag, Keki Adajania

Geeta

11500 ft.; **genre:** Social
pc: Radha Film Co., Calcutta **d/st/sc:** Tincowri Chakraborty **c:** Noni Gopal Sanyal
lp: Lalita Devi, Lilavati, Tincowri Chakraborty, Jahar Ganguly, Kumar

Ghunghatwali

aka **Painted Angel**
11549 ft.; **genre:** Social
pc: Ranjit Film Co. **d:** Nandlal Jaswantlal **c:** Jamnadas Subedar **st:** Chaturbhuj Doshi **sc:** Mohanlal G. Dave
lp: Madhuri, Inamdar, Baburao Sansare, Ishwarlal, Thatte

Gohar Jan

8565 ft.; **genre:** Social
pc: Educational Pictures **d/st/sc:** Hiralal Doctor **c:** Bimal C. Mitra
lp: Raj Kumari

Golibar

aka **Avenging Angel**
10614 ft.; **genre:** Costume
pc: Sagar Film Co. **d:** B.P. Mishra **c:** Sohrab R. Irani **st:** Pessi Karani
lp: Prithviraj, Ermeline, Romila, Mazhar Khan

Gorakhnath

aka **Bhakti Prabhav**
9856 ft.; **genre:** Mythological
pc: British India Film Co. **d:** P.V. Chavan

Gowalan

aka **Gwalan, Milkmaid**
10758 ft.; **genre:** Social
pc: Ranjit Film Co. **d:** Nagendra Mazumdar **c:** G.G. Gogate **st:** Surendranath
lp: Sultana, E. Bilimoria, Manilal

Gulam

aka **Slave**
11030 ft.; **genre:** Costume
pc: Imperial Film Co. **d:** Moti B. Gidwani **c:** Rustom Irani/A.P. Karandikar **st/sc:** Vijay Shankar Bhat
lp: Master Vithal, Manorama, Zaverbhai Kaiser

Gulami Janjir
aka **Bondman**
10679 ft.; **genre:** Costume
pc: Krishna Film Co. **d:** Prafulla Ghosh **c:** Gordhanbhai Patel
lp: Durga, Hyder Shah, Rafiq Gazanavi, Manohar Ghatwai, Takle

Gulami nu Patan
aka **Fall of Slavery**
10627 ft.; **genre:** Costume
pc: Agarwal Film Co., Poona **d/c/sc:** Shyam Sundar Agarwal **st:** Baburao Thatte
lp: Vatsala, Ezak Daniel

Gupta Ratna
aka **Hidden Treasure**
14000 ft.; **genre:** Stunt
pc: Madan Theatres Ltd. **d:** B.S. Rajhans **c:** Mohamed Hanif **st:** Santosh Bannerjee
lp: Kalipada Das, Samar Ghosh, Santosh, B.S. Rajhans, Ramola Debi

Gurjoki Mar
aka **Sword of Allah**
7199 ft.; **genre:** Costume
pc: Surya Prakash Film Co. **d/c:** C.N. Thakore

Haq Insaf
aka **Compromise**
9625 ft.
pc: Kohinoor United Artists **st/sc:** Mohanlal G. Dave

Hanuman Janma
945 ft.; **genre:** Mythological
pc: Asian Film Co.

Hanuman Patal Parakram
7963 ft.; **genre:** Mythological
pc: Shri Kalika Film Co., Calcutta

Hari Maya
10961 ft.; **genre:** Mythological
pc: Mysore Film Co., Mysore **d:** Y.V. Rao
lp: Gubbi Veerana, B. Jayamma, H.L.N. Sinha

Hind Ke Tare
aka **Stars of the East**

7066 ft.
pc: Indian Pictures **d:** Aseer
lp: Niranjan, Maltidevi, L.V. Prasad

His Love Affair
8000 ft.
pc: Karnatak Pictures Corpn., Bangalore **d:** Raphael Algoet
lp: Gubbi Veerana, B. Jayamma, S. Naidu

Hoor-E-Misar
aka **Land of Pyramids**
8456 ft.; **genre:** Costume
pc: Sagar Film Co. **d:** Prafulla Ghosh
lp: Master Vithal, Zubeida, Mr Khurshid

Hoor-E-Roshan
aka **Roshan Ara**
11579 ft.; **genre:** Costume
pc: Ranjit Film Co. **d/st/sc:** Nanubhai Vakil **c:** G.G. Gogate
lp: Madhuri, E. Bilimoria, Ghory, Baba Vyas, Kesari, Ishwarlal

Hridaya Veena
aka **Zindagi, Dance of Life**
9955 ft.; **genre:** Social
pc: Sharda Film Co. **d:** A.P. Kapur **c:** Naval Bhat or A.J. Patel (?)
lp: Zebu, Jairaj, Ata Mohammed

Husna Pari
aka **Queen of Fairies**
8915 ft.; **genre:** Costume
pc: Sharda Film Co. **d:** A.P. Kapur
lp: Mehtab, Jairaj

Intekam
aka **Pitru Roon, Debts of Honour**
8764 ft.; **genre:** Costume
pc: Surya Film Co., Bangalore
lp: Jena, Wamanrao Kulkarni, Peters, Zunzharrao Pawar, Baburao Gade, Manohar Ghatwai

Iraq Ka Chor
aka **Thief of Iraq**
10574 ft.; **genre:** Costume

pc: National Film Co., Hyderabad **d/st/sc:** K.P. Bhave **c:** K.V. Machhwe
lp: Wilma Garbo (Baby Garbo), Master Prem Krishna, Vasantrao Pahelwan, Kotwal

Ishq No Anjam
aka **Kingdom of Love**
10737 ft.; **genre:** Costume
pc: Surya Film Co., Bangalore **d:** Baburao/Sundarrao Nadkarni **c:** D.B. Chavan, Vishnu Sawant, Mohammed **st:** Nanubhai R. Desai
lp: Laxmi, Ganpat Bakre, Zunzarrao Pawar, Baburao Gade

Jadu-E-Mohabat
aka **Magic of Love**
8221 ft.; **genre:** Costume
pc: Sharda Film Co. **d:** A.P. Kapur **c:** Ambadas Pawar
lp: Gulab, Nandram, Salu, Sankatha, Promoth Bose, Balabhai, Miss Nagamma, B. Khan

Jai Vithal
aka **Sant Tukaram**
9956 ft.; **genre:** Devotional
pc: Hind Vijay Film Co.

Jail Ke Parinde
aka **Gaol Birds**
6000 ft.; **genre:** Social
pc: Hindustan Cinema Film Co., Nasik **d:** Munshi Abbas

Jamai Babu
3000 ft.; **genre:** Comedy
pc: Hira Film Co., Calcutta **d/st/sc:** Kalipada Das **c:** Barodekar
lp: Kalipada Das, Sivapada Bhowmick, Parvat Kumar, Radharani, Amulya Bandopadhyay, Rajen Borooah, Sadhnadevi

Jamaika The Fool
1945 ft.; **genre:** Comedy
pc: Poona Comedy Film Corporation, Poona
Remarks: This film is possibly the same film as *Buddu Ki Akkal* that is in the collection of NFAI.

Janma Haq
aka **Birth Right**
8626 ft.; **genre:** Historical
pc: Navjawan Film Co. **d:** P.Y. Altekar **c:** V.V. Date
lp: Roza Hate, Jaswant Vaidya

Jiban Prabhat
aka **Dawn of Life**
10000 ft.; **genre:** Social
pc: Bengal Movie & Talkie Film Ltd., Calcutta **d/st/sc:** Santosh K. Hazara **c:** D.D. Dabke
lp: Dolly Dutta, Kanti Banerjee, Saty Mukherjee, Shanti Gupta, Sushil Mazumdar

Jindagi no Jugar
aka **Gamble of Life**
10852 ft.; **genre:** Social
pc: Surya Film Co., Bangalore **d:** Baburao/Sundarrao Nadkarni
c: D.B. Chavan/ Mohammed/ Vishnu Sawant **st:** Nanubhai R. Desai
lp: Laxmi, Jena, Ganpat Bakre, Wamanrao Kulkarni

Julumgar
aka **Tyrant**
7626 ft.; **genre:** Costume
pc: Mahesh Film Co.
lp: Shahzadi, Malka, M. Udwadia, Khote

Jung-E-Daulat
aka **Lust for Gold**
9986 ft.; **genre:** Costume
pc: Sharda Film Co. **d/st/sc:** A.P. Kapur **c:** Ambalal Patel
lp: Nandram, Mehtab, Nurjehan, Promoth Bose, B. Khan, Narsi, Devsingh

Jungle ke Jawan
aka **Hero of the Wilds**
10862 ft.; **genre:** Costume
pc: National Film Co., Hyderabad **d/st/sc:** Chunilal H. Parekh **c:** K.V. Machhwe
lp: Shankar, Geeta Sundari, Krishna

Kalo Wagh
aka **Black Tiger**
9826 ft.; **genre:** Costume
pc: Mehta Luhar Productions **d:** Harshadrai Mehta c/**sc:** Chimanlal Luhar **st:** Jayant Shyam
lp: Navinchandra, Lobo, Chandrika, Bapurao Apte, Balabhai, Nizam, Kumar Bhagwandas

Kamar-Ul-Zaman
11495 ft.; **genre:** Costume
pc: Imperial Film Co. **d:** Shah G. Agha **c:** A.P. Karandikar
lp: Manorama, Tara, Hansraj, Pramila (Laxmi), Jamshetji, Mazahar Khan, W.M. Khan, Rustam Poonawala

Kanak Kesari
aka **The Lion Hearted**
10892 ft.; **genre:** Costume
pc: Saroj Film Co. **d:** Dhirubhai Desai **c:** G.K. Mehta
lp: Mumtaz, Madhav Kale, Prabhashankar

Karmano Kaher
aka **Toll of Destiny**
10525 ft.; **genre:** Social
pc: Orient Pictures Corpn. Ltd. **d/st/sc:** Pessi Karani **c:** Keki B. Homji
lp: Zubeida, Sultana, Waman Talpade, Jal Khambata, Lavji Lavangia, Master Mac Mody

Karmavir
aka **True Warrior**
9754 ft.; **genre:** Costume
pc: Kohinoor United Artists/Shree Jagdish Film Co.

Kashmir Nu Gulab
aka **Rose of Kashmir**
10626 ft.; **genre:** Social
pc: Young India Pictures **d:** Nagendra Mazumdar **c:** Dwarka Khosla/ V.V. Date/ D.R. Barodekar
lp: Seeta Devi, Madhuri, Tarakumar Bhaduri, Ramesh Niranjan, Indulal Yagnik, Ghory, Madhav Kale, Jairaj, Yeqbal

Kasoti
aka **Supreme Test**
9925 ft.; **genre:** Costume
pc: Surya Film Co., Bangalore
lp: Jena, Bachu, Wamanrao Kulkarni, Baburao Gade, Jamu Patel

Katil Inteqam
aka **Dreadful Revenge**
8855 ft.; **genre:** Stunt
pc: Asian Film Co., Indore **d:** V.H. Palnitkar **c:** M.H. Palnitkar
lp: Shakuntala, H. Benjamin, Nirasha, Ramoo Solanki

Katil Katari
aka **Knife**
10490 ft.; **genre:** Costume
pc: Ranjit Film Co. **d:** Jayant Desai **c:** Jamnadas Subedar **st/sc:** Niranjan Pal
lp: Shantakumari, Inamdar, Thatte, Ishwarlal, Manilal

Katto Dushman
aka **Enemy**
9856 ft.; **genre:** Costume
pc: Sharda Film Co. **d:** Mohanlal Shah **c:** Naval Bhat
lp: Zebu, Jairaj, Ata Mohammed, Ghanshyam, Hanumant Rao

Keranir Mas Kabar
aka **Monthly Budget of a Clerk**
genre: Social short
pc: Madan Theatres Ltd. **d:** Jyotish Banerjee **c:** Jatin Das
lp: Shanti Gupta

Khabardar
aka **Terror**
8953 ft.; **genre:** Costume
pc: Vishwesh Film Co. **d/sc:** Dada Gunjal **c/st:** Ambadas Kasture
lp: Bachu, Muradali, Ganpat, Ramkunvar

Khuda ki Shan
aka **Punya Prabhav, Wrath**
10540 ft.; **genre:** Social
pc: Imperial Film Co. **d/st/sc:** R.S.D. Chaudhary **c:** Adi Irani
lp: Sulochana, R.B. Jagtap, Sushila, Makanda, Salvi, Raghunath, Elizer, Miss Jones
Remarks: The film faced censorship problems because of a character's resemblance to Gandhiji.

Khune Jigar
aka **Within the Law**
9625 ft.; **genre:** Costume
pc: Navjawan Film Co. **d:** Ramakant Gharekhan
lp: Nirmala, Dikshit, Gidwani

Khuni Katar
aka **Sunehri Khanjar, Golden Dagger**
10375 ft.; **genre:** Stunt
pc: United Players Corporation, Lahore
d: A.R. Kardar
lp: Gulzar, Gul Hamid, Nazeer, A.R. Kardar

Kismet
8726 ft.; **genre:** Costume
pc: Maharashtra Film Co., Kolhapur

▲ Das and Sunita Khan in **Kismet**

d: Baburao Patel **c:** D.G. Gune
lp: Sunitadevi, B. Nandrekar, I.T. Nimbalkar, Vasantkumar Das, Sushila Devi, Varde

Kismet ke Herephere
aka **Life After Death**
genre: Comedy
pc: Oriental Players, Lahore **d/c/st/sc:** Roshanlal Shorey
lp: Haider Shah, Kukum Singh, Maqbul, Taj, Zohra, Miss Sirdar, Kamila, John, M. Buksh, B.M. Mehta, Harold Lewis (?)

Kurbani
aka **Martyr**
9629 ft.; **genre:** Costume
pc: Surya Film Co., Bangalore **d:** Baburao/Sundarrao Nadkarni **st:** Nanubhai R. Desai **sc:** Haribhai Desai
lp: Wilma Garbo, Jena, Rozline Garbo, Ganpat Bakre, Wamanrao Kulkarni, Jamu Patel, Jamadagni, Baburao Gade

Kunwari Kanya
aka **Kidnapped Bride**
9105 ft.; **genre:** Costume
pc: Mahavir Photoplays, Hyderabad DN **d:** Latim Mohan Banerjee **c:** Gatubhai Vaidya
lp: Shankar, Miss Mani
Remarks: Earlier version titled *Her Last Dance/Nash Ka Naach* was denied a censorship certificate on 16/12/1930 on the grounds that it was `sordid and revolting'.

Lal Panjo
aka **Fighting Blood**
9835 ft.; **genre:** Stunt
pc: Saroj Film Co. **d:** Dhirubhai Desai **c:** Dwarka Khosla **st:** Nanubhai Desai
lp: Zebu, Chandrarao Kadam, Prabhashankar, Ata Mohamed, K. Budhkar

Last Kiss
11000 ft.; **genre:** Social
pc: East Bengal Cinematograph Society **d:** A.P. Gupta **c:** Azad
lp: Salin Roy, Tuntun, Lalita, Ajamal

Leila
aka **The Star of Mingrelia**
19460 ft.; **genre:** Costume serial in 2 parts
pc: General Pictures Corporation, Madras **d:** R.S. Prakash **c:** Jiten Bannerjee
st: G.W. Reynolds
lp: J. Susheela Devi, Vilochana, M.V. Raju, A. Gafoor Khan

Lost Child
pc: Chitra Art Productions, Nagercoil

The Lover in The Tub
genre: Comedy short
pc: Asiatic Film Co.

Lutaru
aka **Lutera, Dacoit**
10252 ft.; **genre:** Social
pc: Kohinoor United Artists/Saroj Film Co. **d/c:** K.G. Gokhale: **co-d/sc:** Dhirubhai Desai
st: Joshela
lp: Panna, Bulbule, Shakuntala, Rajababu, Dabir, Matin, Jijibhai, Fatma Jr.

Madam Techku
875 ft.; **genre:** Comedy
pc: Patel Bros. **st/sc:** Pijam

Mahasagar nu Moti
aka **Pearl**
10938 ft.; **genre:** Costume
pc: Sharda Film Co. **d:** Mohanlal Shah **c:** Naval Bhat
lp: Zebu, Jairaj, Ata Mohammed, Narsinha, Rashid, Miss Meherbanoo

Maidane Jung
aka **Battle**
9525 ft.; **genre:** Costume
pc: East India Film Co. **d:** Appu A. Mehta **c:** Chaturbhai Patel **st:** H. Joshi
lp: Tara, Surangi, Babi, Aziz, Jehangir, Nizam, Gulab (guest artist)

Marner Parey
aka **After the Death**
8000 ft.
pc: British Dominion Films Ltd., Calcutta **d/st/sc:** A.K. Roy **c:** P. Sanyal
lp: Sabita Devi, Dhiren Ganguly, Radharani, Hem Gupta, Mihirlal, Kalidas

Marthanda Varma
aka **Marthandavarman**
11905 ft.; **genre:** Costume
pc: Shri Rajeshwari Films, Nagercoil **d/sc:** P.V. Rao **c:** P.E. Naik, **st:** based on a novel by C.V. Raman Pillai
lp: Jaidev, A.V.P. Menon, V. Naick, V.C. Kutty, S.V. Nath, Miss Devaki, Miss Padmini, Sundaram Aiyer
Remarks: The film was never released due to a copyright dispute with the publishers of the novel.

▲ A title card from **Marthanda Varma**

MASTANA MEHBOOB
aka **Wild Rose**
8633 ft.; **genre:** Stunt
pc: Krishna Film Co. **d:** Prafulla Ghosh **c:** Gordhanbhai Patel **st:** R.M. Shukla
lp: Miss Sardar, Rafiq Gaznavi, Hyder Shah, Manohar Ghatwai, Durga, Noor Mohamed, Fakir Mohamed

MAYA MADHUSUDAN
8635 ft.; **genre:** Mythological
pc: General Pictures Corporation, Madras **d:** D. Sheshaiah **c:** Jiten Bannerjee
lp: T.S. Mani

MERI MA
aka **Pathani Panjo, My Mother**
8702 ft.; **genre:** Social
pc: National Film Co., Hyderabad **d/st/sc:** K.P. Bhave **c:** K.V. Machhwe
lp: Wilma Garbo, Krishna, Vasantrao Pahelwan

MERI MASHOOK
aka **Divine Girl, Divine Lady**
11643 ft.; **genre:** Costume

pc: Krishna Film Co. **d:** Prafulla Ghosh **c:** Gordhanbhai Patel **st:** Natwar Shyam
lp: Miss Sardar, Hyder Shah, Durga, Madhukar Gupte, Gulam Hussen

Mithi Churi
aka **Eye for an Eye**
10351 ft.; **genre:** Costume
pc: Sagar Film Co. **d:** Madanrai Vakil **c:** Boman Irani **st:** Jitendra Mehta
lp: Zubeida, Sankatha, Salvi, Sakhu, Romila, Mr Khurshid, Vamanrao, Yakub, Gulam Kadar

Mohabat ki Putli
aka **Touch of Love**
9446 ft.; **genre:** Costume
pc: Hindustan Cinema Film Co., Nasik **d:** Ganpat Shinde **c:** Anna Salunke
lp: Kishori Pathak, Shelar

Mojili Mashuk
aka **Desert Damsel**
11311 ft.; **genre:** Costume
pc: Ranjit Film Co. **d:** Nanubhai Vakil **c:** G.G. Gogate
lp: Santakumari, D. Bilimoria, Thatte, Ishwarlal

Mukti Sangram
aka **Vagabond Lover**
11252 ft.; **genre:** Costume
pc: Saroj Film Co. **d/st/sc:** Jayant Desai **c:** Dwarka Khosla
lp: Madhav Kale, Mumtaz, Ghory, Prabhashankar, Husnara, Arab Sandow, Durga

Nadira
5626 ft.; **genre:** Social
pc: Orient Pictures Corpn. Ltd. **d:** Naval Gandhi
lp: Zubeida, Waman Talpade

Nakoga Bai Lagna
aka **Goodbye Marriage**
8956 ft.; **genre:** Social
pc: Aryan Film Co., Poona **d/st/sc:** N.D. Sarpotdar **c:** Y.D. Sarpotdar
lp: Bhaurao Datar, Amboo, Yamuna

Namak Haram Kon
aka **A Bid for the Throne**
10077 ft.; **genre:** Costume
pc: Imperial Film Co. **d:** Madanrai Vakil **c:** Adi Irani **sc:** Zaverbhai Kaiser
lp: Prithviraj, Leelavati, Jilloo, Ermeline, Mubarak, Jagdish Sethi, Zaverbhai Kaiser, Chapla

Nand ke Lala
7816 ft.; **genre:** Mythological
pc: Asiatic Film Co.

Nand Kishore
aka **Krishna Janma**
8775 ft.; **genre:** Mythological
pc: Hind Vijay Film Co.

Nara Narayan
7857 ft.; **genre:** Mythological
pc: General Pictures Corporation, Madras **d:** A. Narayan **c:** Jiten Bannerjee
lp: Vilochana, Tara, J. Susheela Devi, D. Walis

Nari Jaat
aka **Oh Thou Woman**
9745 ft.; **genre:** Costume
pc: Surya Film Co., Bangalore **d/sc:** Haribhai Desai **c:** D.B. Chavan
lp: Ganpat Bakre, Wilma Garbo, Rozline Garbo, Wamanrao Kulkarni, Baburao Gade, Jammu Patel

Nasib ni Balihari
aka **Troubles Never Come Alone**
7406 ft.; **genre:** Social
pc: Punjab Film Co. **d/st/sc:** Niranjan Pal
lp: Seeta Devi, Derrik Rey

Nidrit Bhagwan
aka **Sleeping God**
11975 ft.; **genre:** Social
pc: Indian Film Producing Co., Calcutta **c:** D.D. Dabke **st:** P. Bhattacharya
lp: Bina Dutt

Niradhar Nira
aka **Deity in Distress**
11626 ft.; **genre:** Costume
pc: Mahavir Photoplays, Hyderabad DN **d/st/sc:** Chunilal H. Parekh **c:** Gatubhai Vaidya

Noor-e-Alam
aka **Queen of Love**
12200 ft.; **genre:** Costume
pc: Ranjit Film Co. **d:** Nanubhai Vakil **c:** Pandurang S. Naik **st:** Chaturbhuj Doshi
lp: Sulochana, D. Bilimoria, Thatte, Baburao Sansare (S. Baburao), Baba Vyas, Ghory, Shankar, Prabha, Shantaram Pednekar

Noor-E-Ishq
aka **Light of Love**
10536 ft.; **genre:** Costume
pc: Navjawan Film Co. **d:** Maneklal Thakkar **c:** V.V. Date
lp: Nirmala, Roza Hate, Jaswant Vaidya, Mantri, Khan

Pahadi Noor
aka **Rose of Baluchistan**
10391 ft.; **genre:** Costume
pc: Sharda Film Co. **d:** Arya

Pandav Agnadavasam
aka **Pandav Agnyathavas**
8800 ft.; **genre:** Mythological
pc: General Pictures Corporation, Madras **d:** Y.V. Rao
lp: Tara, T.S. Mani

Pardeshia
aka **Gypsy**
7950 ft.; **genre:** Costume
pc: Indian Kinema Arts, Calcutta **d/st/sc:** Niranjan Pal **c:** Bibhuti Das
lp: Neeta Devi, Binapani, Kalidas Das, Mani Ghosh, Hariram Das, Mihirlal

Pardeshi ni Preet
aka **Warrior from the Wild**
7961 ft.; **genre:** Costume
pc: Sharda Film Co. **d:** Nagendra Mazumdar
lp: Madhuri, Jairaj, Thomas, Miss Vedi

Pavalakkodi
aka **Praval Padmini , Coral Queen**
7926 ft.; **genre:** Costume
pc: General Pictures Corporation, Madras **d:** R.S. Prakash
lp: Vilochana, T.S. Mani, Tara, S.D. Subbulaxmi (?)

Pavitra Pyar
aka **Divine Love**
pc: Shree Vithal Films **d:** Vithaldas Panchotia
lp: Rajkumari, Vithaldas Panchotia, P.R. Joshi

Poladi Farman
aka **Fiats of Steel**
10877 ft.; **genre:** Costume

pc: Surya Film Co., Bangalore **d:** Baburao **c:** Vishnu Sawant **st:** Nanubhai R. Desai
lp: Jena, Bachu, Wamanrao Kulkarni, Baburao Gade

Poladi Pahelwan
aka **Iron Man**
10626 ft.; **genre:** Costume
pc: Paramount Film Co. **d/st/sc:** Jayant Desai **c:** Chaturbhai Patel
lp: Chandrarao Kadam, Nirmala, Salvi, Vijaya, Sultan Alam, Ali Bahadur, Harishchandrarao Kadam

Prem Masta
aka **Heart Thief**
10877 ft.; **genre:** Costume
pc: Sharda Film Co. **d:** R.N.Vaidya
lp: Khalil, Mohini

Prem Vijay
aka **Triumphant Love**
9362 ft.; **genre:** Costume
pc: Orient Pictures Corpn. Ltd. **d:** Naval Gandhi
lp: Panna, Ebrahim, Rajababu, Fatma Jr.

Premi Jogan
aka **Drums of Love**
13477 ft.; **genre:** Costume
pc: Ranjit Film Co. **d:** Nandlal Jaswantlal **c:** Pandurang S. Naik **st/sc:** Mohanlal G. Dave
lp: Shantakumari, D. Bilimoria, Putli, Ishwarlal, Thatte

Premi Pankhide
aka **Love Birds**
11776 ft.; **genre:** Costume
pc: Ranjit Film Co. **d:** Nagendra Mazumdar **c:** Pandurang S. Naik **st/sc:** Maneklal Thakkar
lp: Madhuri, Inamdar, Baburao Sansare, Thatte

Prithviraj
10239 ft.; **genre:** Historical
pc: Sharda Film Co. **d:** R.N.Vaidya **c:** Ambadas Pawar **st:** Prabhulal Dwivedi
lp: Nandram, Mehtab, Nurjehan, Salu, Promoth Bose, Balabhai, Baburao Sankatha Prasad

Priyatama
aka **Redemption**
10626 ft.; **genre:** Costume
pc: Mehta Luhar Productions **d:** Harshadrai Mehta **c/st/sc:** Chimanlal Luhar
lp: Navinchandra, Lobo, Chandrika, Bapurao Apte, Sultan Alam, Mohini, Balabhai

Pujari

9600 ft.; **genre:** Social
pc: Aurora Film Co., Calcutta **d/st/sc:** Niranjan Pal **c:** Dhiren Dey
lp: Moni Ghosh, Bhaskar Pal, Bimladevi, Moni Burma

Raj Bhakt

aka **King's Disciple, Peace Maker**
9976 ft.; **genre:** Costume
pc: Mehta Luhar Productions **d:** Harshadrai Mehta **c/sc:** Chimanlal Luhar **st:** Jayant Shyam
lp: Navinchandra, Lobo, Mohini, Kumudini, Bapurao Apte, Sultan Alam, Manilal

Raj Tilak

aka **Jay Swadesh**
10168 ft.; **genre:** Costume
pc: Imperial Film Co. **d:** Madanrai Vakil **c:** A.P. Karandikar **st:** B. Phatak
lp: Ermeline, Mazhar Khan, Rustom Irani, Elizer, Gohar Jr., Jaydevi, Mehboob, Zaverbhai Kaiser, Miss Shakuntala

Rajnandini

aka **Princess**
9226 ft.; **genre:** Costume
pc: Aryan Film Co., Poona **d:** Dinkar Bidkar **c:** M.D. Wadadekar
lp: Heera Dharwadkar, Bhaurao Datar, P.N. Varne

Rama Janma

1983 ft.; **genre:** Mythological
pc: Asian Film Co.

Ran Haak

aka **His Highness**
10726 ft.; **genre:** Costume
pc: Asiatic Film Co. **d/c:** Saki **st:** Mansingh Salunke
lp: Roshanara, Meherbanu, Sayani, Boman Shroff

Rani Rupmati

aka **Baaz Bahadur, Love Immortal**
9876 ft.; **genre:** Historical
pc: Maharashtra Film Co., Kolhapur **d/st/sc:** Bhalji Pendharkar **c:** R.A. Kamble
lp: Sulochana, Hirasingh Choudhary

Raosaheb

aka **Battalion of the Blunder**
11742 ft.; **genre:** Social

pc: Kohinoor United Artists **d:** Homi Master **c:** V.M. Vyas **st/sc:** Bhailal Upadhayaya
lp: Padma, Bhopatkar, Leela, Malwankar, Pawar

Rathod Kumari
9962 ft.; **genre:** Stunt
pc: Asian Film Co., Indore **d/st/sc:** Bhende **c:** M.H. Palnitkar/M.P. Joshi
lp: Nirasha, H. Benjamin, Indumati, Zohra

Romantic Lovers
2000 ft.; **genre:** Social
pc: Angora Films, Calcutta **d:** Charu Ghosh **c:** Sachindas
lp: A. Husaini, Bina

Ronak Mahal
11316 ft.; **genre:** Historical
pc: Mehta Luhar Productions **d:** Harshadrai Mehta **c/sc:** Chimanlal Luhar **st:** Ramanik A. Mehta
lp: Navinchandra, Lobo, Bapurao Apte, Chandrika, Balabhai, Bhim, Himatlal, Sultan Alam, Fazlu

Rose of Rajasthan
8750 ft.; **genre:** Costume
pc: General Pictures Corporation, Madras **d:** R.S. Prakash
lp: Vilochana, Tara, Devki, Y.V. Rao

Rupsundari
aka **Wages of Sin**
9725 ft.; **genre:** Costume
pc: Sharda Film Co./Mysore Pictures Corporation
lp: Zubeida, Sultana, Shahzadi, Aziz, Captain Kye, R.N.Vaidya

Sahadharmini
aka **Marriage and After**
9885 ft.; **genre:** Social
pc: Rupam Film Co., Calcutta **d:** Anupam Bannerjee **c:** Dhiren Dey **st:** Prabhavati Devi Saraswati
lp: Renubala, Binapani, Jibjyoti, Anima Devi, Rathin

Sainik ke Saitan
aka **Devil's Disciple**
8756 ft.; **genre:** Social
pc: Sun Art Film Studio

Sakhi Lutaro
8000 ft.

pc: Mahesh Film Co. **d:** Vithaldas Panchotia **lp:** Vithaldas Panchotia, M. Udwadia, Bijlee
Remarks: The film was refused a censor certificate.

Saroj Kumari
8500 ft.
pc: Mahavir Photoplays, Hyderabad DN
d: Harilal M. Bhatt
c: Gatubhai Vaidya
Remarks: The film was banned on the grounds that it was `sordid and revolting'.

Satharam
10423 ft.; **genre:** Costume
pc: Associated Films Ltd., Madras
d: Raja Sandow
lp: Leela

Sati Kausalya
aka **Birth of Ramchandra**
9911 ft.; **genre:** Mythological
pc: Associated Films Ltd., Madras **st/sc:** K. Subramanayam
lp: Leela

Sati Mandodari
9885 ft.; **genre:** Mythological
pc: British India Film Co. **d:** Jethalal Joshi **c:** G.K. Karkhanis

Sati Savitri
3960 ft.; **genre:** Mythological
pc: Asian Film Co., Indore **d:** V.H. Palnitkar
lp: H. Benjamin, Zohra

Satyawan Savitri
8865 ft.; **genre:** Mythological
pc: Aryan Film Co., Poona **d:** Dinkar Bidkar **c:** Baburao Shirswade
lp: Heera Dharwadkar, P.N. Varne, Bhaurao Datar, Baburao Athavale

Shadows Of The Dead
11840 ft.; **genre:** Costume
pc: United Pictures Corporation Ltd., Lucknow **d:** Debaki Kumar Bose
lp: Kumar

Shah-e-Jigar
aka **King of Hearts**

8906 ft.; **genre:** Costume
pc: Surya Prakash Film Co. **d:** C.N. Thakore

Shahi Farman
aka **Proclamation**
10324 ft.; **genre:** Costume
pc: Kohinoor United Artists **d:** Homi Master **c:** V.M. Vyas **st/sc:** Mohanlal G. Dave
lp: Panna, Jamuna, Ebrahim, Ganibabu, Chudekar

Shaitan Ka Shikar
aka **Daivache Bhaksh, Victim of Devil**
8952 ft.; **genre:** Costume
pc: Hindustan Cinema Film Co., Nasik **d:** Ganpat Shinde **c:** Anna Salunke
lp: Rajkumari, Kishori Pathak, Gotiram

Shaliwahan
9335 ft.; **genre:** Costume
pc: Sharda Film Co. **d:** A.P. Kapur **c:** Ambalal Patel **st:** Prabhulal Dwivedi
lp: Nandram, Mehtab, Sankatha, Budhkar, Nurjehan, Promoth Bose, B. Khan

Sher Dil
aka **Dashing Devil, Black Mask**
9876 ft.; **genre:** Stunt
pc: Surya Film Co., Bangalore **d:** Haribhai Desai **st:** Nanubhai R. Desai
lp: Baby Garbo, Jena, Jamadagni, Jamu Patel, Zunzharrao Pawar, Roshanali, Bacha

Shivaji No Janma
aka **Rajmata Jijabai, Birth of Shivaji, Shivaji Alive**
10626 ft.; **genre:** Historical
pc: United Pictures Syndicate, Poona **d:** Pandurang Talegiri **c:** R.A. Kamble
lp: Gangoobai, Jairampant Desai, Miss Sharda

Shri Krishna Maya
8527 ft.; **genre:** Mythological
pc: Aryan Film Co., Poona **d:** Gajanan V. Sane **c:** Y.D. Sarpotdar
lp: Durga Korgaonkar, Bhaurao Datar, Lalita Pawar, P.N. Varne, Jadhavrao

Shuri Sinhan
aka **Lioness**
10135 ft.; **genre:** Social
pc: Krishna Film Co. **d:** Prafulla Ghosh **c:** Gordhanbhai Patel **st:** Natwar Shyam
lp: Rampiary, Hyder Shah, Miss Sardar, Rafiq Gazanavi, Madhukar Gupte, Manohar Ghatwai

SHURO SAINIK

aka **Brave Warrior**

10805 ft.; **genre:** Costume

pc: Sharda Film Co. **d:** Mohanlal Shah **c:** Naval Bhat **st/sc:** Chimanlal Luhar

lp: Nandram, Mehtab, Promoth Bose, Prabhashankar

SIGNET RING

8000 ft.; **genre:** Mythological

pc: Associated Films Ltd., Madras **d:** Raja Sandow **st/sc:** K. Subramanayam

lp: Raja Sandow, Leela

SOLANKI SAMSHER

aka **Combat**

9786 ft.; **genre:** Stunt

pc: Mehta Luhar Productions **d:** Harshadrai Mehta **c/st/sc:** Chimanlal Luhar

lp: Navinchandra, Lobo, Bapurao Apte, Bhim, Chandrika, Sawak Shah, Sultan Alam, Fazlu

SORATHI YODDHO

aka **Valiant Warrior**

6835 ft.; **genre:** Costume

pc: Arvind Pictures **d:** Faram Shethna **c:** R.G. Kukde **st:** Nanubhai Bhat

lp: Anwari, Fatma Jr., Ali, Jal Sardar, Yusuf

SUI KA NAKA

aka **Dillagi, The Needle's Eye**

8692 ft.; **genre:** Social

pc: Niranjan Pal Productions **d/st/sc:** Niranjan Pal **c:** D.G. Gune

SWAMI

9100 ft.; **genre:** Social

pc: Films Of The East Ltd., Calcutta **d:** Charu Roy **c:** Debi Ghosh/Panchanan Chaudhary

st: Saratchandra Chatterjee

lp: Tincowry Chakraborty, Phani Burma, Binapani, Renubala, Hingalbala, Manorama, Amar Mukherjee, Ranendra Lahiri

TAJ KE TALWAR

aka **Jaw Breakers**

10852 ft.; **genre:** Costume

pc: Surya Film Co., Bangalore **d:** Baburao/Sundarrao Nadkarni **c:** D.B. Chavan/ Vishnu Sawant/ Mohammed **st/sc:** Nanubhai R. Desai

lp: Jena, Bachu, Jamu Patel, Zunzharrao Pawar, Baburao Gade

TAKAY KI NI HAY

aka **Money Makes What Not**

genre: Social short
pc: British Dominion Films Ltd., Calcutta **d:** Dhiren Ganguly **c:** P. Sanyal
lp: Sabita Devi, Dhiren Ganguli, Nimai Saha

Takhte Toofan
aka **The Rake**
9627 ft.; **genre:** Costume
pc: Kohinoor United Artists/Navjawan Film Co. **d:** Ramakant Gharekhan
lp: Mumtaz, Bulbule

Taranhar
aka **Pride of Hindustan**
10636 ft.; **genre:** Costume
pc: Associated Films Ltd., Madras **d:** Raja Sandow **c:** V.J. Bhave **st/sc:** K. Subramanayam
lp: Raja Sandow, Leela

Teere Katil
aka **Red Archer**
9629 ft.; **genre:** Costume
pc: Surya Film Co., Bangalore **d:** Sundarrao Nadkarni **c:** Mohamed **st:** Nanubhai R. Desai
lp: Jena, Bachu, Baburao Gade, Jamu Patel, Zunzharrao Pawar

Tirandaj
aka **Archer**
9590 ft.; **genre:** Costume
pc: Mehta Luhar Productions **d:** Harshadrai Mehta **c/st/sc:** Chimanlal Luhar
lp: Navinchandra, Lobo, Bapurao Apte, Mohini, Nizam, Bhim

Tofani Taruni
aka **Cyclone Girl**
9110 ft.; **genre:** Social
pc: Sagar Film Co. **d:** B.P. Mishra **c:** Boman Irani **st:** Wamanrao
lp: Ermeline, Jal Merchant, Yakub, Pramila (Laxmi)

Toofan
aka **Children of Storm**
10975 ft.; **genre:** Social
pc: Sagar Film Co. **d:** B.P. Mishra **c:** Boman Irani **st:** Chaturbhuj Doshi
lp: Prithviraj, Ermeline, Fali Merchant

Uthavgir
aka **Bhedi Khavis, Master Villain**

9788 ft.; **genre:** Costume
pc: New Kohinoor Film Co. **d/st/sc:** Behram Vasania **c:** S.N. Patankar
lp: Zebu, Aziz, Jal Sardar, Ata Mohamed, Leena, Merwan

Vanadevi
9869 ft.; **genre:** Costume
pc: Navjawan Film Co. **d:** Ramakant Gharekhan **c:** Bhanu **st/sc:** Surendranath
lp: Manorama, Jaswant Vaidya, Dikshit, Bhagwandas, Khote, Malti

Veer Bahadur
9785 ft.; **genre:** Costume
pc: Kohinoor United Artists/Shree Jagdish Film Co. **d/c:** V.M. Vyas **st:** Shaida
lp: Shakuntala, Ebrahim, Nur Mohamed, Fatma Jr., Gangaram, Dilawar

Ver Na Ansu
aka **Avenging Tears**
9115 ft.; **genre:** Costume
pc: Satyesh Pictures **d:** Faram Shethna **c:** R.G. Kukde **st:** A.K. Pandit **sc:** Dilshad
lp: Nirmala, Rusi Divecha, Kashinath, Ali Mohamed

Vichitra Ver
aka **Tocsin of Death**
10726 ft.; **genre:** Costume
pc: Surya Film Co., Bangalore
lp: Laxmi, Jena, Ganpat Bakre, Roshan Ali, Abbasi, Baburao Gade, Jamu Patel

Vijay Laxmi
aka **Royal Romance**
11566 ft.; **genre:** Stunt
pc: Ranjit Film Co. **d:** Jayant Desai **c:** Pandurang S. Naik
lp: Madhuri, E. Bilimoria, Thatte, Ghory, Kesari, Manilal

Vikral Varu
aka **Wild Wolf**
10623 ft.; **genre:** Costume
pc: Surya Film Co., Bangalore
lp: Baby Garbo, Jena, Wamanrao Kulkarni, Zunzharrao Pawar, Jamu Patel, Doss

Vilasi Atma
aka **Sinning Soul**
10751 ft.; **genre:** Social
pc: Ranjit Film Co. **d:** Jayant Desai **c:** Jamnadas Subedar
lp: Putli, E. Bilimoria

Virni Vibhuti
aka **Goodbye Kingship**
11168 ft.; **genre:** Costume
pc: Sharda Film Co. **d:** A.P. Kapur **c:** Ambalal Patel
lp: Nandram, Mehtab, Salu, Noorie, Sankatha, Promoth Bose

Vishwamitra
9867 ft.; **genre:** Mythological
pc: General Pictures Corporation, Madras **d:** D. Sheshaiah
lp: T.S. Mani, D. Walis, Vilochana, Devaki, Tara

Wafadary
aka **Fidelity**
9875 ft.; **genre:** Costume
pc: Surya Film Co., Bangalore
lp: Baby Garbo, Jena, Manohar Ghatwai, Wamanrao Kulkarni, Jamu Patel, Peters, Zunzharrao Pawar

Zulum
aka **Stolen Bride**
8101 ft.; **genre:** Costume
pc: Prabhat Film Co., Kolhapur **d/c:** Keshavrao Dhaiber **st/sc:** Bhalji Pendharkar
lp: Baburao Pendharkar, Kamladevi, Jai, Ganpat Shinde, Miss Vijya, Smt. Sharma, Miss Shrimatiji

1932

Ankhi Jal
9950 ft.; **genre:** Social
pc: Tarangini Films Syndicate, Calcutta **d:** Kalipada Das **c:** Sachindas
lp: Kalipada Das, Usha Rani, Jibandas, Debibala

Asiai Sitara
aka **Star of Asia**
9821 ft.; **genre:** Costume
pc: Surya Film Co., Bangalore **st:** Nanubhai R. Desai
lp: Baby Garbo, Bacha, Jena, Wamanrao Kulkarni, Jamu Patel, Doss, Jamadgani

Baghdad Ka Badmash
aka **Fighting Vagabond**
11250 ft.; **genre:** Stunt
pc: Ranjit Film Co. **d:** Nanubhai Vakil **c:** G.G. Gogate
lp: Padma, E. Bilimoria, Ghory

Bahurupi Bazar
aka **Vanity Fair**

10321 ft.; **genre:** Costume
pc: Sharda Film Co. **d/st/sc:** Nagendra Mazumdar **c:** Ambalal Patel
lp: Panna, Madhav Kale, Kamla, Kanta, Ghanshyam

Beggar Girl of Agra
9106 ft.; **genre:** Costume
pc: Bengal United Films Co., Calcutta
lp: Mumtaz Begum, Premila Roy, Maya Devi, B. Mitter, Master Karim

Bewafa Katil
aka **Tiger**
9826 ft.; **genre:** Stunt
pc: Standard Pictures **d:** Dada Gunjal
lp: Feroza, Master Bhagwan

Bhagya Laxmi
aka **Goddess of Fortune**
10500 ft.; **genre:** Social
pc: Indian Kinema Arts, Calcutta **d:** Kaliprasad Ghosh **c:** Bibhuti Das **st:** Saratchandra Ghosh
lp: Durgadas Banerjee, Pramathesh Barua, Sabita Devi, Uma, Khitish Roy Choudhary

Bharat Veer
aka **Knight Errant**
9821 ft.; **genre:** Stunt
pc: Mehta Luhar Productions **d:** Harshadrai Mehta **c/st/sc:** Chimanlal Luhar
lp: Yashwant Dave, Chandrika, Bapurao Apte, Lobo

Bhawani Talwar
aka **Sword of Victory**
7556 ft.; **genre:** Historical
pc: Aryan Film Co., Poona **d:** N.D. Sarpotdar **c:** Y.D. Sarpotdar
lp: Bhaurao Datar, Meera, Amboo

Bhedi Khanjar
aka **Three Daggers**
9543 ft.; **genre:** Stunt
pc: Vishwesh Film Co. **sc/d:** Dada Gunjal **c:** Ambadas Kasture **st:** Dilawar
lp: Gulnar, Gulzar, Bachu, Muradali, Ganpat Shinde

Bhedi Rajkumar
aka **Mysterious Prince**
9620 ft.; **genre:** Costume

pc: Sharda Film Co.
lp: Nandram, Madhav Kale, Nurjehan, Sushila

Burkhawala
aka **White Devil**
10551 ft.; **genre:** Stunt
pc: Royal Film Co. **d:** Shanti J. Dave **c:** V.B. Jagtap **st/sc:** Vijay Shankar Bhat
lp: Master Vithal, Nurjehan, Salvi, Gulbanu

Chalta Purja
aka **Passing Show**
10916 ft.; **genre:** Stunt
pc: Royal Film Co. **d:** Balwant Bhat **c:** V.B. Jagtap **st:** Vijay Bhat
lp: Madhuri, Navinchandra, Zaverbhai Kaiser, Rustom, Miss Mayuri

Chhota Chor
aka **Petit Brigand**
9875 ft.; **genre:** Costume
pc: Surya Film Co., Bangalore
lp: Jena, Bacha, Roshanali, Doss, Miss Sultana

Chor ke Vafadar
aka **In Shackles**
9765 ft.; **genre:** Costume
pc: Surya Film Co., Bangalore **d/st/sc:** Haribhai Desai **c:** Mohammed
lp: Jena, Bacha, Roshanali, Bashir, Das

College Girl
3000 ft.; **genre:** Social
pc: Pictorial Club, Calcutta **d:** G. Bannerjee **c:** P. Sandell
lp: Sheiladevi, Sushil Roy Chaudhary

Dagabaz Bhai
aka **Tainted Heart**
7733 ft.; **genre:** Costume
pc: Sharda Film Co. **d:** Asooji **c:** Lallubhai
lp: Yashwant Dave, Chandrika

Dardi
aka **Faithful Heart**
10000 ft.; **genre:** Social
pc: Niranjan Pal Productions **d/st/sc:** Niranjan Pal
lp: Derrick Rey, Aratidevi, Jiten Goswami

Dile Dilar
aka **Stunt King**
8685 ft.; **genre:** Stunt
pc: Surya Film Co., Bangalore **d:** Haribhai Desai **c:** Mohammed
lp: Baby Garbo, Jena, Bacha, Doss, Roshanali

Ekada
2000 ft.; **genre:** Social
pc: Barua Film Unit, Calcutta **d:** Sushil Mazumdar **st/sc:** Pramathesh Barua
lp: Sushil Mazumdar, Prabhavati, Bibhuti Chakravarty, Nirendranath Lahiri

Gir no Gamar
aka **Hill Man**
8803 ft.; **genre:** Costume
pc: Arvind Pictures **d:** Faram Shethna

Gourishankar
10975 ft.; **genre:** Mythological
pc: National Film Syndicate, Calcutta **d/st/sc:** Andymoore Roy **c:** Saroj Mitter
lp: Radhikanand Mukerjee, Dolly Gupta, Ayeshabai, Andymoore Roy, Gesto Pal

Gurjar Veer
10615 ft.; **genre:** Costume
pc: Mehta Luhar Productions/ Sharda Film Co. **d:** Dhirubhai Desai **c:** Chaturbhai Patel
st: Jayant Bhat
lp: Yashvant Dave, Chandrika, Bhim, Himatlal, Ghanshyam, Miss Dorothy

Hind Kesari
9864 ft.; **genre:** Costume
pc: Jayant Pictures **d:** Homi Master **c:** Gajendra Rajgor **st/sc:** Mohanlal G. Dave
lp: Padma, Inamdar, Sultan Alam

Hoor-e-Hind
10526 ft.; **genre:** Costume
pc: Mehta Luhar Productions **d:** Harshadrai Mehta **c/st/sc:** Chimanlal Luhar
lp: Navinchandra, Mira, Lobo, Bapurao Apte, Bhim, Himatlal, Nizamuddin

Jang-e-Jawani
9971 ft.; **genre:** Costume
pc: Navjawan Film Co. **d:** Maneklal Thakkar **c:** V.V. Date
lp: Nirmla, Roza Hate, Gidwani

Jawahir-e-Hind
aka **Modern Hero**

9825 ft.; **genre:** Costume
pc: Shree Ganesh Film Co., Ahmedabad **d:** Dhirubhai Desai **c:** G.K. Mehta
lp: Mumtaz, Inamdar, Ata Mohamed, Bilimoria

Jay Bajarang
10912 ft.; **genre:** Mythological
pc: Jayant Pictures **d:** Homi Master **c:** Gajendra Rajgor **st/sc:** Mohanlal G. Dave
lp: Padma, Inamdar, Vasantrao Pahelwan, Sultan Alam
Remarks: Censors objected to the original title *Vanar Sena*.

Kailas
aka **Land of Martyrs**
9726 ft.; **genre:** Stunt
pc: Kaiser Pictures **d/st/sc:** G.P. Pawar **c:** Baburao Shirswade
lp: Amboo, Ganpat Bakre, G.P. Pawar, Vijaya

Kalo Bhut
aka **Black Ghost**
10927 ft.; **genre:** Stunt
pc: Royal Film Co. **d:** Shanti J. Dave **c:** V.M. Vyas **st/sc:** Vijay Shankar Bhat
lp: Madhuri, Master Vithal, Salvi, Harischandrarao Kadam, Manjula

Kalo Swar
aka **Black Rider**
9726 ft.; **genre:** Stunt
pc: Mehta Luhar Productions **d:** Harshadrai Mehta **c/st/sc:** Chimanlal Luhar
lp: Navinchandra, Chandrika, Lobo, Bhim, Bapurao Apte, S. Baburao, Nizam

Khubsurat Khawasan
aka **Sweet Heart**
10745 ft.; **genre:** Comedy
pc: Sharda Film Co. **d/st/sc:** Nagendra Mazumdar **c:** Naval Bhat
lp: Nandram, Madhav Kale, Nurjehan, Ghanshyam, Nanalal, Master Hanumant Rao, Mona, Rukma

Khyber Falcon
8976 ft.; **genre:** Stunt
pc: Punjab Film Co. **d:** Modhu Bose **c:** Mahendra Malhotra **st:** Niranjan Pal

Kya Baat
aka **Hoop La**
8439 ft.; **genre:** Stunt
pc: Surya Film Co., Bangalore **d/st:** Haribhai Desai **c:** Mohammed
lp: Jena, Ganpat Bakre

Laheri Lutaro
aka **Gay Bandit**
9766 ft.; **genre:** Stunt
pc: Paramount Film Co. **d:** R.N.Vaidya **c:** G.K. Mehta
lp: Harischandra Rao, Padma, Sunita, Nirmala, Jal Sardar, Manohar Ghatwai, K. Budhakar, Ali Bahadur

Lal Swar
aka **Red Rider**
10729 ft.; **genre:** Stunt
pc: Ranjit Film Co. **d/st/sc:** Jayant Desai **c:** G.G. Gogate
lp: E. Bilimoria, Panna, Ishwarlal, Kesari, Thatte

Mahiari
aka **Divine Lovers**
10935 ft.; **genre:** Costume
pc: Jayant Pictures **d:** Homi Master **c:** Gajendra Rajgor **st/sc:** Mohanlal G. Dave
lp: Nurjehan, Inamdar, Vasantrao Pahelwan, Sultan Alam

Mallaraj
aka **Tiger of Rajputana**
10798 ft.; **genre:** Stunt
pc: Paramount Film Co. **d:** R.N.Vaidya **c:** Naval Bhat
lp: C.C. Shah, Nurjehan, Shiraz, Amina, Baba Miyan, Nazir, Master Hanmantrao, Meherbanu, Jamu Patel

Mastikhor Mashuk
aka **Sweet Angel**
9547 ft.; **genre:** Stunt
pc: Shiraz Productions **d/st/sc:** G.P. Pawar
lp: Amboo, Bulbule

Matrubhumi
aka **My Hero**
10676 ft.; **genre:** Costume
pc: Young India Pictures **d/st/sc:** Nagendra Mazumdar **c:** V.V. Date/ Ambalal Patel
lp: Madhuri, Jairaj, Gidwani, Dikshit, Gangu, Babubhai Gharekhan, Fali Cooper

Mohtaj Mashuk
aka **Belle of Baluchistan**
8926 ft.; **genre:** Costume
pc: Indore Picture Syndicate
lp: Shakuntala, H. Benjamin

Mrigjal
aka **Mirage**
8000 ft.; **genre:** Social
pc: Sharda Film Co. **d:** A.P. Kapur **c:** Ambalal Patel
lp: Nandram, Nurjehan, Promoth Bose, Mona

Nakhrali Nar
aka **Naughty Maid**
11250 ft.; **genre:** Costume
pc: Ranjit Film Co. **d:** Nanubhai Vakil
lp: Madhuri, E. Bilimoria

Naukadubi
genre: Social
pc: Madan Theatres Ltd. **d:** Naresh Mitra **c:** Jatin Das **st:** Rabindranath Tagore
lp: Naresh Mitra, Dhiraj Bhattacharya, Shishubala, Shanti Gupta, Kanak Narayan Bhup, Sunila, B.S. Rajhans, Kunjalal Chakraborty, Debbala, Girija Ganguli

Nishir Daak
aka **Phantom Call**
genre: Thriller
pc: Barua Film Unit, Calcutta **d:** Debaki Kumar Bose
lp: Nirmal Banerjee, Prabha, Sheela, Sushil Mazumdar

Poladi Jigar
aka **Dynamite**
9876 ft.; **genre:** Stunt
pc: Chandra Arts Production **d:** Behram Vasania **c:** K.G. Gokhale
lp: Chandrarao Kadam, Harischandra Rao, Bijlee, Ali Bahadur, Pawar

Prabhu na Chor
aka **Four Devils**
11725 ft.; **genre:** Costume
pc: Jayant Pictures **d:** Homi Master **c:** G.K. Mehta **st/sc:** Mohanlal G. Dave
lp: Inamdar, Nurjehan, Vasantrao Pahelwan, Sultan Alam, Bhagwandas, Hiroji, Sunita, Gulzar

Prem Sangam
aka **When Lovers Unite**
8989 ft.; **genre:** Social
pc: Anand Pictures, Kolhapur **d:** Baburao Painter
Remarks: Post-synchronised sound version in 1934.

Raj Laxmi
9764 ft.; **genre:** Costume

pc: Surya Film Co., Bangalore
lp: Baby Garbo, Bacha, Jena, Zunzharrao Pawar, Doss, Jamu Patel, Jamadagni, Roshanali

Rajadhiraj
aka **Omnipotent**
9916 ft.; **genre:** Costume
pc: Surya Film Co., Bangalore **d/st/sc:** Haribhai Desai **c:** Mohamed
lp: Baby Garbo, Jena, Zunzharrao Pawar, Jamdagni, Jamu Patel, Bacha, Roshanali, Doss, Manohar Ghatwai (?)

Ranadevta
aka **God of War**
11945 ft.; **genre:** Costume
pc: Jayant Pictures **d:** Homi Master **c:** D.D. Dabke **st/sc:** Mohanlal G. Dave
lp: Madhuri, Inamdar, Sultan Alam, Gulzar, Vasant, Vijay, Bhagwandas

Rangilo Rajput
aka **Village Warrior**
9525 ft.; **genre:** Costume
pc: Sharda Film Co. **d:** Nagendra Mazumdar **c:** Naval Bhat
lp: Nandram, Zebu, Budhkar

Sandigdha
aka **Her Suspicion**
11500 ft.; **genre:** Social
Radha Film Co., Calcutta **d:** Prafulla Roy **c:** D.D. Dabke/Debi Ghosh **st:** Sourindra Mohan Mukherjee
lp: Lalita Devi, Renubala, Jiban Ganguli, Manoranjan Bhattacharya, Bhanu Banerjee, Amar Mullick

Sati Anjani
aka **Hanuman Janma**
8975 ft.; **genre:** Mythological
pc: British India Film Co.

Shakti Puja
9985 ft.
pc: Chhaya Chitra Pratishthan, Calcutta **d:** Moulie Shastry **c:** Panchanan Chaudhary **st/sc:** Santosh Banerjee
lp: Sarashi, Usha Rani, Santosh, Dwarka, Kalidas, S. Ganguli

▲ Publicity for **Shakti Puja**

Shan-e-Hindustan
aka **India in Glory**
9945 ft.; **genre:** Costume
pc: Navyug Film Co., Indore
lp: Shakuntala, Jaimini, Kumar

Shri Krishna Janma
3560 ft.; **genre:** Mythological
pc: Indore Picture Syndicate, Indore

Sinha Garjna
aka **Lion Man**
9326 ft.; **genre:** Stunt
pc: Young United Players **d:** J.B.H. Wadia c/**st/sc:** Homi Wadia
lp: Boman Shroff, Padma, Sayani, Allawali, Adi Patel, Manchi Thuthi, Gulshanara, Manjula

Sinha Santan
aka **Lion's Cub**
10916 ft.; **genre:** Stunt
pc: Narayan Films Ltd., Ahmedabad/Shree Ganesh Film Co., Ahmedabad **d:** Dhirubhai Desai **c:** Naval Bhat **st:** Ahmedbhai Merchant
lp: Bulbule, Ata Mohamed, Sharda, Nalini, Manilal, Shiraz

Sipah Salar
aka **Captain**
8225 ft.; **genre:** Costume
pc: Ranjit Film Co. **d/st/sc:** Jayant Desai **c:** K.G. Gokhale
lp: Madhuri, E. Bilimoria, Ishwarlal, Ghory

Sneh Veena
aka **Song of My Heart**
10441 ft.; **genre:** Costume
pc: Sharda Film Co. **d:** Nagendra Mazumdar **c:** Ranjikant Pandya
lp: Nandram, Panna

Stree Shakti
aka **Bholi Begum, Super Sex**
9683 ft.; **genre:** Costume
pc: Surya Film Co., Bangalore **d/st:** Haribhai Desai **c:** Mohammed
lp: Baby Garbo, Jena, Ganpat Bakre, Roshanali, Doss, Jamadgni

Toofan Mail
8965 ft.; **genre:** Stunt

pc: Young United Players **d:** J.B.H. Wadia **st/sc/c:** Homi Wadia
lp: Padma, Yashwant Dave, Adi Patel, Manchi Thuthi, J.B.H. Wadia, Narayan Pai, Lalitchandra Arya, Homi Bhujwala, Ganpat, Paul, Edgar Slynn

Vanaraj Kesari
aka **Red Lion**
9899 ft.; **genre:** Stunt
pc: Mehta Luhar Productions **d:** Harshadrai Mehta **c/sc:** Chimanlal Luhar **st:** Jayant Shyam
lp: Navinchandra, Lobo, Bapurao Apte, Padma, Bhagwandas, Bhim, Vasant, Kumar Madhukar

Vishnu Leela
8412 ft.; **genre:** Mythological
pc: National Theatres Ltd., Madras **d:** R.S. Prakash
lp: Jamuna, K.T. Rukmini

1933

Abad Chor
aka **Phantom**
9855 ft.; **genre:** Stunt
pc: Ambika Film Co. **d:** Saki **c:** Badridas
lp: Ermeline, Inamdar, Sayani, K.G. Rao

Annapurna
pc: Bengal Movie Pictures, Calcutta **d:** Anu Mukerjee **c:** Dhiren Dey **st:** Satishchandra Chatterji
lp: Dhiraj Bhattacharya, Radharani, Usharani, Bankim Dutt, Anima Dutt

Azad Abla
aka **Daring Damsel**
9845 ft.; **genre:** Stunt
pc: Ambika Film Co. **d:** Saki **c:** Badridas **st/sc:** S.N. Bende
lp: Ermeline, Inamdar, Shamrao, Hiroji, Sayani, Manilal, Ustad Abdul Hamid

Baap Ka Bol
aka **Faithful Heart**
9857 ft.
pc: Bharatiya Film Co., Ahmedabad **d/st:** Gunjal
lp: Mumtaz, Bhagwandas, Vipin, Ata Mohamed

Badmash Ka Beta
aka **Leather Face**
10971 ft.; **genre:** Stunt
pc: Royal Film Co. **d:** Shanti J. Dave **c:** V.B. Jagtap

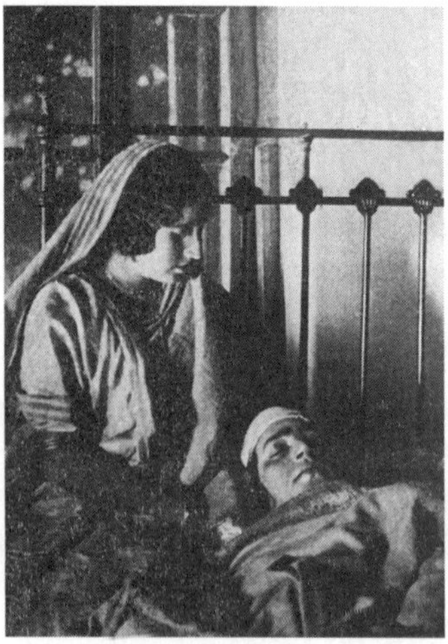

▲ A still from **Annapurna**

st/sc: Vijay Shankar Bhat
lp: Navinchandra, Padma, Zaverbhai Kaiser, Pawar, Manjula

Bhagya Chakra
aka **Taseere Taqdeer, Wheel of Fate**
9953 ft.; **genre:** Costume
pc: Surya Film Co., Bangalore **d/c:** Haribhai Desai **co-d:** Baburao **co-c:** Mohammed
lp: Jena, Tehmul Ankalesaria, Doss, Rohini, Jamadagni, Basheer, Nazir

Bhakta Laxmidas
aka **Adharmodhar**
6996 ft.; **genre:** Devotional

Bhakta Vijaya
9525 ft.; **genre:** Devotional
pc: Shree Ramesh Films, Bangalore **d/st:** Dada Gunjal **c:** Ambadas Kasture

Chandal Chokdi
aka **Gangster**
9744 ft.; **genre:** Stunt
pc: Paramount Film Co. **d:** R.N. Vaidya **c:** G.K. Mehta
lp: Nirasha, R.N. Vaidya, Nazir, Shiraz, Gulbanu, Mansur Ali, Baburao, Shantaram

Chokdi ka Ekka
aka **Ace of Diamonds**
8650 ft.; **genre:** Stunt
pc: Jayant Pictures **d:** Chunilal H. Parekh **c:** Ranjikant Pandya **st/sc:** Mohanlal G. Dave
lp: Shantaram, Lila

Daivi Khajana
aka **Divine Treasure**
10615 ft.; **genre:** Stunt
pc: Chandra Arts Production **d:** G.P. Pawar **c:** Zahur Ahmed
lp: Amboo, Chandrarao Kadam, Master Bhagwan, Batuk

Dare Devil
genre: Stunt
pc: Pratap Pictures **d:** R.N.Vaidya **c:** Khopkar
lp: Chudekar, Ranibala

Dildar
8616 ft.; **genre:** Costume
pc: Navjawan Film Co. **d:** Ramakant Gharekhan
lp: Nirmla, Jashwant Vaidya

Dilruba Daku
aka **Amazon**
9541 ft.; **genre:** Stunt
pc: Wadia Brothers **d/sc:** Ahmed Essa **c/st:** Homi Wadia
lp: Padma, Abdul Haq, Boman Shroff, Manchi Thuthi, Allawali, Sayani, Hasam, Manjula, Minoo Mukadam

Girnar no Simha
aka **Lion of Girnar**
9241 ft.; **genre:** Stunt
pc: Paramount Film Co. **d:** R.N.Vaidya **c:** V.M. Vyas
lp: Tara, Shiraz, Ali Bahadur, Nazir

Gunegar
aka **Culprit**
11876 ft.; **genre:** Stunt
pc: Royal Film Co. **d:** Balwant Bhat **c:** V.B. Jagtap
lp: Padma, Navinchandra, Zaverbhai Kaiser, Pawar, Manjula

Harijan
aka **Untouchable**
7892 ft.; **genre:** Social
pc: British India Film Co **d:** Naval Gandhi
lp: Zubeida, Waman Talpade, Lavji Lavangia, Jal Khambata
Remarks: This film was produced by Oriental Pictures Corp. Ltd. in 1931. Censored in 1933 and released in 1934 under the banner of British India Film Co. The release advertisment carries only the name of Zubeida.

Indian Charlie
7915 ft.; **genre:** Comedy
pc: Elphin Cinema Co.

Jagat Mohini
9940 ft.; **genre:** Costume
pc: Jayant Pictures **d:** Homi Master **c:** Gajendra Rajgor **st/sc:** Mohanlal G. Dave
lp: Padma, Inamdar

Jallad
aka **Chaos**
9441 ft.; **genre:** Stunt
pc: Mehta Luhar Productions
d: Harshadrai Mehta **c/st/sc:** Chimanlal Luhar
lp: Navinchandra, Chandrika, Bapurao Apte, Nizam, Bhim

Jalta Jigar
aka **Flaming Soul**
9911 ft.; **genre:** Stunt
pc: Chandra Arts Production **d:** G.P. Pawar **c:** Baburao Shirswade
lp: Amboo, Chandrarao Kadam, Ghanshyam, Harischandra Rao, Master Bhagwan

Jasal
10250 ft.; **genre:** Stunt
pc: Mehta Luhar Productions/Sharda Film Co. **d:** Bapurao Apte **c:** Chaturbhai Patel
lp: Yashwant Dave, Chandrika, Lobo, Bhim

Kali Waaghan
aka **Wild Tigress**
10911 ft.; **genre:** Stunt
pc: Paramount Film Co./Kumar Films **d:** R.N. Vaidya **c:** V.M. Vyas **st/sc:** H.E. Khatib
lp: Nandram, Prabhashankar, Vijaya, Malwankar

Khofnak Kheladi
aka **Devil May Care**
9715 ft.; **genre:** Stunt
pc: Swastik Pictures **d:** Sanatkumar Vin **c:** Ranjikant Pandya
lp: Harischandrarao Kadam, Sunita

Khoon ka Badla
aka **Avenging Blood**
9875 ft.; **genre:** Stunt
pc: Shree Ramesh Films, Bangalore **d:** Radha Kishore
lp: Laxmi, Ganpat Bakre, Kamala

Laparvah
aka **Undaunted**
9963 ft.; **genre:** Costume
pc: Surya Film Co., Bangalore **d:** Haribhai Desai **c:** Mohammed
lp: Ganpat Bakre, Bacha, Bashir, Rohini, Hansa, Subamma, Jamadagni

Misarnun Moti
aka **Pearl of Egypt**
9911 ft.; **genre:** Costume
pc: Jayant Pictures **d:** Homi Master **c:** V.M. Vyas **st/sc:** Mohanlal G. Dave
lp: R.N. Vaidya, Bachu, Miss Vijaya, Pawar

Nara ke Narayan
aka **Valmiki**

9435 ft.; **genre:** Mythological
pc: Sarosh Film Co.

Nav Bharat
11869 ft.; **genre:** Stunt
pc: British India Film Co. **d/st:** Chunilal H. Parekh **c:** G.K. Mehta
lp: Nurjehan, K.G. Rao, Sunita

Nek Dost
aka **Royal Friend**
9912 ft.; **genre:** Stunt
pc: Chandra Arts Production **d/st/sc:** G.P. Pawar **c:** Baburao Shirswade
lp: Amboo, Chandrarao Kadam, Ghanshyam, Harischandrarao Kadam

Pahadi Swar
aka **Wild Cavalier**
9816 ft.; **genre:** Stunt
pc: Shree Ganesh Film Co., Ahmedabad **d:** Chunilal H. Parekh **c:** Ambadas Pawar
st: Ahmedbhai Merchant
lp: Aziz, Malti, Sadiq, Nazir, Shantaram, Subhadra, Mohamed, Abdul

Parwana
aka **Butterfly**
9515 ft.
pc: New Western India Film Co. **d/st/sc:** H.E. Khatib **c:** Ambadas Pawar
lp: Padma, Ramkunver, Agha Mohamed, Kamla, Rahim, Allawali, Shubi, Kesarsinh

Prem Jivan
aka **Love Life**
7795 ft.
pc: Sarda Rajoo Productions

Punar Janma
aka **Life Divine**
12000 ft.; **genre:** Costume
pc: Mahalaxmi Cinema Co.

Pyari Katar
aka **Beloved Blade**
9897 ft.; **genre:** Stunt
pc: Chandra Arts Production **d:** G.P. Pawar
lp: Amboo, Chandrarao Kadam, Harishchandrarao Kadam, Master Bhagwan

Rajnichandra
aka **Blind Girl**
9714 ft.; **genre:** Social
pc: Ramesh Film Co./Paramount Film Co.
lp: Mehtab, Miss Kapdi, Wagle

Ranbheri
aka **Drums of War**
8652 ft.; **genre:** Costume
pc: Pratap Pictures **d:** R.N. Vaidya **c:** Khopkar
lp: Chudekar, Ranibala, Rajababu, Allawali

Ratna Lutari
aka **Lady Cavalier**
9415 ft.; **genre:** Stunt
pc: Jawahir Film Co. **d/st/sc:** Ata Mohamed **c:** Esmail
lp: Ata Mohamed, Nazir Sr., Nazir Jr., Jayant Acharya, Tara, Dhanvantrao Pahelwan, Manjula

Saitani Chakkar
aka **Satan's Victim**
9453 ft.; **genre:** Stunt
pc: Narayan Films Ltd, Ahmedabad **d:** Ata Mohamed/Dada Gunjal **c:** Ahmed
lp: Ata Mohamed, Sharda, Vipin, Bhagwandas, Fayma

Setu Bandhan
aka **Bridging of Ocean**
13715 ft.; **genre:** Mythological
pc: Hindustan Cinema Film Co., Nasik **d/st/sc:** D.G. Phalke
lp: Yakbal, Malti, Gotiram (?), Phalke
Remarks: Post-synchronised sound version in 1934.

Sher ka Bacha
aka **Happy Warrior**
9216 ft.; **genre:** Stunt
pc: Paramount Film Co./Kumar Films **d:** R.N. Vaidya **c:** V.M. Vyas
lp: Shiraz, Menka, Sakharam, Badshah

Vantolio
aka **Whirlwind**
9876 ft.; **genre:** Stunt
pc: Wadia Brothers **d:** J.B.H. Wadia **c:** Homi Wadia
lp: Padma, Boman Shroff, Allawali, Adi Patel, Sayani, Lovji Lavangia, Manchi Thuthi
Remarks: Only the trailer is available with NFAI.

Vijay Danka
aka **Laurels of Loyalty**
9515 ft.; **genre:** Costume
pc: Shree Ramesh Films, Bangalore **d:** Radha Kishore **c:** Vishnu Sawant
lp: Bhaurao Datar, Laxmi, Gokul, Jadhavrao, Balasaheb Yadav

1934

Ajit Yoddho
aka **Protector**
6857 ft.; **genre:** Costume

Blue Cross
aka **Phulawarno Ekko**
pc: Prithvi Cinetone
lp: Shamshudin Sindhi, Niranjan, Akhtari Lucknowi

Jadui Jung
aka **Phantom Foe, Naag Dand, Khuni Katar**
8904 ft.; **genre:** Fantasy
pc: Colombia Art Productions **d:** R.N. Vaidya **c:** Pranjiwan Shukla
lp: Yashwant Dave, Hira Dharwadkar, Ata Mohamed, Manilal, Sushila, S. Nazir

▼ Trade advertisement for variety entertainment programmes during intermissions

Khajana
aka **Treasure**
9800 ft.; **genre:** Stunt
pc: Ambika Film Co. **d/st/sc:** S.N. Bende **lp:** Ermeline, Harischandra Rao, Nazir Ajmeri, Manjula

Niyoti
10000 ft.; **genre:** Social
pc: Aurora Cinema Co., Calcutta **d/st/sc:** Jogesh Choudhary **c:** Dhiren Dey
lp: Sailan Choudhary, Ajit Bhattacharya, Nripesh Roy, Kamla Devi

Rajadanda
aka **King's Justice**
5900 ft.; **genre:** Costume
pc: Gopal Cinetone Corpn. Ltd.

Sharif Badmash
aka **Invention, Abad Uthavgir**
9885 ft.; **genre:** Stunt
pc: Shree Ganesh Film Co., Ahmedabad **d:** Ata Mohamed **st:** Ahmedbhai Merchant
lp: Ata Mohamed, Manilal, Ganpat, Vasant, Piroja

Sinh ki Pyas
aka **Brave Lion**
8916 ft.; **genre:** Stunt
pc: Daftary Bros.

Tismarkha
700 ft.; **genre:** Comedy
pc: Circle Talkies

▲ Sulochana and Choudhary in **Rani Rupmati** (1931)

FILMOGRAPHY INDEX

Bahare Jindgi, 1931
Baharvatia ni Beti, 1930
Baharvatio Behram, 1930
Bahurupi Bazar, 1932
Baj Bahadur, 1931
Baji Deshpande, 1929
Bajirao Mastani, 1925
Bakawali, 1930
Bal Gopal, 1930
Bal Shringi, 1924
Bal Vidhva, 1925
Balaji Nimbalkar, 1926
Bali Yagna, 1924
Balidan, 1927
Balika Badhu, 1931
Bangabala, 1929
Banke Sanvaria, 1931
Bansari Bala, 1927
Bar ke Pobar, 1931
Barer Bazar, 1922
Basant Prabha, 1924
Be Dhari Talwar, 1929
Be Dinni Badshahi, 1926
Beggar Girl of Agra, 1932
Beghadi Mauj, 1927
Beguman Ashak, 1930
Behula, 1921
Bewafa Ashak, 1931
Bewafa Katil, 1932
Bhadra Bhamini, 1925
Bhadraveshi Gunda, 1926
Bhagva Zenda, 1926
Bhagwata Bhakta Damaji, 1922
Bhagya Chakra, 1933
Bhagya Laxmi, 1932
Bhagyawan Bharwad, 1930
Bhagyodaya, 1930
Bhai ke Kasai, 1928
Bhakta Ambarish, 1922
Bhakta Bodana, 1922
Bhakta Damaji, 1928
Bhakta Kabirdas, 1928
Bhakta Laxmidas, 1933
Bhakta Prahlad, 1926
Bhakta Prahlad, 1926
Bhakta Sudama, 1927
Bhakta Sudhanva, 1923
Bhakta Vidur, 1921
Bhakta Vijaya, 1933
Bhaktha Vatsala, 1931
Bhamto Bhut, 1926
Bhaneli Bhamini, 1927
Bhangela Sikkano Bhed, 1931
Bhanto Bhot, 1930
Bharari the Bandit, 1931
Bharat Ramni, 1930
Bharat Veer, 1932
Bharmaylo Bharthar, 1928
Bharter Fer, 1930
Bhasmasur, 1928
Bhavani no Bhog, 1930
Bhawani Talwar, 1932
Bhedi Khanjar, 1932
Bhedi Rajkumar, 1932
Bhedi Swar, 1929
Bhedi Trishul, 1927
Bhikharn, 1929
Bhim Sanjivan, 1926
Bhimsen the Mighty, 1930
Bhishma Banashayya, 1922
Bhishma Pratigna, 1921
Bhishma, 1922
Bhola Shikar, 1930
Bhranti, 1928
Bhul Bhulaiya, 1929
Bhul no Bhog, 1926
Bhut Rajya, 1931
Bibaha Bibhrat, 1931
Bicharak, 1929
Bidya Sunder, 1922
Bigraha, 1930
Bijli, 1931
Bilet Pherat, 1921
Bilwamangal, 1919
Bilwamangal, 1929
Bimata, 1922
Birth of Shivaji, 1930
Bisha Briksha, 1922
Bisha Briksha, 1928
Bishyut Barer Barbela, 1930
Blood Feud, 1931
Blue Cross, 1934
Bodku Mathu, 1928
Bole te be Khaay, 1927
Bolki Tapeli, 1929
Boltun Bulbul, 1926
Boodha Boobukh, 1922
Briefless Barrister, 1926
Buddha Dev, 1923
Buker Bojha, 1930
Bulbule Paristan, 1926
Bulbul-E-Shiraz, 1931
Burkhawala, 1932
Burkhawali, 1926
Catechist of Kil-Arni, The, 1923
Chabuk Swar, 1930
Chabukne Chamkare, 1930
Chalta Purja, 1929
Chalta Purja, 1932
Chalu Jamana, 1925
Chamakti Chanda, 1928
Champraj Hado, 1923
Chandal Chokdi, 1933
Chandan Malayagiri, 1924
Chandbibi, 1931
Chandidas, 1927
Chandragupta Chanakya, 1923
Chandrahas, 1928
Chandrahas, 1929
Chandrahasa, 1921
Chandrakant, 1925
Chandramani, 1931
Chandramukhi, 1929
Chandranath, 1924
Chandrarao More, 1925
Chandrasena, 1931
Chandravali, 1928
Charitraheen, 1931
Chasar Meye, 1931
Chatur Sundari, 1930
Chaturkanta, 1928
Chaturthicha Chandra, 1925
Chauhani Talwar, 1930
Chhatra Bakavali, 1926
Chhatrapati Sambhaji, 1925
Chhel Batao Ane Rani Mohana, 1927
Chhota Chor, 1932
Chintamani, 1922
Chirage Kohistan, 1929
Chitachor, 1930

Goswami Tulsidas, 1923
Gourishankar, 1932
Govardhandhari, 1921
Gowalan, 1931
Grihalakshmi, 1928
Gul Badan, 1928
Gul Sanobar, 1928
Gulam, 1931
Gulami Janjir, 1931
Gulami nu Patan, 1931
Gulanar, 1930
Gul-E-Arab, 1930
Gul-E-Bakavali, 1924
Gulru Zarina, 1928
Gulzar, 1927
Gunasundari, 1927
Gunegar, 1933
Guniyal Gulab, 1926
Gupta Ratna, 1931
Gurjar Veer, 1932
Gurjoki Mar, 1931
Guru Dronacharya, 1923
Guru Machhindranath, 1923
Hairstorm, 1922
Haiyano Haar, 1928
Hanuman Janma, 1927
Hanuman Janma, 1931
Hanuman Patal Parakram, 1931
Hanuman Vijay, 1930
Haq Insaf, 1931
Haragouri, 1923
Hari Maya, 1931
Harijan, 1933
Haritalika, 1922
Hatimtai, 1929
Hawai Sawar, 1929
Hedimb Bakasur Vadh, 1925
Heer Ranjah, 1928
Heer Ranjah, 1929
Himmate Marda, 1930
Hind ke Tare, 1931
Hind Kesari, 1932
Hira Sundari, 1928
Hirji Kamdar, 1925
His Love Affair, 1931
Hoor-E-Arab, 1928
Hoor-E-Bagdad, 1928
Hoor-E-Hind, 1932
Hoor-E-Misar, 1931
Hoor-E-Roshan, 1931
Hothal Padmini, 1925
Hridaya Jwala, 1930
Hridaya Veena, 1931
Hungry, 1929
Husna ka Daku, 1929
Husna Pari, 1931
Husnara, 1930
Indian Charlie, 1933
Indira, 1929
Indira, 1929
Indrajal, 1926
Indrajit, 1922
Indrakumari, 1923
Indrasabha, 1925
Insaf, 1925
Intekam, 1931
Inteqam, 1930
Iraq ka Chor, 1931
Ishq no Anjam, 1931
Ishq no Umedvar, 1924
Jadu-E-Mohabat, 1931
Jadui Jung, 1934
Jagat Mohini, 1933
Jaheri Saap, 1929
Jai Bhavani, 1928
Jai Shree Shankar, 1930
Jai Vijay, 1930
Jai Vithal, 1931
Jail ke Parinde, 1931
Jaimini and Vyas, 1913
Jakhmi Jigar, 1929
Jal Kumari, 1925
Jalandhar Vrinda, 1920
Jaler Meye, 1925
Jalim Jadugarin, 1930
Jallad, 1933
Jalta Jigar, 1933
Jamai Babu, 1931
Jamaika the Fool, 1931
Jana, 1927
Jane Alam Anjuman Ara, 1927
Jangal ni Jadibutti, 1926
Jang-E-Jawani, 1932
Janjirne Jankare, 1927
Janki Swayamwar, 1926
Janma Haq, 1931
Jarasandha Vadha, 1923
Jasal, 1933
Jawahir-E-Hind, 1932
Jawani Diwani, 1929
Jawanmarda, 1930
Jay Bajarang, 1932
Jay Bharati, 1929
Jay Somnath, 1929
Jayadratha Vadha, 1924
Jayant, 1929
Jiban Prabhat, 1931
Jigarna Gha, 1930
Jindagi no Jugar, 1931
Jobanna Jadu, 1930
Josh-E-Jawani, 1930
Joydev, 1926
Jugal Anguriya, 1929
Jugal Jugari, 1930
Jugari Dharma, 1927
Julia Dalia, 1929
Julumgar, 1931
Jung-E-Daulat, 1931
Jungle ke Jawan, 1931
Kaal Ratrinun Khuni Khanjar, 1928
Kabir Kamal, 1919
Kabir Kamal, 1930
Kacha Devayani, 1929
Kacha Devyani, 1919
Kacha Devyani, 1926
Kailas Kumari, 1927
Kailas, 1932
Kakasahebanchya Dolyat Jhanjhanit Anjan, 1925
Kal Parinaya, 1930
Kala Chor, 1925
Kala Nag, 1924
Kala Pahad, 1927
Kala Pani no Qaidi, 1927
Kalabaj Ashak, 1926
Kali Nagin, 1925
Kali Waaghan, 1933
Kalicha Narad, 1923
Kalidas, 1922
Kalikano Kop, 1930

Madhu Bansari, 1929
Madhu Bansri, 1926
Madhuri, 1928
Maha Sunder, 1929
Mahabharat, 1920
Mahananda, 1923
Maharachi Por, 1925
Maharathi Karna, 1928
Mahasagar nu Moti, 1931
Mahasati Anasuya, 1927
Mahashivratra, 1925
Mahashweta Kadambarimalti Madhav, 1922
Mahathma Kabirdas, 1925
Mahiari, 1932
Maidane Jung, 1931
Malhari Martand, 1928
Mallaraj, 1932
Malti Madhav, 1929
Malvikagnimitra, 1929
Manbhanjan, 1923
Manik Jore, 1930
Mano Vijaya, 1926
Manorama, 1924
Marathyachi Mulgi, 1928
Mard ka Bachcha, 1930
Mard ki Jaban, 1929
Mardna Gha, 1927
Mari Dhaniyani, 1925
Markandeya, 1923
Marner Parey, 1931
Marriage Tonic, 1922
Marthanda Varma, 1931
Masta Fakir, 1930
Mastana Mehboob, 1931
Mastikhor Mashuk, 1932
Mathano Sadhu, 1930
Matri Sneh, 1922
Matrubhumi, 1932
Matruprem, 1925
Matsya and Varah Avatar, 1923
Maurya Patan, 1929
Maya Madhusudan, 1931
Maya Mahal, 1928
Maya Mohini, 1928
Mayabee, 1930
Mayana Rang, 1928
Mayavi Nagri, 1929
Mayilravanan, 1918
Mena Kumari, 1926
Meri Ma, 1931
Meri Mashook, 1931
Mewad no Mawali, 1930
Mewad Pati Bapa Rawal, 1925
Mewadnun Moti, 1929
Milan Dinar, 1929
Minaldevi, 1923
Mira Bai, 1921
Mirza Sahiba, 1929
Misarnun Moti, 1933
Mishar Rani, 1924
Miss Dolly, 1929
Mission Girl, 1927
Mitha Jahar, 1930
Mithi Churi, 1931
Moh Jal, 1928
Mohabat ke Musibat, 1927
Mohabat ki Putli, 1931
Mohabatnun Phool, 1930
Mohini Avatar, 1926
Mohini, 1913
Mohini, 1921
Mohtaj Mashuk, 1932
Mojili Mashuk, 1931
Mojili Mumbai, 1925
Moroo, 1930
Mrichhakatik, 1920
Mrigjal, 1932
Mrinalini, 1930
Mukti Sangram, 1931
Mularj Solanki, 1925
Mumbai ni Biladi, 1927
Mumbai ni Mohini, 1925
Mumbai ni Shethani, 1924
Mumbai no Mawali, 1929
Mumbai no Satodio, 1929
Mumtaz Mahal, 1926
Municipal Nivadnuk, 1924
Muralivala, 1927
Nabin Bharat, 1924
Nadira, 1931
Nag Padmini, 1928
Naharsingh Daku, 1925
Nai Roshni, 1930
Nakhrali Nar, 1932
Nakli Rani, 1927
Nakoga Bai Lagna, 1931
Nala Damayanti, 1920
Nala Damayanti, 1927
Namak Haram Kon, 1931
Nanand Bhojai, 1927
Nand Batrishi, 1924
Nand ke Lala, 1931
Nand Kishore, 1931
Nand Kumar, 1930
Nandanar, 1923
Nandnar, 1930
Nara ke Narayan, 1933
Nara Kesari, 1928
Nara Narayan, 1931
Narad Sansar, 1928
Narasinh Mehta, 1920
Narasinha Avatar, 1919
Narasinha Mehta, 1924
Nari Jaat, 1931
Nari ke Nagan, 1927
Nartaki Tara, 1922
Nasib na Nakhara, 1929
Nasib ni Balihari, 1931
Nasib ni Devi, 1929
Nasib ni Leeli, 1927
Nasib ni Nauka, 1930
Natun Janma, 1929
Naukadubi, 1932
Nav Bharat, 1933
Navalsha Hirji, 1925
Neelam Manek, 1928
Neera, 1926
Nek Dost, 1933
Netaji Palkar, 1927
Nidrit Bhagwan, 1931
Nimak Haram, 1928
Niradhar Nira, 1931
Nirbhagi Nirmala, 1930
Nisha Sundari, 1929
Nishan Danka, 1929
Nishir Daak, 1932
Nisiddha Phal, 1928
Niyoti, 1934
Noore Deccan, 1925
Noor-E-Alam, 1931

Raja Shriyal, 1929
Rajadanda, 1934
Rajadhiraj, 1932
Rajane Gami Te Rani, 1926
Rajani Bala, 1928
Rajani, 1929
Rajarshi Ambarish, 1922
Rajba, 1928
Rajdoot, 1930
Rajeswari, 1930
Rajkumari Budur, 1922
Rajkumari Ni Ranagarjana, 1930
Rajmukut, 1930
Rajnagar Ni Rambha, 1925
Rajnandini, 1931
Rajnichandra, 1933
Rajput Swar, 1929
Rajputani, 1929
Rajrang, 1928
Rajwadana Rang, 1928
Rajyogi, 1925
Raktacha Sood, 1929
Ram Bharose, 1926
Ram Janma, 1920
Ram Rahim, 1930
Ram Ravan Yuddha, 1924
Ram Vanvas, 1918
Rama Doota, 1930
Rama Janma, 1931
Rama or Maya, 1920
Rama Rajya Viyog, 1926
Ramayan, 1922
Ramdas, 1928
Ran Garjana, 1929
Ran Haak, 1931
Rana Hamir, 1925
Rana Pratap, 1925
Ranadevta, 1932
Ranaghelo Rajput, 1929
Ranakdevi ra Khengar, 1923
Ranakdevi, 1930
Ranbheri, 1933
Ranchandi, 1930
Randhir, 1930
Rang Rakhyo Chhe, 1926
Rangilo Rajput, 1932
Rangmahel ni Ramani, 1927
Rani Rupmati, 1931
Rani Saheba, 1930
Rank nu Ratan, 1929
Rank Ramani, 1929
Raosaheb, 1931
Rasili Radha, 1930
Rasili Rani, 1930
Rathod Kumari, 1931
Ratna Lutari, 1933
Ratna Manjri, 1926
Ratnakar, 1921
Ratnavali, 1922
Ratnavali, 1922
Razalati Rajkumari, 1928
Razia Begum, 1924
Reshmi Sari, 1927
Romantic Lovers, 1931
Ronak Mahal, 1931
Roopsundari, 1927
Rose of Rajasthan, 1931
Rukmangad Mohini, 1927
Rukmini Haran, 1921
Rukmini Haran, 1927
Rukmini Haran, 1929
Rukmini Kalyanam, 1921
Rup Basant, 1928
Rupsundari, 1931
Sadevant Savlinga, 1924
Sadguni Sushila, 1924
Sadhu ki Shaitan, 1922
Safadarjung, 1930
Safed Swar, 1930
Sahadharmini, 1931
Sainik ke Saitan, 1931
Sairandhri, 1920
Saitani Chakkar, 1933
Sakhi Lutaro, 1931
Samrat Ashok, 1928
Samrat Ashoka, 1922
Samrat Shiladitya, 1926
Samsher Bahadur, 1930
Samsher Pratigna, 1928
Samsherbaz, 1930
Samudra Madanam, 1923
Samudra Manthan, 1924
Sanam ni Shodhma, 1925
Sandigdha, 1932
Sanmitra ke Saitan, 1929
Sansar Chakra, 1925
Sansar Swapna, 1925
Sansar, 1927
Sant Eknath, 1926
Sant Janabai, 1925
Sant Meerabai, 1929
Sant Namdev, 1922
Sant Sakhubai, 1922
Sant Tukaram, 1921
Sanyasi, 1924
Sarangthara, 1930
Sarfarosh, 1930
Sarla, 1928
Saroj Kumari, 1931
Sarojini, 1928
Sarovarani Sundari, 1928
Satharam, 1931
Sati Anjani, 1922
Sati Parvati, 1920
Sati Anasuya, 1921
Sati Anjani, 1932
Sati Jasma, 1926
Sati ka Shap, 1923
Sati Kausalya, 1931
Sati Laxmi, 1925
Sati Madri, 1927
Sati Mandodari, 1931
Sati Menadevi, 1926
Sati Narmada, 1923
Sati Padmini, 1924
Sati Pingala, 1928
Sati Sardarba, 1924
Sati Sarla, 1930
Sati Saroj, 1926
Sati Savitri, 1927
Sati Savitri, 1931
Sati Simantini, 1925
Sati Sita, 1924
Sati Sona, 1924
Sati Sulochana, 1921
Sati Tara, 1925
Sati Toral, 1922
Sati Ushasundari, 1930
Sati Vijaya, 1930
Sati Virmati, 1923
Sati, 1922

Suvarnamala, 1930
Swadesh Seva, 1927
Swami, 1931
Swapana Sundari, 1925
Swapna Vihar, 1916
Swarga Vihar, 1928
Syamantaka Mani, 1925
Tai Teleen, 1926
Taj ke Talwar, 1931
Tajayali Taruni, 1928
Takay ki ni Hay, 1931
Takhte Toofan, 1931
Tal Bhairav, 1929
Talwar ka Dhani, 1929
Talwar ka Pani, 1930
Taranhar, 1931
Tarun Tapswini, 1929
Tarunina Tarang, 1928
Tati Talwar, 1930
Tawangar ni Talwar, 1929
Teere Katil, 1931
Tehmuras and Temuljee, 1921
Telephone ni Taruni, 1926
Thaksen Rajputra, 1929
The Lover in the Tub, 1931
Thief Entertained, 1921
Thoratanchi Kamala, 1927
Tirandaj, 1931
Tismarkha, 1934
Tofani Taruni, 1931
Toofan Mail, 1932
Toofan, 1931
Toorkey Hoor, 1924
Totayache Bund, 1926
Tridandi Sanyas, 1921
Tukaram, 1921
Typist Girl, 1926
Udantappu, 1928
Udaykal, 1930
Ujaint Kumar, 1925
Ulphat-E-Mohamad, 1929
Umaji Naik, 1926
Urvashi, 1921
Usha Swapna, 1919
Uthavgir, 1931
Vachan Bhang, 1925
Vali and Sugriv Yudh, 1923
Valli Kalyanam, 1930
Valli's Wedding, 1921
Valmiki, 1921
Vaman Avatar, 1923
Vaman Avtaar, 1930
Vanadevi, 1931
Vanaraj Kesari, 1932
Vanaraj, 1930
Vandemataram Ashram, 1926
Vanraj Chavda, 1923
Vantolio, 1933
Vara Chatan Vidhawa, 1928
Vasal ki Rat, 1929
Vasant Bengali, 1930
Vasant Leela, 1928
Vasant Padmini, 1929
Vasantbala, 1926
Vasantsena, 1929
Vasantsena, 1930
Vasavadatta, 1928
Vediya Dhor, 1927
Veer Abhimanyu, 1922
Veer Ahir, 1924
Veer Bahadur, 1931
Veer Baji, 1929
Veer Bala, 1925
Veer Bhimsen, 1923
Veer Bhushan, 1930
Veer Durgada, 1924s
Veer Garjana, 1927
Veer Hak, 1929
Veer Kesari, 1926
Veer Kunal, 1925
Veer na Ver, 1930
Veer Pujan, 1929
Veer Rajput, 1930
Veer Rathod, 1929
Veer Vairagi, 1930
Veer Vijaysingh, 1930
Veerangana, 1928
Veni Bandhan, 1922
Ver na Ansu, 1931
Ver ni Vasulat, 1925
Ver Vasul, 1930
Vichitra Gutika, 1920
Vichitra Ver, 1931
Videhi Janak, 1923
Vidhinu Vidhan, 1926
Vifreli Waghan, 1930
Vigathakumaran, 1928
Vijay Danka, 1933
Vijay Kumar, 1930
Vijay Laxmi, 1931
Vijaya, 1924
Vijeta, 1930
Vikral Varu, 1931
Vikram Charitra, 1924
Vikram Satva Pariksha, 1921
Vikram Urvashi, 1921
Vilasi Atma, 1931
Vilasi Kanta, 1927
Vilasi Vandho, 1928
Vimla, 1925
Vinchucha Dansh, 1924
Vipranarayan, 1930
Vir Bharat, 1924
Virat Parva, 1922
Virni Vibhuti, 1931
Vishnu Avatar, 1921
Vishnu Leela, 1932
Vishva Mohini, 1928
Vishvamitra Menaka, 1919
Vishwamitra, 1931
Vismi Sadi, 1924
Vratasur Vadha, 1923
Wafadary, 1931
Yadav Vinash, 1922
Yashoda Nandan, 1921
Yashodevi, 1925
Yasmina, 1930
Yayati, 1923
Youvan Chakra, 1926
Zagmagti Jawani, 1930
Zalim Zulekha, 1930
Zulum, 1931

APPENDICES

APPENDIX A

This film is not included in the filmography for the reason given in the remarks.

Abhinab

genre: Social

pc: Aurora Cinema Co., Calcutta **d:** Debaki Bose **lp:** Nirmal Bannerji, Sheila Devi, Nripesh Roy, Ranjit Roy, Samar Ghosh

Remarks: This film was probably made in 1932-33 as a silent and shelved. However, a post-synchronised version was released in Calcutta on 15/11/1940 with a running commentary by Ahindra Chaudhary.

APPENDIX B

These films are not included in the filmography for reasons given in the remarks.

1912

An Episode from Ramayan

Cinema De Luxe (Gaiety Theatre)

Remarks: This episode from the *Ramayana* was shown in Bombay with a film titled *The Custom Officer and the Girl* on 2/11/1912. The advertisement states: 'For the first time in India–an episode from Ramayan–The great epic of the Hindoos. This film was taken special (*sic*) for Cinema De-Luxe–will be shown as an extra attraction.' This suggests that it was a topical made during the Dussera festivities.

1921

Wealth or Love

pc: Madan Theatres Ltd. (?) **st:** Aga Hashr Kashmiri (?)

Remarks: This film seems to be a foreign production and not produced by Madan Theatres Ltd. In the advertisement Aga Hashr Kashmiri is given the credit for the story but he probably would have only written the titles. The film was shot in Ceylon.

APPENDIX C

The following films were not released even though they were advertised for a long period. In all likelihood they remained incomplete or had technical faults.

1912

Savitri

genre: Mythological

Remarks: Made jointly by S.N. Patankar, V.P. Divekar and A.P. Karandikar. Unreleased due to technical faults.

1926

Durgesh Nandini

pc: Sudarshan Films **d:** B.P. Mishra **st:** Bankimchandra Chatterjee

lp: Madanrai Vakil, Ermeline, Mazhar Khan

Remarks: This was a joint production of B.P. Mishra, R.S.D. Chaudhary and R.G. Torney.

1930

Sohrab Rustom

pc: Maharashtra Film Co., Kolhapur **d:** Baburao Painter **c:** Yashwant Gune (?) **sc:** Sardar S. Nesrikar

lp: Balasaheb Yadav

1931

Amar Yodho

aka **Immortal Warrior**

pc: Saroj Film Co. **d:** Dhirubhai Desai **c:** Dwarka Khosla

lp: Zebu, Chandrarao Kadam

1932

Jugari

aka **Fortune's Favourite**

pc: Surya Film Co., Bangalore

lp: Baby Garbo, Jena, Zunzharrao Pawar, Wamanrao Kulkarni, Jamu Patel, Doss, Govardhan, Jamadagni

ACKNOWLEDGEMENTS

This newly expanded edition of *Light of Asia* has received the support of many people who helped to make the earlier book possible. Thus, firstly I would like to thank several past and present staff members of the National Film Archive of India (NFAI). Arti Karkhanis, Urmila Joshi, Laxmi Iyer, Seema Vartak, Kiran Diwar and Dilip Rajput were always ready to facilitate the research and viewing of the films. I am also deeply indebted to Prashant Pathrabe, Director, NFAI for his generous support to this project. K. P. R. Nair, who had worked on the restoration of the Baburao Painter films at the NFAI deserves special thanks as without his efforts these invaluable films could not have been saved.

While my friend Anant Vishnu Damle has sadly passed away, I thank his family for once again lending photographs from his collection. I remain deeply appreciative of the late Paul Willemen's help in sending me many of the entries on silent films from the then forthcoming *Encyclopaedia of Indian Cinema*. Paolo Cherchi Usai, my associate editor for the earlier edition, has always been a staunch supporter of this endeavour; and I also thank Piera Patat of Le Giornate del Cinema Muto / Pordenone Silent Film

Festival–who had initially commissioned this publication–for promptly giving the festival's go-ahead for the revised edition.

Ashish Rajadhyaksha has been extraordinarily generous with his time and advice and I am very grateful to him for his valuable contribution to the book. I also thank Virchand Dharamsey for readily agreeing to update the filmography and enrich it with new information and discoveries.

I offer my thanks to Bikash Niyogi of Niyogi Books who recognised the value of a new edition and agreed to publish it in the year of the *Raja Harishchandra* centenary. My gratitude is also due to Mohua Mitra for skillfully editing this book and seeing it through various stages from the time it was intended to only be a reprint to its present expanded form.

Finally, I would like thank my wife Priya Sarukkai Chabria who urged me to work on this project once more. For her constant support and enthusiasm I am very much in debt.

Suresh Chabria

2013

INDEX